MW00776646

Janice G. Raymond is a lo[...] violence against women an[...] [...] [...] [...] abuse of women. She is the author of five books, one edited volume, and multiple articles translated into several languages on issues ranging from violence against women, women's health, feminist theory, lesbian feminism, and bio-medicine. She has published numerous articles on prostitution and sex trafficking and lectures internationally on these topics.

Janice Raymond is Professor Emerita of Women's Studies and Medical Ethics at the University of Massachusetts in Amherst where she was a faculty member since 1978.

For thirteen years, Raymond was the Co-Executive Director of the Coalition Against Trafficking in Women (CATW). CATW is an international NGO having consultative status with the United Nations (ECOSOC), and with branches in many world regions. It was the first global abolitionist network organized to combat sex trafficking, sex tourism, and the international sex industry.

Through her work with CATW, Janice Raymond has been a leader in the campaign to recognize prostitution as violence against women and one of the worst forms of women's inequality. This has included testifying internationally to oppose the legalization of the sex industry, to advocate for governments to provide services and alternatives for women in prostitution and to legislate against the purchase of women and children for sexual activities.

Janice Raymond has also testified before the European Parliament on 'The Impact of the Sex Industry in the EU;' and before the subcommittee of the U.S. Congress on "The Ongoing Tragedy of International Slavery and Human Trafficking." She helped define the UN *Protocol to Prevent, Suppress and Punish Trafficking in Persons, especially Women and Children, supplementing the UN Convention Against Transnational Organized Crime.*

Among other awards, Dr. Raymond received the "International Woman Award" from the Zero Tolerance Trust, in Glasgow, Scotland for her international work to challenge governments and civil society to recognize and oppose prostitution and sex trafficking as violence against women.

Other books by Janice G. Raymond

The Transsexual Empire: The Making of the She-Male (1979/1994)

A Passion for Friends: Toward a Philosophy of Female Affection (1986/2002)

The Sexual Liberals and the Attack on Feminism (co-editor with Dorchen Leidholdt, 1990)

RU 486: Misconceptions, Myths and Morals (co-author with Renate Klein and Lynette Dumble, 1991/2013)

Women as Wombs: Reproductive Technologies and the Battle over Women's Freedom (1995/2020)

Not a Choice, Not a Job: Exposing the Myths about Prostitution and the Global Sex Trade (2013)

DOUBLETHINK

A FEMINIST CHALLENGE
TO TRANSGENDERISM

JANICE G. RAYMOND

First published by Spinifex Press, 2021

Spinifex Press Pty Ltd
PO Box 5270, North Geelong, VIC 3215, Australia
PO Box 105, Mission Beach, QLD 4852, Australia

women@spinifexpress.com.au
www.spinifexpress.com.au

Edited by Renate Klein, Pauline Hopkins and Susan Hawthorne
Index by Karen Gillen
Cover design by Deb Snibson, MAPG
Typesetting by Helen Christie, Blue Wren Books
Typeset in Minion Pro
Printed in the USA

ISBN: 9781925950380 (paperback)
ISBN: 9781925950397 (ebook)

For all those who dare to say women exist. For all those who have courageously resisted the ongoing assault against women and women's rights. For all those who have challenged the disgraceful medicalization of children. And for all those surviors of transitioning who are now de-transitioning. In the hope that others may stand up to this rapid advance of transgenderism that has spread its tentacles into law, government, education and sports.

Acknowledgments

During the years I have been working on this book, and even before, many people on several continents sent me articles and other sources, expressed how important this book would be, and helped with perceptive comments. Many of them are writers with writing projects of their own. For their invaluable courage, support, inspiration and encouragement, I thank Malka Marcovich, Esohe Aghatise, Julie Bindel, Twiss and Pat Butler, Sheila Jeffreys, Anna Zobnina and the Radical Girlsss, Jean Enriquez, Aurora Javate de Dios, Daphne Patai, Nikki Kraft, Rachel Paul, Renee Gerlich, Jan Rivers, Rachel Moran, Max Robinson, Kitty Robinson, Donna Hughes, Melissa Farley and the late Alix Dobkin and Bernice Dubois.

I want to thank the remarkable women at Spinifex Press — among them Susan Hawthorne, Renate Klein and Pauline Hopkins — who dare to publish this book in a climate where dissent from trans orthodoxies is confused with transphobia, and many books that are gender critical are censored. As I have expressed earlier, Spinifex Press is a gift to the feminist movement.

My partner Pat Hynes read the manuscript closely, with her writer's eye, even as she was working on her own book. I can never express my gratitude to her for a loving life of 48 years.

August 2021

Contents

Contents

From Transsexualism to Transgenderism

All that was needed was an unending series of victories over your own memory. 'Reality control', they called it: in Newspeak, 'doublethink'.

—George Orwell, *1984*

I wrote *The Transsexual Empire,* published in 1979, for several reasons. Initially, it was my PhD dissertation. At that time in the early 70s, the feminist women's health movement was evolving and, in the process, challenging many medical practices that were damaging to women such as unnecessary hysterectomies.

Much of my teaching, writing and activism at the time focused on the use of technologies that were destructive to women's bodies and minds — for example, behavior control and modification technologies such as psychosurgery (formerly called lobotomy) and electroshock therapy. My early research and activism led me to question the medical consequences of the bodily mutilations inherent in transsexual surgery and the detrimental effects of taking life-long hormones.

Although it was mostly men at that time who were undergoing transsexual interventions, I suspected that transsexualism, and later its more recent iteration of transgenderism, might change women's lives in ways that would attempt to erase women and brand us with names that are offensive to our ears. But no one would have imagined that transgender activists would have the cheek to rename us as 'cis-women', 'TERFS' (trans exclusionary radical feminists), 'front holes', 'uterus-owners', 'egg producers', 'chest feeders' — even 'non-men' — and, ironically, would keep the name 'woman' for themselves. Even abortion providers have succumbed to modifying their mission statements from that of serving 'women who are pregnant' to 'people who are pregnant'.

Some reviewers of *The Transsexual Empire* called me a conspiracy theorist because of the title that included the word 'empire'. The title was meant to spotlight the gender industry of transsexual counseling, surgery and hormone treatments, an industry that deploys a horde of general surgeons, plastic surgeons, endocrinologists, gynecologists, urologists and psychiatrists in the service of assuring the trans-identified person could 'pass' as the desired sex, which meant conforming to patriarchal sex roles.

The medicalization of gender dissatisfaction I depicted back then has today expanded exponentially into the gender identity industrial complex built on big medicine, big pharma, big banks, big foundations, big research centers, some attached to big universities. Funders like George Soros and Jennifer Pritzker are gifting the trans movement with tremendous resources, helping to subsidize a vast operation that provides transgenderism with legal and policy clout. Although the trans population is small, it is not a fringe movement starved of funding but rather a well-financed global campaign that has helped underwrite laws that enable trans ideology and practices in many countries.

In the late 1980s, trans activists began to challenge the feminist position that transsexualism promoted conformity to regressive sex roles. Instead they argued that transsexualism was a challenge to gender. Also, the language of transsexualism was changing to transgender. Advocates of transgender were making claims that it was trans-identifed persons who posed a radical challenge to gender, transgressing gender expectations and rigid boundaries of binary sex-roles by undergoing hormone treatment and surgeries that promised bodies that would resemble the opposite sex.

In the 1990s, trans activists began to simply appropriate a male or female identity by self-declaration. Surgery and/or hormones were no longer necessary to transitioning.

People sometimes ask me, "What's the big deal about transgender?" and "Why is it such a significant issue, especially in the schema of pressing issues that concern feminists?" As I saw it then and see it now, transsexualism and transgenderism raise questions of what gender is and how to challenge it, questions that have become more critical to ask and answer in this expanding ethos of transgenderism — an ideology and practice that promotes a 'gender identity' different from the sex a person is born with.

In the new wave of transgenderism, gender becomes biology. Instead of recognizing that gender is a social and political construct, trans advocates claim it is a personal issue of self-identification by declaration, with or without hormonal treatment and/or surgical intervention — a biological toggle switch to turn on and off at will. But gender is not a force of nature as trans proponents declare. It can be fashioned to suit the dominant patriarchal power, and that is what is happening today with transgender ideology spreading its sway over almost all institutions including sports, education, law and government.

Looking ahead from 1979, I envisioned that the few university and hospital-based gender identity centers treating adult transsexuals would grow and become sex role control centers for female and male children who deviated from traditional sex roles. I wrote: "Such gender identity centers are already being used for the treatment of designated child transsexuals." In the United States today, the usual figure cited is 60+ gender identity clinics that treat children's 'gender dysphoria'. The gender-mapping project has recently challenged that figure and has located over 300+ clinics in the whole of North America, most in the United States (The Gender Map, 2021).

The current medicalizing of young children is a widespread scandal. A large number of children, who are now seeking transsexual/transgender treatment, are girls. Given the medical model that still governs children's treatment in the gender identity clinics, it is no surprise that drugs such as problematic puberty blockers followed by cross-sex hormones have become acceptable, with virtually no pushback from the medical community.

The good news is that many girls who underwent these treatments — in contrast to boys — are de-transitioning and becoming critics of transgenderism.

Self-declaration has become the dominant ideology of men who insist on confirmation as women and are now leading the campaign for legal recognition. Their mantra is if you self-identify as a woman, you should be treated as one or, more simply, 'men can become women'. In a *Transsexual Empire* chapter called "Sappho by Surgery," I mentioned that men who asserted they were women would also claim to be "trans lesbians."

Before I began writing this book I thought long and hard, knowing that the swarm of trans detractors would gleefully sting me again, only this time it would be more venomous. I had to play catch up on the issues, ideology and practices of the current-day transgender movement, not that the hate messages and censoring I had personally received had ever ceased, but rather that I had gone on to other women's issues that occupied my mind, time and writing.

This book is not *The Transsexual Empire* #2, but it could not have been written without #1. It is much more about girls and women who are transitioning and de-transitioning, whereas there were very few females in the 1970s and 80s who turned to transsexualism and resorted to hormones and surgery.

This book is also about young women who have undergone sexual violence in LGBT+ circles. They are the courageous survivors of trans violence against women who have chosen to speak out about the harm and have braved the silencing and censoring that is rampant in these communities about the sexual exploitation of women. This violence is being ignored and silenced by the mainstream LGBT+ organizations that keep track of violence experienced only by men who identify as women.

This book is also about the biologizing of illusions, i.e. trans obsessions that are fixated on the ways that men might be able to menstruate, get pregnant and lactate. And this book is also about trans newspeak that would strip away from us the very word 'women' yet retain this word for self-declared women, rebranding natal women as cis-women, menstruators, and front holes.

Personal History

I probably have the distinction of being the first named TERF, a dubious title that is now shared with anyone who is a gender critic or abolitionist.

With the advent of the internet, trans activists became ethically unmoored as they captured online podiums, spewed vitriol, and marked any gender critic as transphobic and guilty of a hate crime for repudiating the transgender doctrine that men can become women. Censorship became the first resort for trans activists aimed at mainly feminist critics but also at any therapist, researcher or journalist who conscientiously dissents from the transgender canon.

It took trans activist attacks on male critics who penned some moderate criticisms of transgenderism to jog a bit of public awareness of the misogyny, the threats hurled by cyber trolls, and the silencing that many radical feminists had been experiencing for years. When Jesse Singal wrote a 2016 article in *New York Magazine*, writer Julian Vigo contacted him to ask if he was being harassed. He responded: "I'm a male so I only get a tiny fraction of the harassment women do." More recently, Singal has been getting more than a fraction of trans harassment from a Twitter campaign of lies about him (Kay, 2021).

For me, the censorship happened right from the get-go. In the early 1970s as a graduate student, I had applied for a grant to research and write the dissertation that would become *The Transsexual Empire*. A prestigious US foundation contacted me to say that the grant had been awarded and needed only some pro-forma administrative signatures. Since one bonus of the grant was paid health insurance, they asked me to make an appointment for a health physical, a standard part of the insurance application process

— an exam they paid for and which I promptly underwent. Several weeks later, a colleague who worked at the foundation and who had endorsed my application, informed me that faculty associated with a prominent university gender identity clinic where I had conducted some interviews had complained that my investigation would threaten their work. This was a backhanded compliment and needless to say, they nixed my grant.

In 1995, a trans-identified woman contacted New York-based Columbia Teachers College Press that had reprinted *The Transsexual Empire*, charging that I had 'deliberately' omitted the preface to the original edition of the book in the new edition. The complainant wrote I was guilty of 'scholarly misconduct', a whimsical charge alleging the 1994 version was not a true copy of the original edition. Teachers College editors responded stating it was their decision to cut the original preface from the 1994 reprint for reasons of keeping the book to a specific page length that would include a new introduction.

Not to be dissuaded, the trans accuser contacted my university reiterating the fatuous 'scholarly misconduct' charge and seeking a disciplinary hearing that would confirm a far-fetched denunciation of my 'academic fraud'. After an academic dean told me that the university would conduct such an investigation, I countered that the publisher had already undertaken one and claimed responsibility for the omitted preface. I added I would be compelled to seek legal assistance if the university proceeded with a redundant investigation of such a frivolous claim. The dean promptly reversed his decision and wrote a response to the trans accuser stating that the "proper channel for such expression is not a disciplinary hearing … but rather the scholarly marketplace of ideas."

Also during this same time period, I experienced my first mass protest organized by trans activists at a feminist bookstore in New York City, where I was doing a launch of another book on the subject of new reproductive technologies. The gauntlet of protesters felt very threatening, especially as I entered and exited the store. And I was subjected to many such protests wherever I spoke thereafter. With the advent of the internet, a cesspool of venom aimed at anyone who dissents from the transgender bible went viral, and I began receiving nasty emails.

After 40 plus years of dissenting from transgender orthodoxies, I learned that the Women's Studies Program (now renamed as Women, Gender and Sexuality Studies) in which I taught for 28 years had posted this message on its website:

> Given the persistence of legacies of trans-exclusionary radical feminism, including its presence in the history of Women's Studies at the University of Massachusetts at Amherst, and in response to requests for clarification on this issue from trans communities at UMass and in the Pioneer Valley, we ... categorically reject transphobia in our department, on our campus, and in our discipline.

Although I had retired from the University in 2002, this apology for my unspecified presence in the department felt like a heretic's sentence at her delayed execution. The 'trans-exclusionary radical feminist' was not named probably for legal reasons but was fairly obvious since no one else in the department's history was remotely identified with radical feminism, or with research and writing that challenged the sacred tenets of transsexualism and transgenderism.

And the rest is history, as they say, a history of attempted silencing wherever I spoke and multiple online threats of violence to my person. Regrettably, this is not news to any feminist or trans critic who has expressed disagreement with the trans dogma that men can become women by surgery, hormones or self-identification.

The Trans Canopy and Its Words, Acronyms and Arguments

The trans canopy includes preoperative and postoperative trans-sexuals, those who cross-dress or say they are gender non-binary, those who exhibit any kind of identity or behavior that is self-interpreted as crossing sex, and those who simply 'feel' that they are members of the opposite sex. Some seek hormonal and surgical change of appearance and others, a change of clothing and pronouns.

Combined with a society that is flooded with the fantasies of popular entertainment and virtual reality, the fiction of turning males into females and females into males becomes 'fact'. British journalist Helen Joyce points out that estimates of those who identify as transgender are small and can include men who are 'part-time cross dressers'. She emphasizes that many of these men have not undergone any bodily alterations and don't suffer from so-called gender dysphoria (Joyce, 2020).

When you are privy to those who are part of this 'acronymed' community, you learn there are endless words and short-forms that are used as identifiers such as 'assigned female at birth' (AFAB) or its opposite, 'assigned male at birth' (AMAB), or LGBTQQIAAP. Many of us know what LGBT means, but QQIAAPP stands for 'Queer', 'Questioning', 'Intersex', 'Allies', 'Asexual', 'Pansexual' — whatever the reigning acronyms of the moment. Users view these acronyms as political statements, implying that they don't want to be frozen as 'binary', or simply identified by their sexual preferences. And then there is the hate-filled acronym TERF.

Sometimes I use the term 'gender' interchangeably with 'transgender'. In her insightful book *Gender Hurts*, Sheila Jeffreys chronicles the history of the feminist understanding of gender and its reversal. Before the word gender was widely adopted, "the term more usually used to describe these socially constructed characteristics was 'sex roles'" (Jeffreys, 2014, p. 4). This was the term that I used throughout my early book on transsexualism.

Jeffreys observes that the term 'sex roles' is not as susceptible to "the kind of corruption that has afflicted the term 'gender' and enabled it to be wielded so effectively by transgender activists." Gradually, feminists extended the term gender not only to focus on socially constructed behavior, but on what was called "the system of male power and women's subordination itself, which became known as the 'gender hierarchy' or 'gender order'" (Jeffreys, 2014, p. 4).

As terms like 'male domination' and 'subordination of women' went out of fashion, the agents of women's oppression became invisible, as if it were impolitic to mention men, and especially men who appear as women. Jeffreys wrote that the word 'gender' became a euphemism that disappeared men as the agents in perpetrating violence against women. It also disappeared the term 'violence against women', now generally referred to as 'gender-based violence'. This allowed for official documents and forms to be switched from 'sex' to 'gender'. As Jeffreys puts it, gender became a "stand-in for the term 'sex' as if 'gender' itself is biological" (Jeffreys, 2014, p. 5).

There are other words in the trans vocabulary, some of which have made it into the mainstream media that are insulting to women. 'Cis-women' means natal women, but trans extremists don't even want to acknowledge that women are simply women. It seems to be only self-declared men who can claim to be women unmodified. The trans lexicon is full of other names that are offensive to women's ears such as 'menstruators', people with 'front holes', and — my favorite — 'non-men'.

Note that there are no similar modifiers that are applied to men. I have seldom heard the term cis-men, and never the terms 'back holes' and 'non-women'. And there is no acronym such as TERM that brands trans exclusionary radical men.

It has become politically correct for participants in progressive discussion forums to identify themselves by specifying which pronouns they prefer. Each person can choose from an ever-changing set of preferred gender or neutral pronouns (PGPs) such as 'he', 'she', 'they' in the singular, 'ze' or 'zie'. As one directive states, "Never, ever refer to a person as 'it' or 'he-she' (unless they specifically ask you to)." College presidents are even signing their letters stipulating their preferred pronouns. Oscar Wilde would have riffed that these folks get 'lexically aroused' by pronouns.

'Deadnaming' means we can't reference anyone's pre-trans life. Deadnaming is viewed almost as a criminal act that deserves some of the worst trans vitriol. And you are guilty of 'misgendering' if you dare to call a transitioned 'she' a bygone 'he', especially if you do it intentionally to indicate that no 'he' can become a 'she'. Dizzying, isn't it, and I was an English teacher in a past life!

Many people know that self-declared women are not identical to natal women but won't say so publicly because they fear being shunned as TERFs, bigots or oppressors of trans-identified persons. A number of people have expressed this fear to me privately at various forums or in emails stating, "I admire your courage," but then confess they can't challenge trans ideology openly since they have too much to lose and fear being called transphobic. The numbers of individuals and institutions that have come to accept transgender threats and harassment as normal when aimed at trans critics, especially feminists, have propped up the trans campaign by demonizing the radical feminist opposition and branding it as transphobic.

I have always been critical of the word 'phobia', defined as an irrational or persistent fear of some thing or situation, but often misused to signal hatred of a particular group. Radical critics of transgenderism are not afraid of trans-identified persons nor do we hate them. As writer Suzanne Moore has made clear, "We fear what we have always feared: male violence, in whatever cosplay it chooses. We fear losing our incomes. We fear that womanhood is such a scary place that some young women will be medicated out of it" (Moore, 2020).

What we do hate is the violence, perpetrated by many self-declared women and their allies, against women who reject trans ideology and unwanted sexual overtures.

'Transphobic' is an easy word to throw at someone because the label sticks. Branding a person transphobic appears to rank with being called a racist or fascist. When labels turn people into fearful bystanders incapable of expressing an honest opinion, not just individuals but also institutions are given permission to disparage women, and governments are emboldened to draft (and pass) legislation that codifies gender tyranny and erases women's rights. Many people want to remain ignorant, not the ignorance of innocence, but a chosen ignorance that wills not to know.

It has always struck me as patronizing when intelligent people caution, in a discussion of transgender, that we must distinguish between trans extremists and the alleged majority of trans-identified persons and activists who do not participate in attacks on women. I think of the multiple times feminists have been reprimanded for speaking about misogyny and, predictably, someone would insist, "not all men are like that." Or they might accuse us of hating men when the actual problem is woman-hating.

Gender critical feminists know the transgender community is not a monolithic group. Of course, trans misogynists don't represent the views of everyone. A number of trans-identified persons and their allies — but not enough of them — have criticized the misogyny in their own communities. However, the increasing number of trans cyber and physical attacks on women and lesbians, and the evolving trans ideology that supports these attacks, has come to define the trans movement's political goals.

Be Polite?

People say they just want to be polite by using the language that trans-identified persons call themselves. Journalist and professor Robert Jensen reports that in his conversations with those who use this reasoning, they are at pains not to hurt the feelings of trans individuals. "Sensitivity to others is appropriate, but should it trump attempts to understand an issue? Is it respectful of trans people to not speak about these matters ... based on the belief that the people in the trans community aren't emotionally equipped to discuss the intellectual and political assertions they make?" (Jensen, 2016).

I do not use the pronoun 'she' to describe self-declared women and 'he' to describe self-declared men. I don't believe it is polite to call people something they are not. I wouldn't call a white person Black even if, like Rachel Dolezal, the US woman who insisted she is Black, the person wants to be so named.

What is at stake in the transgender conflict is not just an individual person's 'feeling'. Rather, this anti-woman and anti-feminist ideology is having a far-reaching impact on legislation normalizing that men can be women, often with no input from women who would be harmed by the legislation. Unfortunately, where transgender legislation is on the docket, public opinion lags behind public policy.

We are increasingly bidden to call men women and women men, thereby conforming our language to trans requirements. But when gender ideology infiltrates the legal system, pronouns cannot simply be treated as just a matter of politeness, particularly where the evidence points to the way pro-trans organizations are insinuating themselves into drafting court pronoun policy. In 2020, the British Columbia (BC) Supreme Court issued a 'practice directive' stipulating that all parties appearing in court would be asked to specify what pronouns they want others to use when they are being addressed. "Under this policy, declaring one's pronouns is required when people introduce themselves in court whether they present in keeping with their biological sex or not." If persons appearing before the Court don't specify what "my pronouns are," they will be prompted by a court clerk or judge to comply (Litzcke, 2021).

The policy was presented as promoting 'inclusive behavior' but it sounds more like 'compelling behavior'. The BC bar had not been asked for input and only one group of lawyers belonging to the Sexual Orientation and Gender Identity Committee (SOGIC) had been involved in the drafting. The court "developed the policy with the help of SOGIC," which then served as the media point person for the policy, thereby becoming the public relations arm of the court. When the Chief Justice of the BC Provincial Court was pressed on the implications of the policy, she responded that questioners should go to SOGIC for answers (Litzcke, 2021).

As journalist Karin Litzcke points out: "On more than one occasion, a judge has used male pronouns to refer to girls whose proposed sex change was itself the issue under review. Why have a judicial proceeding at all if a judge's very language indicates that the outcome has already been decided?" (Litzcke, 2021). These changes are taking place in a larger context of court decisions that were settled in favor of children who wanted to transition against the wishes of their parents and "raises questions of whether courts are being co-opted by an ideological movement whose dictates now serve to trump principle of law" (Litzcke, 2021).

In New York City, a business or employer can be fined up to $250,000 for intentionally and repeatedly 'mispronouning' trans-identified persons (New York City, 2002). But you can call a woman 'intentionally and repeatedly' a 'bitch' or a 'cunt' and it won't be accepted and codified as the hate speech that it truly is.

The Ontario Canada Human Rights Commission passed a policy in 2014 stating, "Refusing to refer to a trans person by their chosen name and a personal pronoun that matches their gender identity, or purposely misgendering, will likely be discrimination when it takes place in a social area covered by the *Code*, including employment, housing and services like education" (Ontario Human Rights, 2014).

Yet women do not have similar rights when we are misnamed as 'cis-women', 'menstruators', 'front holes', 'people with cervixes' and 'non-men'. We champion a *Feminism Unmodified* as Catharine MacKinnon has written (1987), although these days she doesn't seem to accept that 'feminism unmodified' must stand on the shoulders of 'females unmodified', i.e. women who refuse to be defined by men.

In progressive organizations, violence against men who identify as women has captured a lot of attention. This is not surprising since men's issues — from men's sports to men who declare as women — usually do command much of the public's notice and resources while women's issues historically have hovered in the background. Men who identify as women are now capturing a primary place in the history of women.

Violence against Trans-Identified Persons

When I told a colleague that I was writing a book chapter on male violence against trans-identified persons, she thought I meant violence directed against trans-identified women (men). She is on the staff of a domestic violence center, and most of the trans victims she helps are men who identify as women. She sees how badly trans women (men) are violated, but I have never heard her mention the violent plight of any woman who identifies as a 'trans man'.

For five years, the Human Rights Campaign (HRC) has tracked reports of 'fatal anti-transgender violence'. But these reports don't log the violence and sexual exploitation that women who identify as men experience, only reporting the violence against men who identify as women. The 2020 HRC report documents that 37 transgender or 'gender non-binary' persons were fatally killed, most of whom were Black and Latino trans-identified women (men) (Human Rights Campaign, 2020a). I suspect the violence directed against women who identify as men or as gender non-binary is a sensitive issue since most of the violence is perpetrated by trans-identifed or gender non-binary men who populate LGBT+ affinity groups.

In Portland, Oregon, journalist Monica Roberts has asked about the trans murders in her community, "who is killing these women and why?" Paige Kreisman, a Portland political organizer who identifies as a woman has found these killings were not random hate crimes where bands of roving fascists seek to murder 'trans women' but rather, "statistically speaking, the most common perpetrators of violence against trans women are domestic partners ... assailants are often aware that their partner is trans; claiming trans panic can be a way for them to avoid admitting they were knowingly attracted to another man who identifies as a trans woman." Most 'trans women' that Kreisman knew were killed by men who knew they were trans (Woodstock, 2020).

In reading this Portland news article and the HRC Report, I wanted to know where the HRC acknowledgment is about violence against women who identify as men. I looked at the HRC website and perused the organization's earlier reports. Nothing. I did a limited search of violence against 'trans men' but couldn't find mention of such violence, but articles kept appearing with reports on violence against 'transwomen'.

With the aid of gender critical blogs, I found online sites that threatened vicious and violent attacks on women, some who were lesbian and gender non-conforming, and some who identified as trans men. A lesbian activist introduced me to a wealth of testimonies of women who once moved in LGBT+ circles and the magnitude of the sexual exploitation of women in these communities, most of it perpetrated by men who identify as women, 'trans lesbians', gender queer, or gender non-binary. Sexual exploitation involved rape, sexual assault and other forms of sexual violence. The activist, speaking as a survivor of male violence perpetrated by men who identify as women, described the persistent presence of male violence in LGBT+ circles. Many survivors of this particular brand of male violence have published their courageous stories in a recent book entitled, *You Told Me You Were Different: An Anthology of Harm* (Kitty Robinson, ed, 2021).

Since the violence against women is perpetrated by men in LGBT+ groups that identify as women in some way, this seems to be one reason we hear so little about this violence and sexual exploitation, and why groups like the Human Rights Campaign won't touch it.

Violence against women by men who identify as women, or as gender non-binary men, is the grimy little secret of the trans movement where women's testimonies are subject to the code of omerta, a code of silence and secrecy that forbids members from betraying their 'brothers'.

Survivors of this violence have reported that women who break this rule of silence about men's violence against women are haunted by the accusation that they are "contributing to the myth of the predatory trans woman," if they speak about the violence done to them. They are told, "even if it's true ... you shouldn't say it" (Kitty Robinson, 2021, p. vii), a flagrant abdication of moral responsibility. The endemic violence against women in these groups is covered up by the 'rape apologism' that excuses it.

In the book *You Told Me You Were Different: An Anthology of Harm*, the editor writes about this "powerful silencing tactic, one that kept many of us silent & trapped for a long time," along with the charge that female victims were contributing to the deaths of self-declared women — 'killing trans women' — if they spoke out about these crimes. "When someone who has been victimized by a male trans person believes that male trans people are the most stigmatized, oppressed, at-risk people on the earth, the act of staying silent about your abuse is positioned as the only morally good option" (Kitty Robinson, 2021, p. viii).

Amplifying the Voices of Survivors of Male Violence against Women

Increasing numbers of those who are now transitioning are young girls on a path to becoming trans-identified men. However, the largest number of desisters and de-transitioners is also girls and young women who have rejected their trans status — many have written eloquently about it. On various online sites and in a few brave books, women who formerly identified as 'trans men' speak movingly about this severance from themselves and other women, their escape from compulsive femininity, their sexual abuse and assaults, the misogyny they experienced growing up, and their journeys in recovering their womanhood (see Max Robinson, 2021, and Chapter 3).

As the #MeToo movement has made men accountable for their abuses of women, principled people have a responsibility to make self-declared women responsible for their ugly behavior. There are trans-identified women who have been honest and articulate stating unequivocally that they are not women and separating themselves from the claims of womanhood expressed by a large segment of the trans community. Unfortunately, this does not change the fact that there is a substantial number of self-declared women and their allies who do attack women with the most vicious language and who want to erase 'woman' by deleting the word from any group or organization that features 'woman' in its title or mission statement.

One of the goals of this book is to amplify the voices of women who have been harmed by the doublethink of transgenderism and to recognize them as survivors of male sexual violence, many of whom identified as trans men, gender non-binary, or queer.

Testimonies of survivors, who have been sexually exploited, raped and violated, have been crucial to other movements such as the feminist anti-trafficking and abolitionist prostitution movement. Survivors are the authoritative voices of women harmed by transgender ideology, practices, and outright sexual violence.

When not censored, websites, blogs, press releases and articles that represent survivors' experiences have been key to public recognition. In their writings and activism, survivors of trans violence against women expose the truth about the transgender industry. They, more than anyone, can unmask the myths about an industry that is severely damaging women and children. Survivors are beginning to speak out as individuals and jointly in challenging the orthodoxies of the transgender empire.

Language Used in This Book

In discussing the wording that I use to refer to those who identify as trans, I do not want to become a language czar comparable to the trans pronoun police. In *The Transsexual Empire*, I created the term, 'male-to-constructed female,' to illustrate the fabrication of trans identities. However, for all its truth-value, this term proved unwieldy and doesn't easily slide off the tongue, or the keyboard.

In some places of the book, I choose the terms 'transitioners' or 'trans-identified men or women', or 'male-bodied women' or 'female-bodied men' and make a judgment call about which of these terms is more appropriate and sheds more clarity on the writing. In other places where the sex is not clear, I add in parentheses the natal sex of the person, for example, 'trans-identifed woman' (man).

Very rarely do I use the terms 'trans persons', 'trans women' or 'trans men' because these words imply that the process of transitioning is a *real* transformation from one sex to the other. It serves to legitimate trans ideology. I do use these terms when quoting. And because most people still use these terms, I retain them in certain contexts to lessen confusion.

I favor the critical honesty of such terms as 'self-declared woman' or 'self-declared man', which challenge trans claims of being 'born in the wrong body' and more clearly describe the self-affirmation involved in transitioning. And where a longer term is warranted, I will write "men who identify as women." But not to worry, I won't 'misnoun' anyone if for some reason, they choose to utilize other terms.

And I use the terms 'gender-critical', 'gender abolitionist', 'gender non-conforming' and 'gender non-compliant'.

∞

In his book *1984*, George Orwell referred to the dystopian land of Oceania's manipulation of language as 'newspeak', the foundation of *doublethink*. His protagonist Winston Smith explained: "Doublethink means holding two contradictory beliefs in one's mind simultaneously ... To tell deliberate lies while genuinely believing in them ... to deny the existence of objective reality ..." (Orwell, pp. 176–77). This is the situation in which many believers/ disbelievers of trans doctrines find themselves in today, as they confront a language that has corrupted reality and a gender industry that sustains it.

Why can't we have an informed and honest conversation in public institutions such as libraries and universities rather than demonizing radical feminist critics and others who won't conform to newspeak? We can't have any conversation when one side — the dissenters from transgenderism — have been labelled transphobic before a dissenter even begins to speak, or are censored by public institutions whose duty it is to encourage free speech. Trans activists seem afraid of debate.

Why should publishers be reluctant to publish articles and books that criticize transgenderism when it is part of their job to encourage critical thinking? In the United States, the record shows that few critiques of transgenderism make it into the commercial book market and mainstream media such as *The New York Times*, and are scarcely found even in progressive electronic journals and university book markets. Thus readers are not aware of the substantial opposition to transgender ideology and issues, the abuse, harassment and violence that have overtaken it, and what is at stake if anyone can now self-declare his or her sex.

Because trans activists are primarily promoting the rights of men who identify as women, much of the trans movement is rapidly becoming part of the larger men's rights movement. The 'trans lesbian' groups that demonize lesbians for rejecting their sexual advances bear comparison to the incel movement, a support group for dissatisfied men who blame women for their dateless status called 'involuntary celibacy', one of the internet's most dangerous cybercultures.

Within the public at large, transgenderism is not well understood. Few are aware what surgical 'reassignment' entails and what is happening to children, among them a rising number of young girls who are being 'treated' in gender identity clinics for alleged gender dysphoria, put on puberty blockers, and encouraged to start hormone treatments at puberty. Most people don't know there is an international debate, especially about medicalizing children who say they are 'born in the wrong body'.

Bystanders may experience genuine concern for youth who are wrestling with their gender identities, and some may believe the trans propaganda that only medicalization will save youth from a worse fate like suicide, but they are not aware of the consequences of a runaway ideology and industry of transgenderism. Nor does the ordinary person understand the costs of legalizing self-identification. Parents are not aware of curricula in their children's schools that 'affirm' a child's new gender identity, and that facilitate a child's hormone treatments without parental consent.

In this book, I have tried to represent facets of the transgender issue that many people may not be aware of. I suspect that most people don't read the various blogs that are concerned with these issues. Although much of this information will be familiar to feminists and others who have long disagreed with transgender orthodoxies, we need to cast the essentials of the feminist critique out to a wider net of people who can understand just what is at stake in this conflict.

CHAPTER ONE

The New Trans Biologism: Female Brains and Female Penises

The meanings we create or learn do not exist only in our heads, in ineffable ideas. Our meanings also exist in our bodies — what we are, what we do, what we physically feel, what we physically know; and there is no personal psychology that is separate from what the body has learned about life.

—Andrea Dworkin, *Intercourse*

In 1979, I wrote that men cannot become women, or women men, via hormones and/or surgery — not only because women or men are born female or male but because of the history, life experience and privilege (male) or discrimination (female) of what it means to grow up in a male or female body.

Amputating a healthy penis or breasts, being dependent on cross-sex hormones, and often embarking on secondary surgical journeys to alter voice or appearance, is a walking tribute to the power of patriarchal definitions of masculinity and femininity, which teach all of us that in a gender-defined culture it is easier to change your body than to change your society.

The traditional understanding of gender was shaped by conservative patriarchal powers. If born a boy, you were allegedly gifted with a biologically assertive and aggressive gender, and if born a girl, you got the crumbs from the master's table — a passive and emotional set of gendered qualities that were to be used mainly in service to men and male-dominant priorities. The traditional gender chart positioned you according to how well you conformed to masculine or feminine standards of behavior. And if women especially failed to take their proper place in the gender hierarchy, they could be subjected to the worst forms of male violence.

In the conservative calculus, gender roles were based on biology and could not be changed by individuals without in some way being punished for it. This punishment fell hardest on gender non-compliant women — many of them feminists and lesbians — who were disciplined for being different and for adopting 'masculine' behavior, considered a hard-wired set of traits intrinsic to male biology. To the extent that men also violated their gendered behavior, they too were chastised but not usually subjected to the sexual violence that women experienced. And if those men who identified as women did experience sexual violence, they were treated *as women are treated.*

Transgenderism is a contrived ideology born of a regressive biologism that, in its latest version, champions men who claim female brains and female penises. It's a rogue idea, an unscrupulous philosophy that, to modify Virginia Woolf's words, serves as a looking glass "possessing the magic and delicious power of reflecting the figure of man" back to himself as the woman he aspires to be (Woolf, 1929, p. 35). Self-declared women (men) spend a lot of time in front of any mirror that reflects their idealized women back to themselves.

The promotion of transgender has become a progressive cause with strong backing from groups who now view it as 'woke'. Progressive organizations have reversed sex and gender, meekly shadowing trans advocates who assert that gender is sex and sex is gender, and thus helping to establish 'gender' as a primary identifier on passports, driving licenses and other official documents replacing sex. 'Sex' is now considered as something to be altered by hormones, surgery or self-declaration.

In *The Transsexual Empire*, I quoted transsexual Angela Douglas who proclaimed:

> Genetic women are becoming quite obsolete, which is obvious, and the future belongs to transsexual women. We know this, and perhaps some of you suspect it. All you have left is your ability to bear children, and in a world which will groan to feed 6 billion by the year 2000, that's a negative asset (Douglas, 1977).

Some have said this was satire, but Douglas dismissed this interpretation. After serving as an FBI informant whose trans surgery left 'her' mutilated, he later reverted to his male status and lived as a homeless man until his death in 2007.

The trans movement today is demanding that women's organizations, especially those concerned with women's health, don't reference parts of the female body because self-declared women feel excluded. Trans activists insist that these groups change references to women's vaginas or breast-feeding and instead call women 'front holes' or 'chest feeders'. Yet it's OK for self-declared women to be preoccupied with natal women's reproductive functions in their quest for womb transplants and ability to breast feed, in trans speak known as 'chest feeding'. Others define natal women as 'menstruators, egg producers, breeders, uterus owners, or non-men', terms that degrade and dehumanize and reduce women to body parts. When feminists resist, we are decried as transphobes. We have come to a point where even those who 'identify' as feminists seem eager to cede the definition of woman to men.

Trans academic and extremist Joelle Ruby Ryan wrote that the term 'female' is offensive, outmoded, sexist and exclusionary (in Keith and Jensen, 2013). Then why seek female status if you have just declared the term offensive and obsolete? Ryan as a self-declared woman feels entitled to appropriate a womanhood that he just scorned, announcing that it is self-declared women who are the rightful women who will usher in a new day.

The irony of this more contemporary wave of men seeking confirmation of their status as women is that they seem to abhor the female bodies of natal women, except when they want to wear one and 'do' woman better. The extremist transgender movement is one more masculinist attempt to colonize women in the interest of appropriating the female body for one's self. It's a superficial preoccupation with women's body parts and with women's bodily functions — not a respect for women's selves.

Trying to 'become' a woman (or a man) affirms, not challenges, the gender binary that trans activists say they have abandoned. If there are no sex categories of male and female, and only a concept of malleable gender expressed as an identity, then the notion of trans becomes contradictory. If there's no biological sex such as male or female, then the terms 'cis' and 'trans' lose their meaning because these modifiers have to modify something.

Transgender claims can affect all our lives. Once biology and the history and experiences of what it means to live in a sexed body is rejected, there is no touchstone especially for children, who are left with the confusion of picking a gender. This confusion encourages a regression to sex-role stereotypes because it's the sex-role markers that are out there and easier to grab onto, the confusion ratified by the effects of puberty blockers and cross-sex hormones. If you like trucks and want to be a fire fighter, you're a boy. If you like dolls and dress up in frilly clothes, you're a girl.

Self-declared women explain the origin of their gender identity by claiming they possess biological female brains. Or, if these men seek to be recognized as lesbians, they claim to sport a 'female penis' that some call 'lady sticks'. They disparage biological womanhood but then locate their need to transgender in their alleged female brains or in some mysterious essence of femininity.

Gender can't become biology because men who claim they were born with a female brain have not lived in female bodies, bodies that carry the history and experiences of oppression common to women across cultures. Women retain not only a common biology but also a unique history as an oppressed class that no man has lived through. Men can't self-identify their way out of their own bodies, history and life experiences into any meaningful definition of womanhood.

Biology trumps transgender in the doctor's office. Personal health history begins with biology but is also influenced by social, political and economic factors, all of which are key to the medical problems that men and women experience in a lifetime. When trans-identified persons seek medical treatment, they have to 'deadname' themselves and reveal they are either a biological male or female. As we grow older, the aging process is a reality check during which gender confronts the health challenges of one's biological corporeality.

For years, women's health advocates have campaigned for women's inclusion in medical research studies and drug trials to ascertain sex-specific risks and reactions. There are multiple health issues that differ by sex, which went unnoticed in earlier medical research.

Women may experience different heart attack symptoms than men. Women and men may react differently to some medications. One study found that "Men who received donor blood from women who had ever been pregnant had a significantly higher mortality rate compared to those who received blood from other men, or women who had never been pregnant" (Starr, 2017). Women have a greater prevalence of autoimmune diseases that are associated with pregnancy or during an extensive hormonal change. When trans persons change their sex identifiers, emergency medical providers may not be able to know immediately the sex of a patient that could delay life-saving medical treatment (Angum, 2020).

When physicians and other clinicians encourage children and adults to undergo transition medicine, it puts these persons in harm's way. As I have written, "No man can have the history of being born and located in this culture as a woman. He can have the history of *wishing* to be a woman and of *acting* like a woman, but this gender experience is that of a transsexual, not of a woman" (Raymond, 1979, p. 114).

This does not mean that there are no differences in women across cultures. It does mean that men cannot claim they are brain-wired as women. That claim comes from the head of Zeus, the mythical god who 'birthed' Athena from his forehead after swallowing her mother Metis, foreshadowing the post-modern mythology of trans biological essentialism.

Science and Pseudo-Science

In *The Transsexual Empire*, I spent an entire chapter disputing the biologism of sexologist and psychologist John Money who at the time was especially influential in promoting a pre-natal theory of gender identity formation in which hormones activate the brain and set the direction of sex differences. Money stated, "Once a sex distinction has worked or been pressured into the nuclear core of your gender schema, to dislodge it is to threaten you as an individual with destruction" (Raymond, 1979, pp. 63–64). Money's genderism flies in the face of feminist theory and activism that challenges the immutability of gendered differences.

Money's work on gender identity formation has led to the more recent rationalizations of the transgendered female brain (although he didn't invent the female penis). As Lierre Keith has eloquently written:

> The strangest part of this whole debate is that feminists are being called biological essentialists … White supremacists are the only people who believe in the 'Negro brain'. But talk of 'lady brains' is completely accepted across progressive communities if it comes from genderists … It's the genderists who claim it's biologically immutable … Yet we are called essentialist? (Keith and Jensen, 2013).

Misty Snow, a Democratic candidate from Utah who ran in the US 2016 Senate elections as a self-declared woman asserts, without citing any evidence, "There is a lot of science that supports the fact that male and female brains are different and respond to hormones differently" (Hedges, 2017). To the contrary, there is *not* a 'lot of evidence' that supports the notion of female and male brains. Brain science provides no proof in defence of the gendered brain.

In a 2019 book entitled *Gender and Our Brains*, author Gina Rippon, a British professor of cognitive neuro imaging, reviews the history of gendered brain studies and examines the recent 'science' on brain differences between females and males. Her key thesis is that scientific knowledge of brain plasticity casts doubt on any 'evidence' of biological differences in female and male brains because boys and girls are treated differently from birth and any variances that do exist don't show up in brain imaging. Imaging of brain activity shows no gendered difference at any age, proving that any alleged evidence about gendered brain differences is in effect dubious. "Rather than 'limitations' imposed by biology' we are looking at restrictions imposed by society"(Rippon, p. 92). You can't examine a brain and distinguish between a girl's brain or a boy's brain, or as I would phrase it, gender may reside in one's head but not in one's brain.

When asked to explain so-called evidence that men can be women, trans activists often allege a wider range of biological sex than simply male or female. Their claim is that scientists now believe that sex is no longer binary but exists on a broader continuum. Trans activists claim biological kinship with intersex persons who have ambiguous sex characteristics, misusing their status to conclude that transgendering persons are the living embodiment of an evolving sex spectrum.

However, only a miniscule percentage of the population is intersex, and intersex persons do not identify as transgender. To be on a spectrum of sex, you would have to demonstrate that a substantial part of the population is intersex and that these individuals are born with chromosomal and/or hormonal anomalies. As biologists Colin Wright and Emma Hilton have written, "… intersex individuals are extremely rare, and they are neither a third sex nor proof that sex is a 'spectrum' or a 'social construct'" (Wright and Hilton, 2020).

Scientists can also be susceptible to transgender pressure to deny empirical facts. A shameful example of denial is the number of medical practitioners who are ready to fast-track affirmation of healthy young transitioning children, prescribing puberty blockers and cross-sex hormones that could cause lifelong infertility. During the eugenics eras, scientists produced 'evidence' that promoted racial inferiority, using the 'proof' of 'scientific' experiments that sterilized vulnerable populations and left many infertile. Government support conveniently accommodated 'scientific' programs and propaganda to justify legislation whose purpose was to eliminate the 'unfit'. As

Donna Hughes has written, "The eugenics movement to breed a better race of people was a fantasy: so too is the trans-sex movement" (Hughes, 2021).

There are scientific outliers writing today in the *Lancet*, *Nature* and *Scientific American* that challenge the binary notion of biological sex lending credence to the idea that men can be women. For example, a 2018 editorial appearing in *Nature* argues, "The research and medical community now sees sex as more complex than male and female, and gender as a spectrum that includes transgender people and those who identify as neither male nor female" (Editorial, 2018).

The *Nature* editorial triggered a letter to the editor signed by scientists associated with the Royal Academy of Medicine in Ireland who stated the following:

> Of particular concern to us is the sight of respected scientific publications, such as *Nature*, now beginning to echo these popular trends ... We regard the claim that sex is neither fixed nor binary to be entirely without scientific merit ... Such politically motivated policies and statements have no place in scientific journals (Hilton et al, 2021).

How ironic that Donald Trump's disregard for science has taken root in progressive circles. If progressive groups continue to assert that there is no biological definition of woman or man, then they cannot credibly fault conservatives for attacking science when conservatives deny, for example, climate change. In their denials, many progressive organizations are erasing the lived experience of women when they reinforce the view that anyone who self-declares as a woman is valid and should be acknowledged as such.

Self-declared women are not women, and attempts to define themselves as such are bogus. Pretending that the female body and the experience of living as a woman are irrelevant — but should be accessible to men — is insulting to women.

Gender identity and so-called gender dysphoria have no biological basis other than what a corporate medicalized system has helped create with its gender identity clinics, treatment guidelines, hormone therapy, surgery for those who want it, and a lengthy history of supporting genderism.

The Medicalizing of Gender: Transsexualism Meets Transgenderism

Gender identity dissatisfaction has been thoroughly medicalized just as much under the new transgender regime as it was under the old transsexual empire. Key to the more recent normalizing of transgender treatment is its development as a clinical entity now requiring only minimal evaluation of self-declaration before proceeding to hormones and surgical intervention, all focused on children.

When doctors and therapists medicalized transsexualism in the 1970s, they played a large role in removing it from public debate, and smothered ethical and political discussion about it. The medical model had a profound influence on the way that people viewed transsexualism. Transsexualism as a medical specialty in a medical empire created the disease of gender dysphoria, and brooked no outside interference or public criticism. If one's basic approach to gender identity is from a psychological and medical basis, then many moral issues, as well as sociopolitical, economic, and environmental problems are transformed into technical problems. And the kind of 'health' values it generates do not encourage a would-be transitioner to recognize that such 'health' may be *unhealthy* in the long run.

Ironically, removing transsexualism from the medical realm actually encouraged trans self-identification. Rejecting transgender as a pathology, self-identifiers began to separate themselves from the medical model and criticize 'dated' clinic requirements. These constraints included proof of ability to pass as women and live in the desired gender for a period of two years. Self-declaration also displaces ethical scrutiny.

However, this severance from the medical model was not total, and the transgender industry failed to fold, because many new trans self-identifiers soon found they needed hormones to achieve their goals of performing masculinity or femininity. Others wanted surgery, but minus the ancien régime's doctor-directed requirement of long-term evaluation. The number of trans self-identifiers increased as prerequisites decreased.

The modern transgender landscape is just as medicalized as the old transsexual empire, but its major clientele is now youth. Like the old system, the new system is dominated by benevolent claims of saving children with gender 'dysphoria' from self-mutilation and suicide if they don't promptly obtain treatment. And big pharma has grown bigger with the onset of the children's market for hormones and surgery. Gender therapists are now promoting transitioning as a 'solution' to childhood gender dissatisfaction, a misguided narrative that leads to rapid affirmation of child self-identification followed by initial treatment with puberty blockers, and later, cross-sex hormones.

The gender identity clinics established for adults seeking sex change in the 1970s and 80s have fast proliferated and have now spawned centers for children, many of them hospital-based. I anticipated that, "As the gender identity clinics expand and the tolerance for transsexual surgery grows, it is conceivable that such clinics could become sex-role control centers ... for the treatment of designated child transsexuals" (Raymond, 1979, p. 136). This has now happened, and 'transitioning' has become a synonym for sex role conformity medicine, which reinforces the patriarchal system that thrives on gender stereotyping.

In the old gender identity centers, clinicians treated mostly young males considered gender 'misfits', whose parents were distressed about their sons' expressions of effeminacy. Parents expected the treatments would enforce conformity to masculinity and fit the boys into the traditional gendered hierarchy.

Although self-declaration no longer requires medical involvement, the new therapeutic model is still a disease model. Affirming young children's gender 'dysphoria' requires a 'therapeutic' regime of puberty blockers, opposite sex hormones and, for some, surgery.

'Dysphoria' is a medical term used to describe the feeling of dissatisfaction with a person's male or female body that is felt so intensely that it interferes with normal life and creates a pathway to medical interventions.

Medical treatments are rampant in gender identity clinics in which gender affirmation often requires a cascade of medical treatments. Practitioners promote gender identity affirmation in which the therapist dispenses with comprehensive evaluations, takes on the role of implementing the child's (or parents') wishes, and avoids gatekeeping the entrance to the new transgender empire.

Recent evidence has confirmed that puberty blockers stunt growth and impair the bone mass density of children who were subjected to the treatment. A nine-year study followed 44 children, aged 12–15, who underwent treatment for gender dysphoria at the Tavistock Clinic in Britain. They found that when puberty blockers were discontinued at age 16, there was some 'reduced growth' in height and bone strength (Carmichael et al, 2021).

For years, trans activists and many clinicians asserted that puberty blockers were 'fully reversible', but the Tavistock Clinic has since updated its guidelines to say the long-term impact on brains and bones is unknown. In November 2020, Tavistock discontinued treatment with puberty blockers for children after the High Court found it was 'unlikely' that children under 16 could give informed consent to these drugs. The decision was the result of a case submitted by Keira Bell, now 23, who had received puberty blocker treatment when she was under 16 and was prescribed testosterone one year later. When puberty blockers are followed by cross-sex hormones, they can cause lifelong infertility. These hormones also increase risks of cancer, liver damage, diabetes, blood clots, strokes and heart problems (Kersten, 2019).

Following the UK path of desisting from using puberty blockers and cross-sex hormones for children, Sweden's Karolinska Hospital has announced it will no longer use them in its pediatric gender services to patients under the age of 18 (SEGM, 2021). This is a breaking point when a major and internationally known hospital acknowledges the risks of treatments that it has prescribed for years and recognizes their potential for harm. The significance of this decision will hopefully prompt other centers to examine their policies of quick affirmation of medical interventions for minors and question the ethics of such treatments.

Unfortunately, the medicalization of children has not been halted yet in most western countries that practice gender medicine. The rush to affirm children's gender non-conforming behavior and treat it with questionable puberty blockers, and cross-sex hormones, is about as medicalized as it gets. Parents are expected to conform to a clinic's speedy schedule of gender affirmation, whether they raise objections or not. In the age of transsexualism, gender dissatisfaction was treated as gender aberration. In the age of transgenderism, it's treated with gender affirmation.

'Gender identity disorder' can be contrasted to similar body-based behaviors such as anorexia and bulimia. In the case of those who counsel children with anorexia, for example, therapists take a long-term view warning (mostly) girls about the harmful consequences of their 'dis-ease' such as low bone density and loss of teeth enamel. The counselor is there not to accept uncritically the views of her/his patients, or baptize the body image of slender girls who think they are obese. And parents are encouraged to take the lead in treatment, not affirm their child's obsession with thinness, or with other unhealthy and dangerous rituals of self-destruction like vomiting and laxatives that girls use to force their bodies to conform to their body fantasies. In the case of gender identity, however, self-perception is sanctified and counselors become deluded cheerleaders of a child's rapid gender affirmation.

For most gender transitioners who desire full affirmation of their cross-sexed bodies, the process still requires some degree of medicalization, such as hormones that help reconfigure the body to wanted and sometimes unwanted body changes. For others, surgery is still on their menu. Although persons who self-declare as trans may not go through all of the medical procedures transsexuals underwent in the past, many are still subject to the risks and complications resulting from long-term hormone treatments.

People may not understand how extreme and irreversible hormonal treatment and surgery are. Males who want to transition are treated with estrogen, which increases the potential for breast cancer. If surgery follows hormones, males can undergo the removal of a healthy penis and castration, followed by more exogenous lifelong hormonal treatments. The skin of the penis can be inverted and used to create an artificial vagina, which then has to be kept open by daily insertion of an object for hours.

Women who identify as males may undergo surgery to remove a healthy uterus (hysterectomy) and ovaries (oophorectomy) and vagina (vaginectomy), all euphemized in newspeak as 'bottom surgery', as well as a bilateral mastectomy called 'top surgery'. Phalloplasty, the construction of an artificial penis, is not satisfactory in most cases because it is very complex, needs a long recovery time, and the results are often not aesthetically pleasing to the transitioner or others.

Both sexes often undergo multiple secondary surgeries to bring the body more in line with their idealized gendered appearance. When the outcome of the surgeries is less than expected, dissatisfaction may result in further frustration and drive a disappointed seeker to undertake more alterations of the body that may ultimately end in regret.

Scott Newgent, a trans-identified man (woman) who transitioned at age 42, creates a picture of the 'brutal process' of undertaking phalloplasty:

> During my own transition, I had seven surgeries. I also had a massive pulmonary embolism, a helicopter life-flight ride, an emergency ambulance ride, a stress-induced heart attack, sepsis, a 17-month recurring infection due to using the wrong skin during a (failed) phalloplasty, 16 rounds of antibiotics, three weeks of daily IV antibiotics, the loss of all my hair, (only partially successful) arm reconstructive surgery, permanent lung and heart damage, a cut bladder, insomnia-induced hallucinations – oh and frequent loss of

consciousness due to pain from the hair on the inside of my urethra. All this led to a form of PTSD that made me a prisoner in my apartment for a year. Between me and my insurance company, medical expenses exceeded $900,000 (Newgent, 2020).

Newgent addresses not only the effects of surgery but also the long-term consequences of medical treatment. Hormonal therapy shortens lives and has been "associated with an increased risk of heart attacks, pulmonary embolisms, bone damage, liver and kidney failure and mental health complications." Warning parents of 'gender dysphoric' children not to be naively lured into "walking their children into gender-treatment centers," Newgent calls out the propaganda that features medicalization as the solution to child distress (Newgent, 2020).

It defies understanding that, after Newgent has listed all these dangerous consequences of 'his' own medical transitioning as an adult, as well as setting out some of the research and data that undercuts the pretty picture of trans treatments, Newgent tells us: "Medical transition is for adults," not for children, but in a contradictory sentence he relates how "as the years go on, reality sets in, and you have to face up to the reality of biological health, not to mention the health issues. This is not a life of glitter bombs" (Newgent, 2020).

There are few other medical settings in which major surgery is done on healthy organs and where the pathology is actually *created* by the treatments. In traditional medicine, an existing physical pathology is the reason for the treatment. In transgender medicine, the cart goes before the horse. Hormone treatments and surgeries are performed without reference to any traditional standard of bodily need that requires that organs are injured or ailing in some way before removal. In other words, there is no customary medical reason for hormone treatment and surgery. In medical ethical terms, these treatments were traditionally recognized as bodily mutilation and called iatrogenic, or doctor-induced disease.

Like its older counterpart of transsexualism, transgender has come to be defined as legitimate medical territory. As a wide swath of conduct and personal struggles are labelled as psychological problems or syndromes requiring medical solutions, all sorts of behaviors are treated with drugs, surgery and other technical means. More and more ethical and social conflicts are defined as medical problems when they are actually human problems in living incongruent with social norms. Approaching these problems from a disease perspective discourages a person who is dissatisfied with her or his body from seeing treatment in a social or political framework based on challenging gender and its expectations.

Is it beneficial to those seeking help that the only solutions they are offered are hormones and surgeries at odds with physical reality? Are such treatments the only avenue that relieves gender distress? Or should clinicians point the way for their patients to learn how to exist in their bodies that don't involve the risk of harmful consequences they may live to regret. The latter question can't be answered by medicine but rather is an ethical question about how to inhabit the body you were given.

Public philosopher Max Robinson analyzed her 'choice' to become a man.

> Where did this idea come from, that becoming a man was better than being myself? Transition was presented by other FTMs (female to male transgender people, otherwise known as trans men) as a cure for the distress I felt about being female. I saw myself inside the framework of gender dysphoria because of the basic assumptions that I needed fixing and that hating being female is something that can be medically cured through obscuring physical signs of femaleness. This approach to addressing a woman's distress around her sex relies on a fundamental lack of faith in the ability of gender non-compliant women to live meaningful lives. I 'chose' transition because I did not understand that life as a gender noncompliant lesbian was a real option (Robinson, 2021, pp. 7–8).

At first, Max writes, it felt good. She viewed transition as 'empowering'. She could dress as she wanted and wear clothes that confirmed her sense of masculinity. It felt good to have clinicians affirm her pain and distress. It felt good to look different and have strangers treat her as competent. But ultimately she came to realize that this was not meaningful empowerment.

No one told her that changing her viewpoint from medical to political and becoming a feminist could change

> … the entire framework in which the distress around my sex existed. There is little incentive for professionals to research or inform others about the relief that can be found far outside the relationship between medical provider and patient, relief that may indeed come in part from challenging the value of transitional medicine (Robinson, 2021, pp. 11–12).

Gender as Presentation

For men who identify as women, gender is a presentation, an exhibition of *feeling* like a woman in possession of a *female brain* and/or a *female penis*. The exhibition becomes noticeable with the medicalized aid of hormones and surgery, or by assertions of self-identification and the thrill of passing.

Unlike other actors, those who self-declare as trans are not participants in a discrete performance during which the audience suspends belief for the duration of the show. Rather, the audience is being commanded to suspend belief in perpetuity as a moral obligation and, in some jurisdictions, a legal imperative, where anyone who performs femininity and identifies as a woman is thus a woman. Trangenderism urges us to collude in this incineration of truth.

One survivor of male violence wrote that men's gender presentation as women feels like

> … watching children playing pretend, fueled by their imaginations into thinking they're dinosaurs or pirates or fairies, but these are grown adults, believing that if they do X or Y, that they can know what it is to be a woman as if they had been swaddled in pink from the day they were born. What a luxury it would be, to arrive to womanhood so late in the game (Eve, in Kitty Robinson ed, 2021, p. 108).

Self-declaration, hormones and surgery become political tranquilizers reinforcing gender conformity. In spite of the belief that transgenderism and transsexualism challenge gender role definitions, both actually reinforce conventional gender roles. They do so by fortifying society's norms of masculinity or femininity.

In an early 1978 women's movement publication, feminist artist and writer Jeannette Muzima lamented the thinking that, "[W]henever we feel different or strange, or as the 'other', ... we are conditioned to look inside ourselves to find the 'problem'. Something must be wrong with us, certainly not with the outside 'real world'" (Muzima, 1978).

'Men can be women' is such an audacious claim that it could only come from men who are models of male entitlement. When I asked some plainspoken women what they think of men who 'feel' they are women, one responder said that 'transwomen' want to define us. "I don't think any man can wipe away his masculinity and simply clothe himself with womanhood. Men cannot experience what women are by taking hormones or undergoing surgery." Another woman responded, "Their ideas about what constitutes a woman are very superficial" (pers. com., 2020).

Few of the people that I speak with about transgenderism really believe that men can become women. They might acquiesce in public and go along with the woke trans police who monitor the politics of gender so as not to be outed as transphobic, but in their hearts do not consider that self-declared women are really women. People are skeptics even where there is legislation, as in Canada or New York City, where a gender critic could suffer legal consequences if a person intentionally misgenders or mispronouns a trans person.

When we are compelled by law to call men women, we are forced into lying. In an era when lies have boldly become truths, we have no reason to believe in the lie that men can be women. There is no moral reason to call these lies truth, especially if one knows the lies are not true.

Responding to an excessive alleluia to genderism by Carol Hay that appeared in a *New York Times* feature, one reader (Zawicki) commented:

> At a time when women's reproductive rights are being taken away; where women are victims of rape and domestic violence; where women die in childbirth, why are we debating what it is to be a woman? The answer is, and always has been very simple: a woman is an adult human female (Hay, 2019).

Another reader (cfaye) warned:

> To gaslight women into believing that identifying as a woman is more real and more valid than being biologically female has its cruel side, and carries the potential to harm both women and trans people alike. This is not happening to men … where's the similar uproar about the definition of men? (Hay, 2019).

One answer to this last question is: because self-declared women (men) are afraid of other men and could never get away with the dictates they try to impose on natal women.

As self-declared women, many men say they *fear* using men's bathrooms, men's changing rooms, ending up in men's prisons and competing in men's sports. Trans activists cite the risk of physical harm to self-declared women in men's spaces as one justification for appropriating women's spaces, yet trans activists have no concern for natal women and girls who need our own safe spaces now threatened by legislation. If trans-identified women are afraid of men's spaces and increasingly being protected by legislation, why don't women who have been subjected to male violence throughout our lives, get the same legal protection?

Women in the United States had to fight for many years for women's bathrooms in public buildings. United Nations (UN) reports on female refugees and migrants highlight the need for separate women's toilets, and humanitarian workers in conflict zones presume that women are vulnerable to male violence without these facilities. But progressive organizations continue to ignore women's rightful need for single sex toilets, domestic violence centers and other separate venues. Instead they call out women and women's organizations as trans exclusionary radical feminists, i.e. as TERFs.

The Women's Liberation Front (WoLF), a US front line organization that "fights vigorously against the ongoing attack on the rights, privacy, and opportunities of women and girls," featured this statement in a Declaration of "No Confidence in LGB Movement Leadership":

> The advice given by development agencies to poorer nations looking to increase girls' literacy rates ... or reduce sexual assault rates in areas lacking toilet facilities is to provide safe sex-segregated toilet facilities. But this advice is turned on its head by gender activists who seem to think that men in majority white countries ... do not pose any kind of harassment risk to women ... and so don't need to be kept away from areas where we might be undressing (WoLF, n.d.).

Is it only men in refugee camps who perpetrate violence against women? Do we exempt men in whiter and richer countries, just because they declare themselves to be women and should get a pass into women's separate spaces? Should we presume that men who declare they are no longer men will not perpetrate violence against women if invited by law into women's toilets or women's dressing rooms? The presumption that only poor and migrant men violate women's spaces carries racist overtones when men anywhere can and do offend.

If we accept the claim that some men can identify themselves into womanhood, it is the beginning of no end as the boundaries of women's biology, history, and life experiences will prove assailable and the violations continue to multiply.

What Is a Woman?

In 2016, the Young Greens, a part of the UK Green party, used an old trope about women when they issued an invitation to 'non-men' to join their Facebook group. The negative response was immediate, but the Green Party Women came to the defense of the Young

Greens tweeting that, "Green Party Women, as a whole, are happy with terms such as 'non-men' to be used." As feminist Caroline Criado Perez countered, "Women are not non-men ... you do not include people by establishing men as default human" (Beale, 2016).

Feminism makes women proud of *who* we are.

Simone de Beauvoir wrote: "... if [woman] did not exist, men would have invented her." Far less quoted is the second part of de Beauvoir's statement that reads: "But she exists apart from men's inventiveness" (de Beauvoir, 1949, p. 174). The radical feminist critique of transgenderism is a testimony to women, who are neither the products of male conceit nor the man-made 'other' of de Beauvoir's *Second Sex*.

The trans-identified woman is a product of male invention.

The debate about Rachel Dolezal, a white woman who declares herself Black and was formerly the president of the US National Association for the Advancement of Colored People (NAACP) in Spokane, Washington, created lots of commentary. Dolezal has even used the term trans to support her status. "I feel like the idea of being *trans-black* would be much more accurate than 'I'm white'" (Aitkenhead, 2017). Her insistence that she is black is relevant to trans assertions about purported womanhood. Trans activists reject any analogy between transgender and what has been called trans-black or trans-racial. However, calling yourself a trans woman or man is just as inaccurate as calling yourself trans-black.

Trans activist Misty Snow denies this comparison:

> Bringing up Rachel Dolezal ... is a false equivalency that has no relevancy when talking about transgender people ... Gender dysphoria is a very real and documented condition with a *biological* basis and very specific treatment guidelines and a long history behind it. Transracial and trans-black are terms with no history that Dolezal has made up and cannot be equated with the experiences or realities of transgender people (in Hedges, 2017, italics mine).

However, the Dolezal incident holds great relevance in the debate over transgender.

A person who has lived as white her whole life and later asserts she is Black has no credible claim, because she has no lifelong experience of the racism that Black people live with. And "Black women — real ones — live at the nexus of that oppression and enduring sexism" (Harris, 2015).

Many African American commentators view Dolezal's claim to be both arrogant and insulting. African American artist and writer Pippa Fleming argues, "Imagine if white folks ran around claiming they were black or demanded access to our affinity spaces. They would be called deluded racist fools" (Fleming, 2018). Unfortunately, with the transgender intrusion into women's spaces, reality is reversed, i.e. those who 'run around' claiming they are women and demanding access to women and women's spaces receive accolades and public approval, including the approval of many women.

Andrea Dworkin: Biological Essentialism vs. Political Materialism

After feminist writer Andrea Dworkin's death in 2005, considerable attention has been paid to Dworkin's opinions about transgender. Dworkin's life partner, John Stoltenberg, has channeled and championed Dworkin as a trans ally, singling me out as guilty of the biological essentialism that Andrea would have abhorred.

With the backing of Stoltenberg, who is also Dworkin's executor, gay writer Martin Duberman wrote in his 2020 biography of Andrea:

> For a time … she had been somewhat friendly with Janice Raymond, whose *transphobic* 1979 book *The Transsexual Empire* … deplored the 'medicalization' of gender that encouraged surgical intervention to create 'a woman according to man's image." Stoltenberg claimed that Andrea "*deplored* my view and let me know at length" (Duberman, 2020, p. 161, italics mine).

Andrea and I had several conversations in the mid-1970s when I was writing *The Transsexual Empire*, and I don't recollect any 'at length disagreement' with my critique. In the Acknowledgments to my book, I thanked Andrea who had commented particularly on Chapter IV and in fact, it was *The Transsexual Empire* that precipitated our friendship. Dworkin read the manuscript in process and contributed an endorsement published on the cover of the paperback edition that read:

> Janice Raymond's *The Transsexual Empire* is challenging, rigorous, and pioneering. Raymond scrutinizes the connections between science, morality, and gender. She asks the hard questions and her answers have an intellectual quality and ethical integrity so rare, so important, that the reader wants to *think*, to enter into a critical dialogue with the book.

Hardly a 'deplorable' view of my work!

I spend some time in this chapter refuting Stoltenberg's interpretation of Andrea's opinion on transgender because he has become the mediator of Dworkin's views; views she did not publicly align herself with after writing her first book, *Woman Hating*. Stoltenberg's version of Dworkin as a trans advocate stands in stark contrast to the rest of her writing in which Andrea conveyed that female bodies matter. In a 1989 interview, Dworkin said, "So much of what happens to women happens to us not just *in* our bodies, but *because* of our bodies ... if you cannot deal with the reality of what it means to physically exist as a woman in this world, then you can't know anything" (Jenefsky, 1998, p. 105).

If Dworkin spoke those words today, trans advocates would brand her a biological essentialist. In the same interview, Dworkin states that the oppression of women happens, "because" of our material bodies. And when you take away everything else, "what you have left as a woman is your body: it is your commodity, your existence ... *it's what people violate you for*" (Jenefsky, 1998, p. 105, italics mine). It is women's body parts, especially breasts, which are hyper sexualized and ruthlessly objectified.

Self-declared women (men) claim *a womanhood* based on fanciful notions of the female body. Many spend years trying to construct the female body they wish for. Whether by surgery or self-declaration, they especially "cannot deal with the reality of what it means to physically exist as a woman in this world" (Jenefsky, 1998, p. 105).

Transgenderism is an ideology that defines women by essentializing whatever men think women are or should be, and in so doing not only erases our bodies but also our oppression. Women's oppression cannot be separated from women's bodies.

Dworkin recognized not only that female bodies matter but also are composed of female matter, i.e. women's bodies materially exist and significantly affect the conditions of our lives. The 'matter' of female bodies is imbued with a history about what it means to be born in a female body — a set of experiences that men don't possess because of their sex, including the history of menstruation, the history of childbirth and abortion, the history of certain bodily cycles and life changes, the history of rape and sexual assault and most significant, the history of female subordination in a male-dominant society.

Writing about the trans appropriation of women's sex, Sarah Ditum puts it this way, "For women, it means their sex is increasingly cast as a matter of feeling, not fact — no minor thing when your sex is the one that takes the brunt of pregnancy, maternity discrimination, unpaid domestic labour, sexual harassment and rape" (Ditum, 2018a).

In 2016, Cristan Williams, the founder and editor of *The Trans Advocate*, interviewed Stoltenberg. Williams has used the magazine to attack radical feminists and our positions on transgender. In this interview called 'Radical Feminism's Trans-Affirming Roots', Stoltenberg asserts he is disturbed that some radical feminists support a biologically essentialist notion of "real womanhood." Stoltenberg mediates Dworkin's alleged views on transgender, insisting that "she was trans-affirming" (in Abeni, 2016).

Stoltenberg reiterated his accusation of essentialism in an article published on the fifteenth anniversary of Dworkin's death, asserting that the radical feminist position on transgender is a betrayal of

Dworkin's work and telling radical feminist women what is wrong with our analysis:

> The fundamental problem with radical feminism's obsession [*sic*] with biologically defining the category woman is that it unwittingly enables a politics that is profoundly reactionary ... it completely misses the point about how male supremacy actually functions to construct the category of 'real manhood' (Stoltenberg, 2020).

I can't quell the thought that Stoltenberg joins the crowd of mansplainers who tell women that we don't know what we are doing and explain to us what is wrong with our 'obsession'. But at the same time, I know that Andrea Dworkin understood the difference between biological essentialism and a *political materialist analysis* that recognizes women have sexed bodies that no man can simply wear.

Dworkin affirmed this materialist analysis in her book *Intercourse*:

> The meanings we create or learn do not exist only in our heads, in ineffable ideas. Our meanings also exist in our bodies — what we are, what we do, what we physically feel, what we physically know; and there is no personal psychology that is separate from what the body has learned about life (Dworkin, 1987, p. 139).

This is not a biological essentialist analysis of women's sexed bodies but a *political materialist* analysis in which women's oppression is grounded in women's bodies, which are often occupied by men and male interventions.

Women have learned a lot about life through our bodies. Our life history has been lived in our sexed bodies. Dworkin knew that the 'learning' women gain from our lives is not some feeling, essence, or 'ineffable idea' that men can claim. This learning about a woman's life is not driven by biology but also not detached from our biology, a material condition in which our bodies help shape the circumstances of our lives.

Our bodies are the sites of our oppression.

For centuries, women were denied access to education, jobs, and all kinds of legal rights, losses that were determined by a variety of essentialist pretexts such as, 'women are irrational', 'women have a natural drive to reproduce', 'motherhood is women's destiny'.

Radical feminists understand only too well the burden of biological essentialism, and this is why different waves of feminism have historically fought against it. We have consistently argued that women are more than our biology and not determined by it, rejecting an ideology that reduces women to only our bodies.

It's disappointing that Stoltenberg continues his biological essentialist branding of radical feminists who oppose transgenderism. "I have no doubt that Andrea would now be excoriating ... the biological essentialism of anti-trans radical feminists" (Stoltenberg, 2020). Stoltenberg references the last chapter of *Woman Hating* where Dworkin wrote:

> Every transsexual has the right to survival on his/her own terms. That means that every transsexual is entitled to a sex change operation, and it should be provided by the community as one of its functions. This is an emergency measure for an emergency condition (Dworkin, 1974, p. 186).

On this same page, Dworkin notes, "More probably transsexuality is caused by a faulty society" (Dworkin, 1974, p. 186), not a biological given, as trans proponents today argue. If transsexuality is an "emergency measure for an emergency condition," it is not permanent. So the question could be asked, why are trans activists and Stoltenberg helping to prolong the emergency rather than ending it? Those who refer to Andrea Dworkin's positive position on transsexuality seldom quote these last lines in which she sees transsexuality as temporary.

Furthermore, Dworkin argues that a

> ... community built on androgynous identity will mean the end of transsexuality as we know it. Either the transsexual will be able to expand his/her sexuality ... or, as roles disappear, the phenomenon of transsexuality will disappear ... (Dworkin, 1974, pp. 186–87).

These words present a challenge to how Stoltenberg has channeled her views.

Stoltenberg has maintained that, "In the 31 years we were together those views did not change; she never retracted them" (in Abeni, 2016). Not quite correct! Actually, Dworkin did express doubts about this very section in *Woman Hating*. In 1989, when Cindy Jenefsky interviewed her she asked Dworkin about her controversial last chapter, and Andrea admitted that she no longer agreed with it. She told Jenefsky, *"I think there are a lot of things really wrong with the last chapter in* Woman Hating" (Jenefsky, 1998, p. 139, italics mine).

In the final chapter of *Woman Hating*, Dworkin had also affirmed incest and bestiality. Jenefsky wrote that this chapter centered on a multisexual paradigm that Dworkin believed at the time were repressed practices and should be accommodated in an 'androgynous world'. Dworkin admitted she was wrong in her last chapter of *Woman Hating* so it's doubly wrong that Stoltenberg is perpetuating an analysis of transsexualism that Andrea would not have affirmed today. Funny, I don't see him defending her early views on incest and bestiality, both of which Dworkin had supported in her last chapter.

Dworkin wrote that it was mainly through getting responses to *Woman Hating* and in developing her future writings that she became critical about this final chapter (Jenefsky, 1998, p. 139). In 1977, I wrote one of those responses in an article called 'Transsexualism: the Ultimate Homage to Sex-Role Power'. I quoted Dworkin and said that in her "otherwise insightful" book, *Woman Hating,* she stated that sex-change operations should be provided by the community as one of its functions (Raymond, 1977). Dworkin only objected to my words, "otherwise insightful."

To Stoltenberg and others who are misrepresenting radical feminist critics with their tiresome charge of biological essentialism, I say: Stop casting us as biological essentialists when the real biological essentialism permeates the trans movement of self-declared women who argue they are women because they allegedly possess female brains and female penises. Read this incisive statement about this nonsensical charge of biological essentialism directed at feminists written by the *Radical Girlsss Young Women Movement* of the European Network of Migrant Women:

> The radical feminist position is wilfully misinterpreted as supporting biological essentialism. This is a deliberate tactic in order to 'prove' that radical feminism is outdated and belongs to the 'white feminists' of the second wave. This narrative foil makes way for a third wave of feminism that is supposedly more intersectional, more progressive, and more open minded than any wave which came before it — and in doing so promises to eradicate the failures of feminist history. In fact, if those who claim that radical feminists are biological essentialists would actually engage in the history of this debate, they would find that the radical feminist position has always been clearly against biological essentialism. We believe that gender expression is not linked to biology, as we believe that nobody is inherently conforming to just masculinity or just femininity (Radical Girlsss, 2020).

I believe that Andrea, were she alive today, would have recognized and named the dangerous direction that transgenderism has taken and would never have condoned the sexual objectification, sexual abuse, the rape and death threats, the medical mutilation and the denigration of natal women on which the transgender movement is built and which Stoltenberg has decided to disregard.

Gender-Critical Trans-Identified Persons

Some trans-identified women have supported the feminist position by questioning the whole idea of self-declaring as females because it does not rely on objective evidence. Debbie Hayton, a defender of trans rights, argues that self-identification destroys honesty. "I am not female and I know that I cannot become female, but I can and do live in a way analogous to the way that women live. I make no claims I cannot justify and my life is better for it." Hayton criticizes the convoluted language invoked by the trans activists and cautions, "Trans people have to live in the real world, where people do not need torturous language to distinguish between men and women" (Hayton, 2018).

Trans-identified Kristina Harrison was banned from Twitter after tweeting that "sex and gender are not the same." In an *Economist* article, Harrison expanded this tweet to an explanation of why women and some trans-identified women should be concerned about a legal system of gender self-identification.

> Perhaps you can begin to understand the concerns of many women when it is increasingly being asserted in practice, if not fully in law, that simply identifying as a woman means being able to access women's and girls' private, formerly single-sex, spaces — toilets, rape-crisis centres and so on. We worry about the nature, influence, methods and implications of the ideology at the heart of this transgender movement. We are also opposed to any proposal which would mean that a man is legally recognised as a woman if he makes a simple self-declaration that he is, and vice versa (Harrison, 2018).

In an essay called 'Transwomen and Narcissistic Rage', one brave trans-identified person targeted the narcissistic rage of many self-identified women. "I'm sick and tired of what I see in the trans community, the community of which I am supposedly a part. I'm tired of the misogyny and narcissistic rage I see directed at women, and other transwomen."

The author, a trans-identified woman, points to the voluminous posts and tweets directed at women that contain vile accusations. "This has to stop … We are not women … We will get nowhere by badgering everyone into agreeing with us."

Talking directly to the 'ragers', the author continues:

> The world doesn't owe you anything … I fail to understand how so many who believe they are women, who want to be women, can treat women so terribly … This should cause every self-identifying transwoman shame. They should look at their community, their peers, and their 'sisters' and be horrified by what they see … Attack dogs are praised or ignored. The truly harmful, the mentally unstable, are embraced and cloaked in an extra layer of victimhood. Transwomen

should call on fellow transwomen to stop harassing women (Gender Apostates, n.d.).

'Transwomen and Narcissistic Rage' is a unique essay. In its final paragraph, the author goes to the heart of the matter in a rebuke to beta male misogynists who declare they are women. "What you are feeling is … entitlement. Being raised male, we are taught how to view women … you will find that the first step towards transitioning away from masculinity is to stop acting like a man" (Gender Apostates, n.d.).

In an early online post from a transsexual woman entitled, 'Was Janice Raymond Right? Why Trans People are Often Their Own Worst Enemies', Cathryn Platine talks about the irrationality of transgender ideology where "Penises become feminine, up is down, black is white and reality can completely be ignored." Platine states:

> 'Penis-wielding women' insist that they are women, much to the confusion of many in the outside world and of many who find this bizarre identity an article of faith in 'trans-wonderland' (Platine, 2007).

Helen Highwater, a British accountant who underwent transitional surgery, now rejects the idea that he is a woman. Highwater believes that the 'trans women are women' dogma sets up trans-identified women for "failure, disappointment, and cognitive dissonance." He continues, "I've not experienced the things women have experienced. I've not been brought up that way. So why on earth would I want to claim that I'm a woman as much as any other woman?" (in Goldberg, 2015).

Another trans agnostic is UK writer Miranda Yardley who Highwater met at a meeting of radical feminists. Yardley states that transitioning vastly improved his life, but that it didn't make him a woman. "I'm male, I own it," he says. Yardley and Highwater began dating and describe themselves as a gay male couple. "We don't identify as lesbians" (in Goldberg, 2015).

Highwater and Yardley represent a growing number of trans-critical trans who are rethinking their identities and past beliefs, a group that is despised by others who identify as transgender.

In 2012, Corinna Cole from Indianapolis, Indiana, founded a trans-critical blog, which she was forced to shut down because of cyber bullying, harassment and threats. "I am more afraid of my community harming me that I am of society harming me" (in Goldberg, 2015). Like others who identify as trans persons, they reject that they are, or can become, members of the opposite sex.

Many of these trans critics transitioned before the recent stage of transgender activism and its promotion of self-declaration. They see the dangers of self-declaration and understand how removing all boundaries leaves natal women open to male violence. Sarah Ditum adds another caveat, "if the problem is male violence, then trans people have every bit as much interest as all women do in keeping bad-faith claims from gaining legal force" (Ditum, 2018b).

I welcome the perspectives of those trans-identifed women (men) who recognize the dangers of self-declaration. I appreciate the public statements they have made in criticizing the excesses of the contemporary trans movement. And I admire their courage in making these statements public. But I also question why some gender critical trans-identified persons do not recognize and discuss their own supporting roles in generating this current trans movement.

Jennifer Bilek explores these contradictions. The 'good trans-women', as she calls them, "have all changed their sex markers to that of the opposite sex. Even if they call themselves gender critical … they always seem to miss the objectification" of themselves and of women and womanhood involved in their transitions, first of all in dissociating from their own bodies and then in the process of "passing" or identifying, at least initially, as women (Bilek, 2020a).

In other words, you can't be a convincing critic if you are still embracing and conforming to sex-role stereotypes. And you can't be a convincing critic if you are appearing on television saying to those who may be considering hormones and surgery by giving the brand of advice that cautions not going through these procedures "although it did work for me."

The 'good transwomen' are seldom like their female counterparts whose de-transitioning process is based in a deep reflection of coming to terms with their own missteps. The 'good transwomen' are not de-transitioning like the hundreds of young women who formerly identified as trans men and who are now de-conforming. These women, who are coming back to themselves, have recognized that a detoxing process begins with changing themselves. As important as the 'good transwomen's' critiques of the contemporary trans movement are, they rarely reflect personal changes.

There is no corresponding *movement* of 'good transwomen' who have taken the plunge of de-transitioning. Trans-critical 'trans women' have met the problem of gender halfway, whereas women who identified as men but have de-transitioned have taken the whole way forward to reclaiming their womanhood. As Bilek puts it, "It is astonishing that they get so close to grasping it, how destructive it is in society, eloquently describe it to others, and still be unwilling to part with it. They still call themselves 'transwomen.'"

It is important that trans-identifed men who have become gender critics recognize a parallel obligation to confront the systemic transgender industry by involving themselves in addressing political transformation. At the very least, why aren't they criticizing the medicalization they have undergone and that is now damaging many children? The early wave of transsexuals served as the antechamber to self-declaration and led many others who came after them into the dangers of medicalization.

Academic Babel

Journalist Helen Joyce has written critically of transgenderism:

> Developed by academics in gender studies and 'queer theory,' a hard-to-define offshoot of postmodernism that sees almost everything as discursively constructed ... it regards 'gender identity' [as] the

> supposedly innate sense of which sex you are … it is the identity that is understood to be the true self. The body is something to be moulded accordingly (Joyce, 2020).

Trans essentialist theories are rampant in former Women's Studies departments, now called Women, Gender, and Sexuality Studies (WGSS). WGSS programs have become laboratories of transgender research and activities that produce student activists who treat dissent from transgender ideology as a cardinal sin. Among academic women who write and teach on 'gender, sexuality and women', transgenderism trumps radical feminism any day. Radical feminism was never popular in academic Women's Studies departments, but attitudes had not degenerated to the point where critics of transgender were being censored and couldn't speak.

African American writer Pippa Fleming confirms that this academic trend is not accidental:

> The educational establishment was the lead car when it came to shake up women's studies and replace it with gender studies. That damn radical feminism was a thorn in the side of patriarchy and they needed some heavy-duty tweezers to pull it out. All those trickle-down theories of gender trumping sex strike like lighting and folks are charged by the idea that they can identify however they please, even if it means co-opting lesbian identity (Fleming, 2018).

Academic gender and sexuality programs and departments bear disturbing responsibility for the silencing of dissenters who do not accept that men can be women and women men.

Not confined to WGSS departments, other academic women and men have become gender conformists and defend an essentialism that feminists fought against in the 1970s and 1980s and are still opposing. The rush to silence these critical voices is troubling in a context where free speech should be the norm, but is not always the reality. A significant number of universities are caving in to trans censorship, with students and faculty members who challenge trans orthodoxies, targeted for attack.

In the earlier quoted *New York Times* feature 'The Stone', philosopher Carol Hay wrote an article entitled 'Who Counts as a Woman?' 'The Stone' is billed as "a forum for contemporary philosophers and other thinkers on issues both timely and timeless." Hay's piece didn't evince much thinking, but it did make many wonder what has become of philosophy and philosophers who on Twitter jubilantly refer to their own writing as "terf-bashing."

For example, rather than engage with my work, Carol Hay is more anxious to tell her readers that I am a 'TERF' and a purveyor of hate speech.

> It all started with Janice Raymond's controversial book, *The Transsexual Empire: The Making of the She-Male*, published in 1979. Reissued in 1994, the book continues to inspire 'gender-critical' or 'trans-exclusionary radical feminists' — TERFs, for short. For the record, while some consider the acronym derogatory, it is a widely accepted shorthand for a literal description of the views these feminists hold; also for the record, many of us who are critics of TERFs consider Raymond's book to be hate speech (Hay, 2018).

It certainly can't be said that this article created any deep respect for feminist philosophy and feminist philosophers when the author, and other women academics, have so little to say about the realities of real women's real lives.

If Hay thought her article was a triumph, the actual record of comments showed that the majority opposed her 'philosophy'. Here are a few more of the responses to *The New York Times* piece:

> There is something deeply disingenuous about female academics following this train of thought. These 'philosophical' problems of what constitutes a woman are little more than semantics for most women: Being paid 1/3 less than a man for equal work or having your body politicized by government are not philosophical problems resulting from an over-indulgence in female performativity. These are realities that academic feminists have decided are beneath them to discuss … academics like Butler and Halberstam [and] show just how pointless academic feminism is for the vast majority of the world's women (Elsie).

What Ms. Hay promotes is NOT feminism and it is not 'progressive'. If you disagree with Ms. Hay you may very well be a radical feminist; welcome to the club! (Anne).

Ms. Hay's argument is patently obtuse. Sexism is the air we breathe, the water we swim in from birth (Cgtwet).

One commentator argues,

In my view, this is not honest philosophy. This is using philosophy in service of sociopolitical ends instead of using philosophy to seek the truth (ilmerlo).

Another reader breathes,

Whew! By the time a reader gets about two paragraphs into Ms Hay's piece, it becomes glaringly obvious that she is an academic (and one with lots of time on her hands as well). News flash Carol; there's such a thing as overthinking your subject and, when that happens, readers can be forgiven for identifying the author as an ideologue, which you seem to be. TERF, intersectional feminism and cis women indeed (Cactus Jerry).

Trans activists who demand that women pledge allegiance to trans truths have launched a new age of inquisition. Women are being silenced, shunned and assaulted for speaking the truth that men cannot be women.

CHAPTER TWO

The Rapid Rollout of Transgenderism: How Did It Happen?

The system of male supremacy comes down hard on non-conforming men and women ... While switching gender identity may alleviate some problems on an individual level, it is not a political solution.

—37 Radical Feminists, *Forbidden Discourse*

C ritics of transgender ideology have been perplexed at its rapid acceptance. Even supporters of transgenderism such as Mara Keisling of the US National Center for Transgender Equality have been surprised that the transgender movement has made "faster progress than any movement in American history," an assertion that resonates in Britain and in many parts of the globe (Sarah Ditum, 2018b).

In the United States, most influential were the strategic early alliances trans activists made with the mainstream LGB organizations, such as the Human Rights Campaign, Lambda Legal and GLAAD, who gave them an equal place at the table and then allowed them to preside at the head where they hammered the 'T' into the original LGB. There doesn't seem to have been any time at which the majority of lesbians and gay men were able to register an opinion on the policies and programs of the mainstream LGBT+ agenda.

Hitching their wagon to the mainstream corporate gay and lesbian organizations, transgender advocates were very shrewd in organizing support for their issues. In a relatively short time, we have all been plunged into the alphabet swamp of the LGBT+ environment and are sinking there. LGBT+ fusion has taken root particularly in campus-based gender communities and departments, especially in former Women's Studies Programs now renamed Women, Gender and Sexuality.

In an analysis of a report called *Only Adults? Good Practices in Legal Gender Recognition for Youth,* British journalist James Kirkup reveals in detail the strategy that has made the transgender platform successful. He has outed a strategic report written by Dentons, an international law firm, in conjunction with the mammoth Canadian media giant, Thomson Reuters, and with NGOs such as the International Lesbian, Gay, Bisexual, Transgender, Queer and Intersex Youth & Student Organization (IGLYO) (Kirkup, 2019b).

Kirkup documents how transgender activists pushed the legal envelope in various countries to achieve legal changes that allow young children to change their gender "without adult approval and without needing the approval of any authorities." The report contains an explicit acknowledgment that it was written so that activists can use the tactics listed to advance transgender youth rights. It includes various 'best practices' to achieve transgender goals and some specific recommendations that help youth to transition and circumvent parental and legal approval such as the following:

> "States should take action against parents who are obstructing the free development of a young trans person's identity in refusing to give parental authorisation when required."

> "Get ahead of the government agenda."

In many transgender campaigns where NGOs were proactive and intervened early, they had 'far greater ability to shape the government agenda' than if they let the legal authorities develop their own policies and laws.

> "Tie your campaign to more popular reform."

In the United States, transgender advocacy historically was tied to the campaign for gay rights and marriage equality. This strategy provided a "veil of protection" in locations where gender identity wasn't on most people's radar.

"Avoid excessive press coverage and exposure."

Early on, limiting publicity gave transgender activists initial success avoiding bad press and pushback from others (Kirkup, 2019b). Now, transgender supporters don't have to worry about the press, mainstream and progressive, which seem to play a cheerleading role in the transgender juggernaut.

I would add that another tactic that trans lobbyists have used to their utmost advantage is to *stifle debate*. Trans activists are experts at branding dissenters transphobic and guilty of hate speech so that their opponents can be discredited and not allowed to speak for themselves. Activists are no-platformed and critics boycotted when they are scheduled, for example, to speak in universities or public libraries — those fictional paragons of free speech, which ironically, of all places, have easily capitulated to trans demands, even when speakers are not talking about transgender issues.

With the help of this rapid advance strategy, transgender activists won public acceptance and often, their preferred legislation. "Faster than rights for blacks; faster than rights for women; faster than rights for homosexuals; way, way faster than rights for Down syndrome kids … [I]n most Western countries, trans rights have become the new civil rights" (Cook, 2018).

Framing Rapid Transgender Treatment for Children as 'Emergency Health Care'

Rapid gender affirmation at gender identity clinics, also called 'gender health centers', has channeled multiple youth into puberty blockers and hormones. It is estimated that between 60 to 300 US clinics have been established in almost all states at a brisk pace within a period of several decades. As one saying goes, "if you build it, they will come."

The American Academy of Pediatrics (AAP), an allegedly non-partisan organization whose portfolio would not be expected to adjudicate sports policy, promotes gender identity as a health issue for children. Wading into the debate about allowing boys who identify as girls into girls' competitions, the list of AAP false claims reads like a pro-trans lobbying document. The policy includes directives such as: prohibiting boys from girls' sports is "harming transgender youth"; and state legislatures that are passing legislation to limit girls' sports to natal girls have "the sole purpose of threatening the health and well-being of transgender youth" (Bartosch, 2021).

Advocates of rapid child gender affirmation treatment, along with professional medical associations, have framed trans health policy as 'lifesaving medical care' or 'necessary health care'. The exact opposite is true as more female de-transitioners tell their stories of what should be more appropriately defined as 'unnecessary health care' (see Chapter 3).

In a rush to affirm every young patient's self-diagnosis of cross-sex identity, US transgender lobbyists have promoted hormonal and surgical transitions for 'gender dysphoric' youth. And as we have seen from the strategy outlined by LGBT+ organizations in concert with international law firms that have made the transgender platform successful, this rapid approach is working in the United States while being more effectively challenged in Britain.

Writer and campaigner for women's rights, Josephine Bartosch, has called this US child transgender juggernaut "America's Creation of the Transgender Child," asserting that "the transgender child industry has outstripped policy." Comparing the UK and the United States, she writes, "The obvious difference is that in the United States healthcare is dominated by the private sector who have an obvious motive to promote drugs and surgeries," whereas in the UK the private incentive is mostly missing, given the existence of a National Health Service (Bartosch, 2021).

Other country differences include a robust UK feminist resistance with successful political clout. In the United States, the transgender debate has divided feminists, and the feminist opposition that exists has only recently been politically visible. Also, the British media environment is much more accepting of critical views that get more of a hearing. In the United States, by contrast, "once the *New York Times* and *Washington Post* have decided to promote transgender kids, then there is no scope for dissent" (Bartosch, 2021).

The Suicide Threat

The spectacle of suicide hovers over any discussion that is critical of trans ideology and practice and has been influential in accepting not only quick gender affirmation of children but also its rapid public acceptance. Proponents especially of child transitioning, use the threat of suicide when clinicians warn parents seeking help for their child that transitioning is necessary for his or her health; and that reluctance to approve puberty blockers might result in more suffering and self-harm, perhaps even leading to suicide. Parents who hesitate to subject their children to risky treatments are cruelly asked, "Do you want a live son or a dead daughter?"

Claire, now a 19-year-old student, began her hormone treatment at age 12 because she loathed her female body. "I felt it was the only option, especially with the insistence that having dysphoria meant you were irrevocably trans, and thus you will probably kill yourself if you don't transition." When Claire came off testosterone, she embraced her life as a lesbian, desisted and is furious at the industry that gave her only one 'choice' (*The Economist*, 2020).

Writer and transgender survivor, Max Robinson, notes that the narrative of "transition or die miserable, sooner or later" (2021, p. 11) retains a hold on those who identify as trans, their family members and medical professionals.

But it simply isn't true … there is a very simplistic roadmap provided to patients diagnosed with gender dysphoria. The patient is in severe distress and the medical professional will alleviate that distress through prescribing hormones, performing surgery, or directing the patient to another medical professional who will facilitate these medical interventions (Robinson, 2021, pp. 11–12).

The suicide threat is emotional blackmail that particularly exploits the guilt of parents who might not want their children to go through quick affirmation of medical treatment with puberty blockers and cross-sex hormones. The clinical message is that waiting or withholding treatment from youth transitioners may increase suicidal thoughts or actual suicides.

The looming ghost of suicide haunts parents. For example, the attention-getting number of 48 percent of Australian trans youth who *attempted* suicide, is a statistic that comes from the 2017 *Trans Pathways* report of the Telethon Kids Institute in Perth, Australia — a report constantly cited by trans advocates and clinicians (Strauss et al, 2017, italics mine).

Hasci Horvath, an American epidemiologist and expert in research methods, who has written, "for 13 years I 'masqueraded' as a woman" and has now de-transitioned, says trans advocates use convenience samples to inflate suicidality, a research method that polls subjects who are easy to reach in some way. This kind of testing is questionable because it can cause under- or over-representation of a certain segment of the research population; use a selective group of people chosen to be interviewed; and may result in biased conclusions (Horvath, 2018).

As evidence of this bias and how it changes the outcome of studies, Horvath cites a California clinic's government-funded research where the federal grantors stepped in to require a more rigorous design. The grantors instructed the clinic to include a representative sample of California's adolescents, as well as using trained interviewers who would test suicidality claims. The result: "Only three percent of 'highly gender non-conforming' kids reported attempted suicide," a far distance from the Pathway numbers (Lane, 2019b).

Suicide messaging is regularly but irresponsibly used in trans culture, ignoring the National Action Alliance for Suicide Prevention appeals for responsible messaging to avoid the spreading of suicide contagion. "Many groups ... routinely disseminate messages about suicide in websites, social media, educational materials, and other print and digital communications. It is important that this information be conveyed in ways that support suicide prevention rather than increase risk" (National Action Alliance, n.d.). But trans activists continue to exploit fears of suicide especially to defend the medicalization of children.

Transgender activists accuse feminists and other critics of depriving children of 'life-saving medical care'. Even legitimate parental concerns about their child are dismissed with warnings that their reasonable hesitations could lead their child to suicide. Trans activists invoke children's rights to promote questionable puberty blockers and cross-sex hormones and call elective surgery for adults a 'life-saving treatment' when in fact it can be medically risky to undergo such treatments.

In 1980, I was commissioned to prepare a report on the social and ethical aspects of transsexual surgery for what was then a division of the Federal US Department of Health, Education, and Welfare, called the National Center for Health Care Technologies (NCHCT). When the report was publicized, trans advocates accused me of denying "medically necessary psychological and medical care" insurance coverage for those who identified as transsexuals. The suicide propaganda was deployed even then as trans activists asserted: "One of the most severe results of denying coverage of treatments to transgender insureds ... is suicidal ideation and attempts" (The TERFS, n.d.).

I was accused of leading the charge against what trans activists constantly frame as 'medically-necessary healthcare': "It was only after the NCHCT pushed Raymond's bigotry in 1980 that the US government reversed course in 1981 and took up Raymond's views and rhetoric. Raymond's hate became the government's stance ..." (The TERFS, n.d.)."

Outsize claims of trans suffering and death were laid at my door. Allegedly, my paper:

- eliminated federal and state aid for indigent and imprisoned transsexuals;
- engineered the purported anti-trans stance the US government adopted in the 1980s;
- collaborated with Senator Jesse Helms, an extreme right-wing politician to deny coverage for sexual reassignment surgery under Medicare;
- and finally — "the reason why many trans people lay the death and suffering of untold numbers of trans people at the feet of Janice Raymond, PhD" (The TERFS, n.d.).[1]

My accusers listed several studies that claimed to support their statements about suicide. They asserted, "Studies provide overwhelming evidence that removing discriminatory barriers to treatment results in significantly lower suicide rates" (The TERFS, n.d.), but their studies contained many methodological flaws, including low numbers interviewed and little long-term evaluation.

However, studies consistently reach the opposite conclusion about trans suicide claims. In 2011, a Swedish long-term follow-up study of 346 persons who underwent transsexual surgery found that, "persons with transsexualism, *after sex reassignment*, have considerably higher risks for mortality, suicidal behaviour, and psychiatric morbidity than the general population." Suicides and suicidal attempts were more prevalent *after surgery* than before. Their findings concluded that transsexual surgery "may not suffice as treatment for transsexualism. And the Swedish findings support a judgment that surgical treatment could be the cause of, not the solution to, suicidal feelings (Dhejne et al, 2011, italics mine)."

Meanwhile, trans activists and many clinicians continue to exploit the medical necessity of cringe-worthy gender treatments.

---

1   I have extensively debunked all these claims on my website in a section called 'Fictions and Facts about *The Transsexual Empire*' at janiceraymond.com (Raymond, 2014).

Dubious Evidence and Doctor Advocates

Dependence on dubious studies has helped to fast-track the rapid acceptance of transgender ideology and treatments. It is ironic in an age that has criticized doctors for giving hormonal replacement treatment (HRT) to post-menopausal women and testosterone to men and young boys trying to bulk up their muscles, that any gender clinic would even consider giving cross-sex hormones to children who want to appear as the opposite sex.

The Dutch Protocol

Most claims for prescribing puberty blockers and hormones rely on one single Dutch study called the *Dutch Protocol*. It is quoted widely to support rapid gender affirmation hormone treatment of children. However, the respected UK Society for Evidence Based Gender Medicine (SEGM, 2020) points out that in coming to its conclusions, the Dutch study used a small cohort of 55 interviews with only 40 completing the process; little follow-up; and no health evaluation of consequences. One participant died due to post-operative complications, and several others experienced health issues due to the hormonal treatment. There was no control group, yet the study concluded after only one year that the medical interventions used were successful (SEGM), 2020).

Although the Dutch study claimed that participants' 'gender dysphoria' improved, SEGM debunked that claim and found that many participants' body image problems went unchanged or worsened (SEGM, 2020). Equally disturbing is that one of the Dutch researchers, Dr Annelou de Vries, published a commentary in the medical journal *Pediatrics* that the Dutch model was never intended for treating children, and that it is being wrongly applied to any population of children under 18 years of age (*The Economist*, 2020).

Added to the poor quality of methodology and evidence proffered by the Dutch Protocol is the fact that it did *not* encourage early childhood transitioning, nor did it include a cohort of young people. Yet it is constantly cited by clinicians who treat children (*The*

Economist, 2020). SEGM director Dr Carl Heneghan has stated that child gender treatment with hormones is not supported by high-quality evidence, or in many instances, provides no evidence at all (Kersten, 2019). Heneghan has called use of hormones on children an "unregulated live experiment on children" (in Sinnott, 2019).

The American Academy of Pediatrics' (AAP) Bogus Evidence

Another dubious report is the AAP's 2018 policy statement, which claimed of the 11 academic studies that have been conducted on approaches to help children with gender dysphoria, that all of them support the rapid gender affirmation model. But in a fact-checking rebuttal to this claim, Dr James Cantor, director of the Toronto Sexuality Centre, found that these studies did not say what the AAP alleged they did. "In fact, the references that the AAP cited as the basis of their policy outrightly contradicted AAP policy and repeatedly endorsed 'watchful waiting'" (Cantor, 2018).

Cantor researched his rebuttal by examining in detail all the studies the AAP cited to support its policy and found it is "based on evidence that is demonstrably false. For example, where the AAP policy claimed that a particular review of the literature endorsed gender identity affirmation, it was actually a review of the *sexual orientation* research. The AAP also based its reasoning on the belief that conversion therapy is being used to delay affirmation and to prevent children from identifying as transgender. Fact-checking revealed, however, that all 11 of the AAP's original sources said the opposite, i.e. "delaying affirmation should *not* be construed as conversion therapy or an attempt to change gender identity" (Cantor, 2018, italics mine).

The AAP "provided recommendations entirely unsupported and even in direct opposition to that research and opinion" (Cantor, 2018). Their distortions of the actual evidence are not simple mistakes or misunderstanding an unclear source, but rather their recommendations appear to be based on a purposeful misrepresentation of the evidence.

The Center for Transgender Health and Development at the Children's Hospital in Los Angeles

Even with the lack of high-quality evidence, the US medical industry is flourishing, particularly targeting children, when several decades ago, you could count on both hands the number of gender identity clinics. Dr Johanna Olson-Kennedy, the Director of the Center for Transgender Health and Development at the Children's Hospital in Los Angeles (LA) — the largest children's gender clinic in the country — has been one of the most influential voices for lowering the age of child eligibility for puberty blockers and cross-sex hormones.

Olson-Kennedy conducted a five-year research study of the effects of cross-sex hormones on children, for which she received $5.7 million from the National Institutes of Health (NIH).) It is alarming that midway through this federally financed study, the researchers lowered the minimum age to receive cross-sex hormones from 13 to eight (2019). The lack of a control group in Olson-Kennedy's study almost guaranteed that she would get the results she wanted.

Olson-Kennedy's gender pediatric center has performed mastectomies, renamed as chest surgery, on young girls. In reviewing the study's results in a medical journal article that documents her NIH study, it is evident that the LA gender pediatric center has performed mastectomies on girls as young as 13. "The mean (SD) age at chest surgery in this cohort was 17.5 years (range, 13–24 years), with 33 (49%) being younger than 18 years. Of the 33 postsurgical participants younger than 18 years at surgery, 16 (48%) were 15 years or younger" (Olson-Kennedy et al, 2018a).

When questioned in a *YouTube* appearance about child mastectomies and the possibility, whether, when older, girls might change their minds, Olson-Kennedy played down the surgery and its consequences. "If you want breasts at a later point in your life, you can go and get them" (Olson-Kennedy, 2018b). Like the ads that flood us with all sorts of consumer goods, Olson-Kennedy advertises the female body as product and the consumer as buyer who can purchase various body parts — a consumer 'choice'.

Until the Tavistock hormone treatments were put on hold in late 2020, the leadership of the UK clinic had spoken quite openly in favor of encouraging the country to adopt the same rapid affirmation system of 'care' as in the United States. This would mean that a girl as young as eight could receive puberty blockers and testosterone and be subjected to a mastectomy at age 13. It is fortunate that the Tavistock gender services have been reined in at this time.

Part of the LA program involves a team of health educators who go into communities where there are schools and churches, "where the youth are," and procure five new youngsters weekly to attend the clinic (Transgender Trend, 2019). I find this procuring of young girls for experimental treatment with hormones and surgery a pathway to exploitation. To Olson-Kennedy, children seem like test subjects for her theories and unethical experimental treatments since girls in early puberty are undergoing hormone and surgical treatments that may be irreversible.

The Center's services, in addition to providing puberty blockers, cross-sex hormones and surgery to those who want these treatments, also provide support groups for youngsters and family members, including a playgroup for little kids. Fourteen hundred 3 to 25 year olds who are 'gender diverse' have used various aspects of the LA service.

Like a fundamentalist preacher who gives impassioned speeches and believes in the faith of gender identity transformation, Olson-Kennedy disdains the heresy of "watchful waiting," i.e. taking the process of transitioning slowly, and derides this process calling it "do nothing and wait" (Transgender Trend, 2019). She sees no validity in being cautious.

Ironically, recent US medical institutions like the Children Minnesota clinic have followed the LA model and launched their facilities for pediatric gender 'care' just as Britain's premier pediatric clinic was closing some of its services, with multiple clinicians resigning "as a matter of conscience" from the Tavistock Center's

Gender Identity Development Service (GIDS) (Kersten, 2019). The Center had been known for accelerating children through its gender identity program and ignoring reports on the risks of puberty blockers. After the 2020 UK High Court ruling, Tavistock cannot refer new patients for puberty blockers and has suspended these treatments. Tavistock has appealed the decision.

The history of medicine has recorded many treatments that ended in ruinous long-term results, for example "the past use of thalidomide, lobotomies, and the recent opioid epidemic. The 'gender affirmative' model commits young people to lifelong medical treatment with minimal attention to the etiology of their conditions, and the psychosocial factors contributing to gender dysphoria" (SEGM, 2020).

Sex and Transgender Industries of Exploitation

The sex industry has numerous links with the transgender industry. Both have built edifices of exploitation based on misogyny and the downgrading of women's rights. Both are sold to women as empowerment, liberation and consumer choice. And both are industries that have managed to expand by protecting men's rights.

Like the sex industry, the US transgender industry is thriving and has been assessed as a legitimate consumer industry in market watch forecasts. The transgender business outlook has predicted long-term growth based on increased public awareness of transgenderism and favorable government legislation launched in various cities, states and countries. The *Market Watch* calculations forecast an expanding population that will soon be seeking sex change treatment and procedures that will be worth US $1.5 billion by the year 2026 (Market Watch, 2021).

Based on data from the American Society of Plastic Surgeons (ASPS), 3,200 trans surgeries were performed in 2016. The number of those seeking surgery increased almost 20 percent from 2015 to 2016 (American Society of Plastic Surgeons, 2017).

Another study in the *American Journal of Psychiatry* maintains that transgender surgery improves mental health problems, yet they wrote:

> Compared with the general population, individuals with a gender incongruence diagnosis … were about six times as likely to have had a mood and anxiety disorder health care visit, more than three times as likely to have received prescriptions for antidepressants and anxiolytics (anxiety drugs), and more than six times as likely to have been hospitalized after a suicide attempt (American Society of Plastic Surgeons, 2017).

Why are clinicians sending all these people in distress, including children, into hormones and surgery?

There is no conclusive evidence that gender surgery improves trans lives. Actually, the evidence is to the contrary.

> Many people remain severely distressed and even suicidal *after* the operation … [I] n a review of more than 100 international medical studies of post-operative transsexuals … the study found no robust evidence that gender reassignment surgery is clinically effective (Batty, 2004, italics mine).

An outsize number of those who underwent surgery remain traumatized.

When many of the studies that claim gender surgery improves trans lives were reviewed, it was discovered that more than half of their participants dropped out and *most* studies were poorly designed, which skewed the results that claimed surgery is beneficial. The elevated drop-out rate could indicate high levels of dissatisfaction (Batty, 2004). Yet despite this evidence that interrogates the efficacy of surgery, increasing numbers of gender identity clinics have encouraged a rising medicalized population of young children in which the sheer availability of these clinics will attract those who seek therapy and body changes.

Looking at the medical marketplace, the first US clinic for childhood gender dissatisfaction opened in Boston in 2007. In 2021, estimates of the number of North American gender identity clinics vary from 60 to over 300. Medical institutions are designing new medical specialties and training doctors in medical schools to cover the increased demand for trans treatments.

Turning children into permanent consumers of transgender medicine has become big business in the United States. The pharmaceutical industry is raking in millions from puberty blockers and cross-sex hormones. Puberty blockers cost up to $20,000 a year and if the young person proceeds with cross-sex hormone treatment, that treatment can be lifelong (Clary, 2018).

Self-declared women are paying to enlarge their breasts, whereas self-declared men want to remove theirs. Breast amplification for self-declared women (men), or breast removal for self-declared men (women), costs around $10,000. Inverting the skin of a penis and fashioning an imitation vagina costs up to $30,000; constructing a faux phallus out of skin stripped from the forearm, costs $20,000-$150,000 (Clary, 2018).

'Facial feminization' surgery, which disguises some of the changes caused by male puberty, ranges from $20,000 to $50,000 and above, depending on the number of procedures performed (Clary, 2018). Facial feminization is a surgery that involves the cosmetic modification of facial characteristics, undertaken by men who want assurance that they are recognized as women. The goal is to soften masculine features into a more feminine façade. Many insurance plans in the United States are covering both the hormones and the surgeries, thus promoting treatments to more subscribers who will undergo more treatments since the plans finance a significant amount of the cost.

Although recent transgender proponents argue that the majority of trans-identified persons are self-declared and *not* seeking medical transitions, especially surgery — as indicated in the terminology shift from transsexualism to transgenderism — the economic trends reveal a medical model that has become sizeable enough to be tracked as an industry with a large market share.

The Market Watch data also challenges dominant opinion that the numbers of women/girls who are transitioning rivals the numbers of men/boys — a conjecture derived from the exponential number of young girls in the last decade seeking gender transition treatment. Nevertheless, in assessing the broader arc of all those seeking gender transition treatment — both children and adults — it appears that this increase in young girls undergoing surgery has not dramatically changed the traditional ratio of four males to one female. More recent figures move the needle down only one point with a ratio of three males to one female, and it may go lower with the numbers of girls de-transitioning.

> According to recent studies, the number of gender confirmation surgeries from male to female are 3 times more than female to male surgeries. In 2019, male to female sex transition surgery accounted for a revenue of over USD 184.6 million. The growth can be attributed to the rise in medical insurance coverage for male to female transition procedures along with the availability of expert opinions on the medical necessity of gender transition (Market Watch, 2021).

It appears that significantly more males than females are still seeking more surgical procedures as indicated by *Market Watch*.

A Civil Rights Issue or a Promo for the Gender Industry?

In a groundbreaking investigative article that questions whether the trans movement is a civil rights movement for the oppressed or an 'ad campaign' for transitioning, writer, blogger, and environmental activist Jennifer Bilek states, "It's hard to imagine a civil rights movement so indelibly tied to the capitalist marketplace that it could be used to sell fashion, makeup, hormones, surgery, cosmetology services, movies, TV series, mental health treatment and women's underwear" (Bilek, 2018b). At the same time that billionaire philanthropists are subsidizing transgender organizations and events, they are investing in pharmaceutical industries, major tech corporations, and banks, all of which have connections to the transgender industry.

Bilek has 'followed the money' in researching billionaire funders such as investor and philanthropist Jennifer Pritzker and trans humanist Martine Rothblattt, the creator of Sirius XM satellite

Radio. Both men identify as trans women, invest large amounts in biomedical companies, and are trans stakeholders who bankroll various transgender organizations. Others like philanthropists George Soros and Jon Stryker are also giving LGBT+ organizations enormous amounts of money (Bilek, 2018a), but it is hard to determine what part of the funding goes to the LGB part of this alliance and is not totally swallowed up by the T. It is also difficult to know how much of this money benefits those who seek direct services from these organizations and is not used in lobbying for legislation.

The 2017–2018 Global Resources Report tracks global philanthropic funding for LGBT+ issues and organizations. Over a two-year period of 2017 and 2018, "funding for LGBTI issues totaled more than $560 million — an increase of $57 million, or 11 percent, since the 2015–2016 reporting period" (Wallace and Kan, 2020).

The amount given to the foundations these men favor is relatively small when compared to their personal fortunes, which are principally invested in the technology, medical and pharmaceutical industries. These investments provide a substantial economic foundation for institutionalizing and thus normalizing transgenderism, and the LGBT+ organizations offer a civil rights shield that helps to distract from the actual medical industrial complex — the transgender empire — that is being built and strengthened.

Jennifer Bilek has demonstrated that in almost every section of the global marketplace, but mainly positioned in the medical industrial complex, it's misleading to call the trans movement a campaign for human rights. She writes of those who identify as trans and their allies who have a daunting presence in Hollywood on Oprah and several TV series. Whoopi Goldberg has started her own trans modeling company presented as the "future of modeling" (Bilek, 2018b).

Alas, *The New York Times* jumped on the transgender bandwagon with a 12-page fashion article on "new options in trans underwear." The entire article is focused on self-declared women's (men's) underwear that is luridly preoccupied with how to "tuck your dick!" And why is this news? Because the majority of men who identify as women is evidently large enough to merit "a market for a functional pair of underwear that should assist with the process of tucking the genitals" (Pajer, 2019). Most trans-identified women (men) avoid 'bottom surgery' and choose to preserve a functioning penis.

The *Times* article features trans models displayed in trans feminized underwear that is advertised as sexy but comfortable for penis-tucking 'women'. Companies are making a new line called 'tucking undies' that relieve men who declare themselves women of 'folding back genitalia'. One doctor, Rixt Luikenaar, who appears to serve as a medical and fashion consultant for the *Times* article tells readers, "Women [i.e. men] who tuck often hold in their urine because they have to untape in order to urinate," which can cause bladder infections. Dr Luikenaar's standard for a pair of trans feminine 'tuckies' is underwear that "allows someone [men] to tuck, slide on, and feel pretty in the process" (Pajer, 2019). What free advertising from *The New York Times*!

As an example of the lengths that the medical markets will go to promote their products by supporting the transgender movement, Tampax advertises its product as 'gender inclusive' and has erased the word woman from its ads. In September 2020, Tampax tweeted, "Fact: Not all women have periods. Also a fact: Not all people with periods are women. Let's celebrate the diversity of all people who bleed."

> This language obfuscation is part and parcel of the burgeoning gender identity industry ... Purportedly this is to make people comfortable who think they are, or wish to present themselves as the opposite sex. Trans-identified individuals make up approximately .06% of the population. ...Tampax doesn't mind making women, who make up more than 50% of the population, and 100% of their consumer base, uncomfortable (in Bilek, 2020b).

The Trans Pornography Industry

Writer and trans-identified woman Cathryn Platine contends that if one does an internet search of issues related to transsexuals, "it would be … wading through literally thousands and thousands of she-male porn sites and crossgender vanity pages … they are often done up in the same provocative outfits found in pornography or as a reflection of some poor woman they sexualized" (Platine, 2007).

The pornography industry feeds on women's hatred of their bodies. Young girls learn to hate their bodies at an early age, and many take eating disorders to the point of starvation. Some engage in cutting. Others are pressured into sexting and self-sexual objectification, which has become a free trade in teen pornography. For a number of girls and young women, these disorders are a prelude to cutting off their breasts to identify as men (see Chapter 3).

Cosmopolitan Magazine has joined in the whitewashing of pornography by featuring the claims of Foxhouse Films to produce it in an "ethical and sustainable manner … made by ethical producers who don't fetishize trans bodies, and actually pay their actors." The *Cosmo* article provides a list of "the best places for trans and gender non-binary people to find 'legitimately' good pornography" (Windust, 2018). All of this is promoted as individual 'choice' to mask the market manipulation.

Trans pornography has captured a substantial part of the market, appealing to men who have bizarre sexual proclivities. Men have historically always been interested in impersonating women whether they are cross-dressers or trans. Many men who are self-declared women want to look ultra-feminine, and trans pornography provides a template for their gendered dress (or undress) and behavior.

In 1993, *The Advocate* published an article that championed the allure of gender ambiguity and the polymorphous sexuality exuded by many trans-identified women — the "hyperfeminine and hypersexual chick with a dick scene, is said to attract many men." Trans pornography appeals to a cohort of men who want their pornographic actors "to have penises as well as breasts" (Greenberg, 1993).

Users of this genre of pornography get off on viewing the mix of genitalia and the actors being violated. One pornography user advised,

> ... just Google '*bihardcoreporn*,' and you'll find a web site whose home page lists some 300+ porn videos showcasing guys who are getting off with each other and with girls, because, damn boy, you are so riled up not getting any boy-boy action with boy-girl action and girl-girl action, your brain can't think straight!

My brain couldn't think straight after reading this sentence![2]

On one *bihardcoreporn* site, a commentator stated that most trans porn is actually marketed to and consumed by primarily "hetero trans fetishists. It sells precisely because it's trashy, objectifying, and offensive. They're marketing trans people as a naughty taboo for bored straight people."

Even users of trans porn sites express (somewhat) unfavorable opinions about the pornography industry. One user confirms, "There's also the sad reality of the fact that discrimination is a way to make a lot of money quickly. I know a number of trans women who've used porn as a means to pay for piecemeal surgeries they otherwise wouldn't be able to afford." Trans pornography like trans prostitution, as dehumanizing as both are, makes money for numbers of young men who self-declare as women. Much of this sexual objectification and exploitation is romanticized.

Although some of these pornography users recognize that trans-identified persons are being sexually exploited, they call it 'workplace discrimination', leaving the 'workplace' itself intact to harm others. These users believe, "Until we address the problems of workplace discrimination and insurance coverage for transitioning, trans porn, no matter how vilely it's marketed, is going to remain an important part of many young transwomen's reality."

---

2   All examples of the pornography, or the users' comments, quoted in this section come from the 'bihardcoreporn' sites, unless otherwise noted.

Other users mention that a substantial number of trans-identified women who are subjected to trans pornography come from poor countries where they are led into 'shemale' porn — a genre populated by participants who are engaged in pornography for economic subsistence:

> The vast majority of trans porn comes from 3rd world countries like Brazil and Thailand, but the distribution (including marketing and naming of it) is largely controlled by non-gay men in the US. And the majority of 'trans women' seen in 'shemale' porn are from countries where there are few economic or educational options for them.

Another user recognizes the indignity of pornography but bemoans the fact that porn has gotten so bad that he can't enjoy it anymore.

> It's gotten to the point where I can't really enjoy real porn. I just think 'There's no amount of money I'd be okay being paid for that,' and then feel awful for the people so abused or desperate that their dignity is worth so little [that] they're okay with being humiliated on screen for the amusement of jack-offs everywhere.

In recent years as demand increased, trans pornography has become more popular.

> The pornography typically involves men wearing lingerie and engaged in 'forced feminization' — eroticizing the illusion of being made to 'become women' through dress, makeup, and sexual submissiveness, and the fetishizing of the humiliation this brings.

This genre of porn sends the appalling message that "getting fucked makes you female because fucked is what a female is" (Gluck, 2020).

So-called 'sissification' pornography communicates to the viewer that being a woman is essentially degrading, and users can be turned on through 'forced feminization'. "In these scenarios, the penis is referred to as a 'clitty', and the anus as a 'pussy'. Prostate orgasms are referred to as 'sissygasms'" (Gluck, 2020). While trans advocates deny that these 'sissified' men are part of the trans community, the overlap between the trans-identified woman community and the 'sissy' community is evident on trans pornography sites.

Writer Genevieve Gluck who authored an article on trans pornography concludes that as all of us become more saturated with social media, so too do men who identify as women and want more accessibility to online streaming of pornography. "The phenomenon and trend is too great to ignore" (Gluck, 2020).

Alliances between Transgender and Pro-Sex Work Advocates: Promoting Decriminalization of Prostitution

Those trans activists who are shouting the loudest are often the same ones who are pro-sex work and campaigners for decriminalization of prostitution. Between activists who are pro-prostitution and those who are pro-transgender, there are many alliances with decriminalization advocates who partly populate the trans movement. By demeaning feminists who oppose the sex trade as SWERFs (sex worker exclusionary radical feminists), a term that derives from our earlier branding as TERFs, trans activists and pro-sex work advocates have joined at the hip to invoke another one of their derogatory terms to describe the radical feminist opposition to prostitution.

Organizations promoting transgender ideology are promoting full decriminalization of prostitution and the sex industry, which means decriminalization of pimps, brothels and sex buyers. In a *Slate* article covering LGBTQ life, prostitution decriminalization is acknowledged as the centerpiece of trans rights (Urquhart, 2018).

The more mainstream LGBT+ organizations such as Lambda Legal and the Gay and Lesbian Alliance Against Defamation (GLAAD) — which is now known by its initials to include bisexual and transgender issues — and others such as Amnesty International and the American Civil Liberties Union (ACLU), have publicized their support for decriminalization of prostitution, buying the pro-sex work line that current laws put women in prostitution at risk of violence. But it is decriminalization that puts women at risk of violence with proponents providing no recommendations for exiting prostitution, romanticizing pimps as third party business agents, and championing sex buyers as cordial clients.

Of course, prostituted women should be decriminalized. This has been a central message of feminist prostitution abolitionists. However, proponents of full decriminalization contend that it's necessary to decriminalize the entire industry by glamorizing the perpetrators — pimps and sex buyers — as 'protectors'. This is like asking the fox to protect the proverbial henhouse.

According to the 2015 US Transgender Survey, 19 percent of all trans-identified people and 47 percent of Black trans-identified women have engaged in what the survey calls 'sex work' (James, 2016).

Police harassment aimed at many men who identify as women is widespread. Many turn to prostitution to make a living, especially at the beginning of their 'transition'. Bias and discrimination, especially experienced by trans-identified women of color, limits their access to employment, and many end up in poverty without housing and health care. Forty-eight percent of trans-identified women who have engaged in prostitution also report they experienced homelessness. Eighty-six percent report being harassed by the police. Many are driven into 'survival sex' (Fitzgerald, 2015). Similar statistics are not published for women who identify as 'trans men'.

However, the term 'survival sex' does not explain the broader context that clarifies *why* many self-identified women (men) enter the sex trade. For some, it is to support their hormonal and surgical transitions. For others, it is part of the discovery process of becoming a 'woman', a validation of femininity, and an idealization of trans sex that unfortunately, for many, ends in violence, injury and death.

Not every trans person who engages in 'sex work' does so to avoid homelessness or to survive economically. Ally Brinken, a self-identified 'transfeminine genderqueer' person talks about entering prostitution because it is a "profession … [S]ex work as a community is very trans positive. It's profitable, and it's good for us, allowing us to use our bodies and our sexuality that society so often stigmatizes" (in Urquhart, 2018).

Ally originally got into prostitution when in graduate school to supplement his income and then started to enjoy being his own boss and pro-domme [pro-dominatrix] of a sex business. With the help of a pro-domme guide advertising practices for learning the 'business', Ally became a professional dominatrix. "You'll learn how to brand yourself, how to advertise, how to vet clients as well as how to sustain your business" (in Urquhart, 2018).

The policy recommendations of a 2015 report entitled *Meaningful Work: Transgender Experiences in the Sex Trade* highlight decriminalization of prostitution as the first step in what policy makers and legislators should do to assist transgender 'sex workers'. The recommendations claim that decriminalization will

> strengthen them by focusing resources on the real problem and making it far easier for sex workers to screen clients, report violence, access social services, and find employment outside the sex trade without the burden of a criminal record (Fitzgerald, 2016).

A study entitled *Prostituted Youth* found that 50 percent of all streetwalking prostituted minors in New York City were Black, and an additional 25 percent were Latino. A different study found that up to 67 percent of those in prostitution in New York were Black youth, and another 20 percent were Latinos (Gragg, 2007). Since African Americans make up 26 percent of the population in New York City, these numbers are extremely disproportionate.

Pro-transgender and pro-prostitution activists in the United States are using such numbers to exploit criminal justice reform and racial justice efforts – efforts to counteract police abuse and killings of African Americans. Organizations are using such campaigns as wedges to promote decriminalization of prostitution.

ACLU Trans Justice Campaign Manager, LaLa Holston-Zannell has written an essay entitled 'Sex Work is Real Work and It's Time to Treat It That Way'. She writes that police regularly target, harass, and assault "sex workers or those they presume are sex workers" such as trans women of color. Listing reasons to decriminalize 'sex work', she states, "Trans women of color feel the impact of criminalization the most, whether or not we are sex workers." Placing her reasons in the context of the Black Lives Matter Movement she argues,

"Decriminalizing sex work would promote the message that Black trans lives matter" (Holston-Zannell, 2020).

Links Between Feminist Activists Who Fight Against Prostitution and Transgenderism

As there are alliances between trans activists and 'sex work' activists, there are alliances between the opposition, with much crossover between feminist activists fighting to abolish prostitution and the sex industry, and those opposed to transgenderism and the transgender industry. The US Women's Liberation Front (WoLF) has taken a leading role in the opposition to transgenderism in its *Declaration of No Confidence in LGB Movement Leadership.*

WoLF has spearheaded opposition to LGBT+ leadership for its part in supporting the sex trade by opposing laws that penalize sex buyers and instead promote legalization and decriminalization of the sex industry. "Movement leaders have presented this support for the sex trade as part of the culture of the LGBT+ community, as if being desperate, excluded from the regular economy, or sexually exploited, were somehow innate to any of us." Calling this a "cynical abdication of the urgency of fighting sexual exploitation," the Declaration calls on organizations to stop justifying the sex trade (WoLF, n.d.).

In an article in *Medium*, the international Radical Girlsss Movement has made their resistance to transgenderism clear in an article supporting J.K. Rowling who has been a stalwart and influential opponent of transgenderism. The article pointed out "People have come to use the word gender ... when they really mean sex. This leaves us with a shaky foundation on which to make sense of male violence and femicide ... This distinction between sex and gender is essential in order to understand the root of women's oppression" (Radical Girlsss, 2020).

Many of the writings of the Radical Girlsss link the global sex trade to male violence against women. They turn a critical spotlight on the commodification of women's bodies that promotes "historical class inequalities between men and women and instead offers a brave new world in which women and girls can choose their way out of their own subjugation through the offerings of exploitation-based industries" (Radical Girlsss, 2020).

The UK Women's Human Rights Campaign (WHRC) is a global group of women committed to protecting "women's sex-based rights." It includes academics, writers, organizers, activists, and health practitioners, and aims "to represent the total breadth of the human female experience."

The WHRC created the *Declaration on Women's Sex-Based Rights* to lobby nations to maintain language protecting women and girls on the basis of sex rather than 'gender' or 'gender identity' and re-affirms these principles.

- We re-affirm motherhood as an exclusively female status.
- We re-affirm women's and girls rights to physical and repro-ductive integrity and oppose their exploitation through surrogacy and related practices.
- We re-affirm women's rights to freedom of opinion and expression, peaceful assembly and association, and political participation.
- We re-affirm women's rights to fair play in sports.
- We re-affirm the need to end violence against women and girls, and to protect rights of children (WHRC, n.d.)

The Declaration reaffirms the rights of women, described in the UN *Convention on the Elimination of all Forms of Discrimination against Women* (CEDAW). CEDAW requires ratifying countries to enact policies that reject sex-role stereotypes and affirm the rights of women and girls.

In another key feminist statement published in 2013, 37 radical feminists authored a manifesto entitled *Forbidden Discourse: The Silencing of Feminist Criticism of 'Gender'*. Among the signers were a global and racially diverse coalition of prominent feminists and writers from five countries including Laura X, Margo Jefferson, Michelle Wallace, Merle Hoffman, Faith Ringgold, Marge Piercy, and Christine Delphy. After the original statement was published, more signers were added.

Recognizing that "the system of male supremacy" has no tolerance for those who are gender non-conforming, the statement acknowledges that transitioning may ease an individual's pain but "it is not a political solution … Furthermore, a strong case can be made that it undermines a solution for all, even for the transitioning person, by embracing and reinforcing the cultural, economic and political tracking of 'gender' rather than challenging it" (37 Radical Feminists, 2013).

The statement concludes with a forward-looking message:

> We look forward to freedom *from* gender. The 'freedom *for* gender movement,' whatever the intentions of its supporters, is reinforcing the culture and institutions of gender that are oppressing women. We reject the notion that this analysis is transphobic (37 Radical Feminists, 2013).

The 37 Radical Feminists' statement was prescient in rejecting charges of transphobia anticipating perhaps that the statement would be removed from internet platforms once it was branded as 'transphobic'. Twitter and Facebook were in their early stages, but radical feminist criticism of transgenderism was being forcibly removed from websites and blogs that were at that point more widely used means of communication. The 37 Radical Feminists' statement was indeed taken down from its original internet platform, after a debate about its legitimacy was used as a ruse for censorship (37 Radical Feminists, 2013).

Many radical feminists have opposed both the global sex trade and transgenderism in their writings and activism and include: Germaine Greer, Julie Bindel, Renate Klein, Susan Hawthorne, Robin Morgan, Sheila Jeffreys, Pippa Fleming, Phyllis Chesler, Kathleen Barry, Donna Hughes, Lierre Keith, Pat Hynes, Anna Zobnina, Heather Brunskell-Evans, Meghan Murphy, Renee Gerlich, Julia Long, Twiss and Pat Butler, Nikki Kraft, Natasha Chart, Esohe Aghatise, Malka Marcovich, Cherry Smiley, Julian Vigo, Alix Dobkin, Raquel Rosario Sanchez, Drisha Fernandez, Nina Paley and Rachel Moran, some of whom have been quoted in this book and many others who have worked tirelessly for women's rights.

And numerous survivors of male violence, perpetrated by men who identify as women or non-binary, are beginning to make their voices heard in luminous books (see Chapter 4).

Celebrity Modeling of Sexual Objectification

When celebrities speak out in favor of an issue, many people listen and are influenced. When former Olympian Bruce Jenner underwent transsexual surgery, he became an icon of feminine fashion and was celebrated as a gender-transitioning hero on the cover of *Vanity Fair*. Jenner's fashion statement — appearing in a sexy bustier — was picked up by numerous media that portrayed the transformed Caitlin as a champion who had the courage to go public with a conversion from a male Olympics decathlon winner to a sexy feminized poseur.

Jenner won the Arthur Ashe award for courage at its 2015 event, making one wonder what counts as heroism anymore. A public exhibition of an artifactual feminized body displayed in a classic pin-up pose? When you are publicly awarded for a gender transition, and when you appear on the cover of a national magazine celebrating your 'courage', you have a public presence for better or for worse.

In an article entitled 'The Price of Caitlyn Jenner's Heroism', Rhonda Garelick has written: "Caitlyn's transition is more than a private matter. It is a commercial spectacle on an enormous scale, revealing some disturbing truths about what we value and admire in women" (Garelick, 2015). With the help of hormones and surgery, it is also a vivid sexualization of a constructed feminized body superimposed on a male body and 'dressed to kill'.

A basic tenet of feminism is that women shouldn't be treated as sexual objects, but Jenner objectifies himself for the viewing public. Jenner's rewarded appearance as a cover girl epitomized an image of woman that is alluring to men and reveals the man-made femininity and the hypersexualization of the trans movement.

Men have always fetishized parts of the female body, the fetish used as an erotic battery — a sexual turn-on — including a fixation on women's breasts, or small feet in the Chinese tradition, or certain articles of female clothing, such as women's underwear. Now self-declared women are fetishizing the whole female body. Jenner has helped to provide a template for the ideal trans feminine body that men who identify as women wish they could possess. Fetishizing women and our body parts objectifies women and serves as another prop for men's sexual gratification and the dehumanizing of women.

Sexual objectification dictates women's images in art, in advertising, and in the cosmetics, fashion, and pornography industries, where men have constructed their versions of women's bodies. It infects the images of women called forth in men's language such as cunt, pussy and slut.

Historically, women have lost control of our own bodies — from the violation of women's reproductive rights to the inability to walk down public streets without being sexually harassed or assaulted. The right of sexual access to women's bodies has historically been a shared male entitlement — droit de seigneur — to sex on demand of the patriarch. Male entitlement generates the deception that women consent to being violated, as is alleged of rape victims and women in prostitution.

Permeating the construction of man-made femininity is the age-old patriarchal perception that women's bodies should be made available to men — sexually and reproductively. Trans self-declaration is a peculiar variation on this theme of access, and its most recent manifestation is of self-declared women (men) demanding sexual access to lesbian bodies. Men who self-declare as lesbians not only argue they have female brains but also some claim female penises.

The Transgender Movement and Its Erasure of Lesbians

The fast-moving transgender campaign influenced the rapid erasure of lesbians. Girls who would have become lesbians in a former time were pressured to transition, beginning with the using of male hormones. Over a decade ago, in speaking with a group of young informed lesbians at a conference, I learned that the big question among girls and young women immersed in LGBT+ circles is "are you on hormones or have you transitioned yet?" Many older lesbians are asking where have all the lesbians gone.

The last several decades have seen young girls increasingly self-identifying as male and seeking male hormone treatment, with some proceeding to surgery. When *The Transsexual Empire* was first published in 1979, such 'transitioning' would have been anathema to lesbians who understood the construction of gender and its dissatisfactions from a feminist political perspective.

LGBT+ groups have displaced lesbian communities and become the primary affinity gatherings for socializing and 'educating' young girls about their gender dissatisfactions, and for channeling them into identifying as self-declared men. Not only has 'lesbian' been swallowed up in the word 'queer' but also naming one's self a lesbian has become a dirty word in LGBT+ groups. Young women who identify as lesbians are accused of being transexclusionary, transphobic and 'vagina fetishists'. Julie Bindel has written, "Not only do lesbians have the least clout in the 'queer' world, on account of being mere women, the word 'lesbian' is becoming synonymous with 'transphobia'" (Bindel, 2018a).

A number of self-declared women (men) purport to be 'trans lesbians' and have stepped up the pressure on lesbians to have sex with them. If lesbians refuse, they are accused of sexually discriminating against trans-identified women. Bullying young lesbians that rejecting sex with 'trans lesbians' is transphobic is an appalling example of sexual harassment and intimidation based on contempt of lesbians.

Self-declared lesbians (men) have also used the internet to viciously attack lesbian events and gatherings where trans-identified women are not welcome. African American performance artist and writer Pippa Fleming focuses on the dwindling presence of lesbians in the African American community — that "a war is being waged against female-to-female love and that lesbian identity is fighting for its life" (Fleming, 2018).

Trans activists argue that men can appropriate lesbian identity. Their battle cry is "men can be lesbians too." Fleming argues that trans activists have especially undermined black lesbians.

> Whether it be in feminist studies, gender studies or the history of gay pride, black lesbians often go without their names or sexual orientations being mentioned … to brand everyone and everything as queer and transgender, means black lesbians are rendered invisible … lesbians have a right to say no to the phallus, no matter how it's concealed or revealed (Fleming, 2018).

It appears that women's bedrooms are now the topic du jour of the transgender press and blogosphere. Certain forums have been organized specifically to discuss and strategize how lesbians could be pressured to date and have sex with self-declared lesbians (men). The epitome of this absurdity is the claim that these men possess a lesbian penis or (seriously!) a 'lady stick'.

For many years, lesbian feminists have been sharply critical of the view that men can be women and have rejected the male fantasy of 'male lesbians'. As early as the 1990s, singer and lesbian activist Alix Dobkin, who died in 2021, wrote about the ways she and other lesbian feminists who opposed the demands of 'trans lesbians' were disinvited even from certain lesbian events because they dissented from the view that men could be women, never mind that men could be lesbians (Dobkin, 1998).

Dobkin also pointed out that many women are implicated in their own erasure when they too readily are willing to cede a female identity to men. These women not only concede that men can be women but are also championing male lesbians. "In the Lesbian community, 'diversity' used to be code for the coming together of Lesbians from a variety of racial, ethnic and class backgrounds." But with the acceptance of so-called male women and male lesbians, diversity now means accepting men as women and "the 'inclusion' of, you guessed it: 'nice men', 'supportive men', 'curious men', 'questioning men', 'ex-men' and anyone with a 'sexual minority' credential" (Dobkin, 2000a).

Dobkin realized that acceptance of the fantasy that men can become women is 'cultural appropriation'. "Everyone has a right to self-definition so long as other people's boundaries are respected, and this means recognizing when certain identity claims disrespect the identity claimed" (Dobkin, 2000b).

Cultural appropriation has been widely condemned when, for example, someone takes on a Native American identity, tradition, or dress and adopts it as his/her own. But when men who identify as women claim they are women or lesbians, too many women disregard this appropriation of a female identity that is increasingly co-opted by men. Germaine Greer issued a similar warning. "Women's lack of choosiness about who may be called a woman strengthens the impression that women do not see their sex as real, and suggests that perhaps they too identify themselves as not-male, the other, any other" (Greer, 2000).

CHAPTER THREE

Self-Declared Men, Transitioning and De-transitioning

In the LGBT+ community, "Anyone who dares to say they regret transitioning is told they are committing actual violence towards trans people."

—Max Robinson

Trans activists are not equal assailants of both sexes. They seldom confront natal men who are preserved from the vitriol and abuse aimed at female critics of transgenderism. Overwhelmingly, the emerging lexicon of transgender activists is designed to degrade women. According to trans speak, we can't name ourselves women anymore and, instead, must accept that we are *cis-women, front holes, persons with cervixes,* or *non-men.*

This branding of women comes from a trans vocabulary that gets zanier and zanier, insulated from ordinary conversation and often located on the edge of rationality. Those who are attacked in a particularly vicious way are women who transitioned into trans-manhood and then ultimately chose to de-transition, de-conform and reject masculine identity.

Trans activists are not trying to impose their offensive vocabulary on natal men. There is no matching campaign to undermine men, and rarely does the term *cis-men* appear. I have never heard men referred to as *back holes, non-women, or sperm producers.* Trans energy is not invested in targeting men, nor is there any corresponding goal of trans activists to modify manhood. But womanhood and women's rights are up for grabs.

It is seldom women who identify as men that are launching the linguistic missiles targeting gender critics. It is seldom women who identify as men that hurl insults and threats at women. It is seldom women who identify as men who weaponize words like TERF and gleefully belittle women who are critical of transgender orthodoxies. And it is seldom women who identify as men who soak up all the media attention.

Trans activists target women as easy marks knowing that many women will simply accommodate them. It is women who are being gaslighted into accepting men as legitimate women.

The thrust of trans activism has by and large been reserved for women and organizations dedicated to assisting women. Trans activists have exerted no comparable pressure on men's clubs or organizations to admit self-declared men as members. Their attacks on women's organizations and events have no counterpart of invading men's single-sex venues. Men's clubs and events are left alone while trans activists are aggressively picketing women's groups and events.

Why aren't trans activists vilifying all TERMs, 'trans exclusionary men' who are engaged in the actual murders of trans-identified persons, rather than demonizing radical feminists who get accused of hate speech, transphobia and outright violence against 'trans women'? While some women's organizations have caved into labelling themselves cis-women, avoiding the very word woman unless it is modified, men's organizations refer to men as men, not as cis-men, nor do they use other trans-generated terms.

Trans activists have laid claim to women's sports. Men who identify as women may not shine against other male competitors, but they can excel in women's sports. Thus self-declared women, such as cyclist Rachel MacKinnon, are demanding inclusion and the right to participate against women in women's athletic events. But self-declared men are not demanding entrance into men's sports because most women — which is what they are — would be at a biological disadvantage: the same disadvantage that exists when they are compelled to compete in women's sports against biological men who claim to be women.

The Invisibility of Women
Who Self-Declare as Men

Women who identify as men have little visibility in the US and international media compared to men who identify as women. Because there is so much attention demanded and given to self-declared women, self-declared men seem to be largely left out of the mainstream narrative. As CJ Atkinson observed, "the story told about the trans masculine experience is often a footnote, an addendum to the experience of trans women, as though all trans people experience things in exactly the same way" (Atkinson, 2018). So even when women become 'trans men', like women everywhere they are second-class.

One exception to this invisibility of 'trans men' is Stephen Whittle. Whittle, a legal scholar and Professor of Equalities Law at Manchester Metropolitan University, is a prominent campaigner in the transgender community in Britain and has also been president of the World Professional Association for Transgender Health (WPATH). A natal woman, Whittle has written widely on gender issues, and after the Gender Recognition Act came into force in 2004, Whittle achieved legal recognition as a man and was able to marry her female partner. Before her sex change, she was described as 'a radical lesbian'.

Whittle has been credited with almost single-handedly inventing the legal switching of sex with gender identity and is also known for convening a self-appointed group of scholars and activists who came together to draft a set of legal principles relating to transgender, now called *The Yogyakarta Principles*. While not having the authority of a UN convention or declaration, this document has been used as an influential source on gender identity, especially for proponents of transgenderism, because it establishes a definition in international law that describes gender as a "felt internal and individual experience, which may or may not correspond with the sex assigned at birth." *The Principles* have been widely quoted in academic articles, bills, resolutions and reports and serve as a legal basis for making gender into sex.[3]

Self-declared male Aydian Dowling, in googling the word transgender, pulled up 402 images on page one of the search. Mostly all the photos were of self-declared women. *TIME* magazine featured Laverne Cox on the cover of its 2014 cover. Netflix favorite Janet Mock was awarded a three-year multimillion-dollar contract, the first self-declared woman to make such a deal with a major film company. Caitlyn Jenner, formerly Bruce, winner of the men's Olympic decathlon, debuted as a sexy woman plastering the cover of *Vanity Fair* magazine.

Media have rendered women who identify as men invisible except in one area, that of abortion. One article headlined, 'Not Everyone Who Has an Abortion Is a Woman'. It featured the need for women's organizations that provide abortions to women to insure that self-declared men who are biologically female can also obtain them, while still declaring themselves as men. The strategy was to pressure women's groups to change their mission statements (Rankin, 2013).

New York Abortion Access Fund (NYAAF) was one of the first US pro-choice groups to change its mission statement arguing for what they call 'gender inclusivity':

> NYAAF's belief in physical autonomy is a core link between our belief in the right to an abortion, and our belief in the rights of transgender and gender nonconforming people to access holistic health care and services. We recognize that people who identify as men can become pregnant and seek abortions; we strive to meet the needs of all people who seek our funding (NYAAF, n.d.).

---

3   See Brunskell-Evans (2020) and Hawthorne (2020) for further feminist critiques of *The Yogyakarta Principles*.

It's a baffling task to disentangle the meaning of this statement, which can confuse those who don't follow the intricacies of transgenderism. In a US Democratic presidential primary debate in 2019, Rep. Julian Castro underscored his support for abortion rights by mistakenly admonishing viewers not to forget "someone in the trans community — a trans female." He continued, "Because a trans female is poor, doesn't mean they shouldn't exercise that right to choose" (in Kitchner, 2019). No wonder that Castro confused self-declared men with self-declared women when the maxim in some abortion service organizations is, 'Men can get pregnant too'. Understanding requires not only a linguistic leap, but also a leap of logic and a brain that must work overtime to sort out just what this slogan means.

Senator Kamala Harris, when she ran in the same primary for president, was attacked for affirming that pregnancy is a women's issue. She and her campaign were blamed for not upholding the reality-defying dogma that 'men can get pregnant too'. Anyone not prepared to accept that self-declared men can have abortions is guilty of 'cis-sexism'.

Ignored is the truth that a woman who identifies as a man is in need of an abortion precisely because she remains a biological woman. *Because* 'he' is a biological woman who has become pregnant, that is why 'he' seeks an abortion.

Transgender activists argue that abortion organizations should not only change their language and mission but in doing so, reach out to the LGBT+ organizations so that self-declared men don't feel excluded and can count on locating sympathetic places where they can go to receive an abortion if needed.

Pregnant Men?

There is an underlying sub-text that explains why trans activists won't use the term 'pregnant woman' and instead talk about 'pregnant persons'. A small but vocal contingent of self-declared women is demanding the 'right' to get pregnant. Since self-declared women are biological men, they argue this term excludes them and their efforts to become pregnant. There is an outspoken faction of the transgender movement that is clamoring for new reproductive technologies, such as womb transplants.

In 2018, the first womb transplant from a deceased female donor to a live woman was successful — news that came four years after another womb transplant had taken place from a live donor woman to another woman who experienced a subsequent successful birth. Transgender advocates view womb transplants as potentially achievable for men who identify as women who want to get pregnant.

An article in the *British Medical Journal* expressed openness to furthering the future of male pregnancy:

> We discussed the potential medical steps necessary and associated risks for uterus transplantation in *genetically XY women*. Presently, the medical technology does not exist to make uterus transplantation a safe and effective option for genetically XY women, however this group should not be summarily excluded from participation in trials (Sampson et al, 2019, italics mine).

In 2018, Dr Richard Paulson, former president of the American Society for Reproductive Medicine asserted, "there is no anatomical reason why a womb could not be successfully implanted into a transgender woman." It could happen tomorrow, he claimed, and barring "additional challenges," he doesn't see any problems that would prevent it.

> I personally suspect there are going to be trans women who are going to want to have a uterus and will likely get the transplant ... As womb transplant surgery is further improved and perfected, it's vital trans women are not excluded from the conversation, as it could immeasurably improve a great many lives (in Lavender, 2019).

If the medical community accepts this treatment for self-declared women, it would be a short hop to resolving legal issues for men who claim a 'right to give birth' — a 'right' that could not legally be denied. There are no regulations that would prevent a self-declared woman with a womb implant from having in vitro fertilization (IVF) treatment followed by caesarian birth (Lavender, 2019).

Reproductive specialists and transgender doctors have worked together at some points. In 1966, medical psychologist John Money, together with Howard Jones of in vitro fertilization (IVF) fame and a team of other clinicians, founded the gender identity clinic at Johns Hopkins University in Baltimore, Maryland — the first prestigious medical institution in the country to offer what was then called 'change of sex operation'. The Hopkins gender identity clinic closed its doors in 1979 when pressure from members of the faculty found that "sex change surgery conveys no objective advantage in terms of social rehabilitation" (Hamby, 2017).

Forty years later, Johns Hopkins Hospital experienced a resurrection and reversed its policy on what they call "transgender health … moving forward to take care of transgender people in a supportive, affirming way that's grounded in evidence-based medicine" (Hamby, 2017). With pressure from 600 students, faculty members, interns, alumni and others at the medical school who signed a petition calling on Hopkins to develop a new Center of Transgender Health, "the hospital has stated that it strongly and unambiguously supports the LGBT community but acknowledges the right of individuals associated with Hopkins to express views contrary to its official policy" (Hamby, 2017). Today, the Center is a fully functioning clinic that offers an assorted menu of trans services.

In 1985, Money began talking about male pregnancy that precipitated journalists Dick Teresi and Kathleen McAuliffe's article in *Omni* magazine asserting there were almost no intractable problems that would prevent a man carrying a baby to term. The article dismissed the hormonal, ovarian and womb difficulties that other physicians said were barriers to male pregnancies (Teresi and McAuliffe, 1985).

The New York Times revived its interest in male pregnancy featuring a 1994 article by Dick Teresi who had raised private money for a reproductive experiment. Bob Guccioni, the pornographer who owned *Omni*, agreed to finance an experiment in womb implants, but Teresi quietly dropped the project when the experts agreed, "it would be more appropriate to try the technique on women who have had their uteri removed" (Teresi, 1994). Wouldn't you know that proponents of male pregnancies would first use women as their experimental subjects/objects in the interests of advancing male motherhood!

As of this writing (August 2021), only 'people with ovaries and a uterus', i.e. natal women, can get pregnant unless you also count self-declared men who are biological women if their fertility has not been damaged by the male hormones taken in transitioning.

The De-transitioners: A Long Line of Self-Declared Men Recovering Their Womanhood

Recent research has indicated that the majority of those who are transgendering currently are young girls on a path to becoming trans-identified men. It is also the case, though not frequently mentioned in academic sexuality studies courses or the media, that the greatest number of de-transitioners are girls or women who have rejected their current trans status — many who have powerfully written about it.

De-transitioning challenges the conventional trans narrative, prompting trans activists to suppress any discussion of it. Any revelations about the numbers of young women who have chosen to take back their womanhood after transitioning is never examined openly.

Although there is not much credible epidemiological research on the number of self-declared men who are reclaiming their womanhood, another authoritative kind of community-based research can be culled from multiple YouTube videos, blogs, Twitter, Facebook and other writings on social media. On such sites, women who formerly identified as trans men speak movingly about this severance from themselves and other women, and why many have de-transitioned and taken back their womanhood.

De-transitioners: In Their Own Words

There are misconceptions about what de-transitioning is all about, and the many different ways of experiencing and describing it. Although a commonly accepted definition of de-transition is "the cessation or reversal of a transgender identification or gender transition whether by social, legal, or medical means" (Wikipedia, n.d.), personal accounts shed a brighter light on this complex process. My definition of de-transitioner is a person who is a survivor of transgenderism, most of whom are born female.

One common definition of survivor is 'a person who manages to live through a situation that often causes death'. What we are witnessing in the de-transitioning movement is women's resurrection from a type of living death that sentenced their womanhood to oblivion.

Some survivors of transitioning question the term de-transitioning. A survivor whose pen name is Satan Herself observes, "I don't know how I feel about the term de-transition. I prefer to call it recovery" (in Joyce, 2020). Others have pointed out that de-transitioning is better described as *de-conforming*.

The testimonies that follow feature various reasons why women who identified as men began to de-transition, underscoring the complexities of their individual journeys. In a collection of writings called *Blood and Visions: Womyn Reconciling with Being Female* and published by Autonomous Press, women unpack their journeys going from female to self-declared male and back to female. Numerous de-transitioner stories are also published on sites such as *Post Trans, Gender Apostate, 4thWaveNow* and other such online venues frequented by trans-identified men and de-transitioners.

Self-Declared Men in a Man's World

Some de-transitioners talk about transitioning as giving them a passport into a world where they were treated as equals. Others said it was a survival strategy and the antidote to 'compulsory femininity', a remedy for the gender distress they experienced.

> Men shook my hand without being gentle and looked at me face-to-face instead of giving me a full body scan. I had discovered white male privilege. The grass was even greener than I could have imagined … (Autonomous, 2015, Staring Back & Man Made Trans).

> People were definitely nicer to me after I transitioned and they saw me as a man instead of a butch dyke … Transitioning was a kind of a survival strategy. … I got a lot of very harsh, negative messages about what it meant to be a woman … Living as a man provided a kind of refuge until I was ready to dive into all that (Herzog, 2017).

> I could speak with authority … in the gas station, on the phone, to the waitress, to the bartender, to the landlord. I was taken seriously by perfect strangers (Autonomous, 2015, Staring Back & Man Made Trans).

Self-declared men who have not chosen the path of de-transitioning and remain as self-identified men also open a unique window into how men talk about women. Much of what they say provides an insider's view of how women who identify as men are treated in the real world:

> If I'm going off-the-cuff, no one really questions it. It's taken as, 'He's saying it, so it must be true.' Whereas while I was practicing [law] as a female, it was, 'Show me your authority' (Alter, n.d.).

> All of a sudden, I'm the golden child. I have been with this company for 6 years, no one ever recommended me for management. Now I'm put into a managerial position where I could possibly be a regional director (Alter, n.d.).

> As a female I felt I had to smile all the time, just to be accepted. As a male I don't feel a sense of having to be pleasant to look at (Alter, n.d.).

I've heard men saying things about slapping a woman or cheating on women in the most brutal ways and think it's OK. Being privy to the conversations that men have amongst themselves really does give me an indication of how they think about women. And sometimes it can be really scary (Alter, n.d.).

Women who decide to remain as trans-identified men have many observations about their changes, especially as they become conscious of the ways in which they take on male privilege. Journalist Charlotte Alter sums up the ways that the world views them as men and treats them differently: "They gained professional respect, but lost intimacy. They exuded authority, but caused fear" (Alter, n.d.).

When self-declared men say their words and opinions are more easily accepted and less questioned, transitioning becomes tangible. Their self-perceptions change as they become more decisive and assertive. Compared to their natal female colleagues, women who identify as men are judged as more competent than the women they work with.

Many who still identified as men talked about the glaring difference in the way men talk about women to other men. As part of the male club, self-declared men were party to the crude humor men used to sexualize women.

Misogyny: External and Internal

Reasons why women transition are radically different than men's motives for transitioning. A substantial number of female survivors of transgenderism report that they shifted identities from female to male because of the misogyny they experienced as girls and women. Recently, survivors have also come to grips with the way they internalized misogyny, a consequence of the social pressure to transition in a society where becoming a self-declared man is often more accepted than being a natal women, especially a lesbian.

Conforming as male meant hearing the word 'rape' used as a synonym for domination, humiliation, or asserting authority — and not being able to say anything … Being a man meant bragging about 'getting pussy' and listening to over-dramatized fantasy versions of my co-workers' sexual exploits. It meant laughing at the misogyny saturating my world and profiting from it … this was one I could not swallow … though I tried for three years via a deepening subconscious hatred of my own sex (Autonomous, 2015, Staring Back & Man-Made Trans).

So how did I get to where I am today? I was sexually molested from the age of 8 to the age of 12. After all, I bought the lies. At one point I believed the gender craze, I advocated for the trans community, I did the TV circuit, and I wrote a book (when I lived as a male called Mark [Cummings] entitled the *The Mirror Makes No Sense*. I believed that I was born wrong.

Growing up in a female body wasn't easy for me. Friends told me I should lose weight. I couldn't leave the house without men whistling after me and people talked to my breasts instead of talking to my face (Post Trans, Nelle's Story).

I regret it all … There's a very strong narrative that if you don't transition you are going to kill yourself (in Joyce, 2020).

In reading these accounts, patterns emerge of past sexual abuse and harassment, eating disorders, discomfort with — even hating — their bodies, and rejection of 'compulsory femininity'.

The Complexities of De-transitioning

De-transitioning is not always an immediate desisting from a gendered body and/or mind. It's a process that may take time, and those involved may be betwixt and between for several years. A small number who have made efforts to de-transition still declare as 'transmen'.

In adolescence, Cecile Stuart loathed her developing female body. She became Michael in her 20s, because she was constantly under stress about going to the toilet, "living a lie," and "pretending to be a man." She got to the point where she had to make a decision about her life and resolved, "Okay, this is ridiculous. You're not a real man: you're just presenting to the world as a man. I decided I'd try to be comfortable in the body [female] I'd originally been given" (in Dumas, 2015).

De-transitioners exit in many different ways and for diverse reasons. Laura, who is now the mother of a young toddler, has a YouTube channel where she talks about her de-transition and why she left a trans life behind.

> Eventually, I got sick of living a lie. When I transitioned, I was isolated and did not know how to help myself. I had spent the better part of a decade forcing friends and family to support my transition and cutting people out of my life who refused to play by my rules ... I don't see myself as a victim, and I want to take accountability for my mistakes. Part of that means speaking out against this harmful ideology (Post Trans, Laura's Story).

Others mention difficulties coping with their situations and of being in-between identities.

> I suppose I would have to admit that I am not coping yet ... I still bind my breasts. I still want top surgery ... my discomfort predates puberty ... I don't expect to ever make sense of it. I can live with that (Autonomous, 2015, Coping).

> When FTMs express distaste for de-transition ... They assume I am accepting the female gender role ... Of course it is unappealing to think about going back to the performance that was so painful that evacuation was necessary. I am not going backwards. I am living in a completely different way than I did before or during transition because now I know I can opt out of both forms of gender conformity (Autonomous, 2015, De-transition Is De-programming).

When the domestic chores need to be done in trans activist circles, ironically self-declared men are stereotypically treated as the biological women that they are. They do all the jobs necessary to organize events, make the coffee, mediate arguments and take on the tasks that natal women usually assume.

> I've been in lots of rooms with men ... I have not found one avenue of activism or one professional context where the grunt work ... did

not fall to women. Except in trans activism. In trans activism, young men (women) do all that ... Young men ... make the phone calls. Young men burn themselves out ... So now I'm out of the trans scene (Autonomous, 2015, Girl).

Where Have All the Lesbians Gone?
The Trans Trap

The increase in girls identifying as males is related to the disdain in which both society and the trans movement hold women who are lesbians. Julie Bindel has written that lesbians have the "least clout in a queer world" (Bindel, 2018b).

Of all the women and girls who have undergone the transitioning process that brought them to the point of identifying as male, lesbians have been intimately marked by their journeys to and through the promised land of manhood. Many speak of the ways in which bullies and others undermined their female sense of self. Most presented as not feminine in appearance during childhood and in adolescence, more of a 'butch' appearance.

As some describe it, 'butch' is not another stereotype of masculinity but more of a way of accessing qualities that have been reserved for men.

> I call myself butch, but it's not an identity ... it's just a descriptor of how I fit into a gendered world. Butch isn't masculine. I work on my habits of performing masculinity and femininity on a daily basis ... I'm not keeping score anymore, because gender is a game rigged in favor of men (Autonomous, 2015, De-transition Is De-programming).

> Shortly after beginning my transition, my mental and physical health spiraled. It changed my life in ways I wish I could take back. I know I'm simply a butch lesbian. I feel at home with myself and have begun repairing my relationship with my body. I thought for so long we were two separate things, but now I know my body is actively me, and I am not outside it ... (Post Trans, Eli's Story).

People who would have said awkward and offensive things to me about my sexual orientation only three years ago are now coming up to me at parties to ask my pronouns and tell me how brave I am. I suspected all along that straight people would like me better as a man ... than as a butch lesbian, but seeing them admit to it is hurtful and shocking (Autonomous, 2015, Coping).

Others spoke about the lack of role models and social networks that existed in their growing lives.

There were no lesbians around to guide me, to speak to me. To help me unpack my past ... my relationship to the world ... Of course I'd think I was a man, what other words did I have? I am a woman, I am a lesbian ... It simply is the factual truth of my existence ... and my body doesn't need to change to house me happily within it (Post Trans, Andy's Story).

Meeting other de-transitioners was a revelation ... Where have these women been all my life? ... It was just so normal to be a lesbian and a masculine woman and I've never felt that, ever (in Joyce, 2020).

Leaving the Trans Life Behind

De-transitioning for Max Robinson became a possibility when she and a group of friends began to read a wide variety of radical and lesbian feminist literature "... and to discuss and debate it at such length and with such depth that it began to change our lives ... becoming a feminist and tangibly living my feminism in community."

In her groundbreaking book entitled *Detransition: Beyond Before and After*, Robinson writes about her journey:

I 'chose' transition because I did not understand that life as a gender non-compliant lesbian was a real option. Without the understanding and awareness of misogyny and patriarchy I have now — that is a feminist consciousness — I saw transition as 'empowering' and named it to myself and others as such ... [but] my transition was not empowering. It required no community of women, and it accomplished nothing for other women (2021, pp. 6–7, p. 8).

Others discovered sister de-transitioners and lesbian feminist commonalities on the internet, read feminist books and articles, and were encouraged to write about their experiences.

> De-transition was a shock to my system that woke me from a fantasy, and I couldn't be more thankful I found the community of de-transitioned women online (Post Trans, Eli's Story).

> Being trans was an idea that made [past] absolute sense to me … to … cut pieces off of yourself to claim your rightful identity … I created a new me … I never got to finish creating him. I found the de-transitioners first and realized I had much in common with them … I respect her [herself] … She's not embarrassed that she likes girls. She doesn't lie or apologize (Autonomous, 2015, Backstory).

> Other people have dictated my comfort level most of my life, and I am so pissed off that I have internalized the putrid message that what I am is not meant to be natural or acceptable. I am not a man, I cannot be a man, and I shouldn't need to be a man for my 'masculinity' to be acceptable. I am exhausted from punishing myself for being the sort of woman I am (Autonomous, 2015, What's Wrong with Being Butch?).

> One of the (many) mindfucks of de-transition is the feeling of deception/double life. I don't think of myself as a man. Plenty of people who see me think I am one, though, and I spent about four years trying my hardest to be one (Autonomous, 2015, Womanhood Still Feels Like It Doesn't Belong to Me).

> All the pain, all the trauma is left behind and to have to turn around and dig that back up while having to deal with the existence of gender is extremely difficult. Rather than cling to an appealing but overwhelmingly false notion of what gender is and how it works. I imagine it would be far easier to simply stay detached and keep gender from getting into your head in the first place (Autonomous, 2015, Passing the Damage On).

> For me, I couldn't pursue the aesthetic changes to my form via medical intervention. Without medical intervention to change my aesthetic sex characteristics and a staunch disbelief in brain sex theory, there was nothing left to point to that defined me as male … Female with

a history of transition and de-transition, but female the same as all females (Autonomous, 2015, Thought Exercises).

For Jackie, instead of talking to therapists about de-transitioning, she found an online community of women. She felt clinicians lean towards wanting to help people transition since they don't want to be seen as gatekeepers or labelled as transphobic.

> I started to think the whole concept of transitioning was regressive ... I didn't really feel like I could talk to my counselors about de-transitioning in the way I wanted, because they have specific political views, and I felt like if I said I had these criticisms of the whole concept of transitioning, they would have thought I was being brainwashed by transphobic bigots (Herzog, 2017).

Women Returning to Themselves or Not

> I regret it all ... There's a very strong narrative that if you don't transition you are going to kill yourself (in Joyce, 2020).

> In translandia, I'd parroted a lot of drivel ... Half-truths that wouldn't stand up to a moment's scrutiny ... Now my future self is the woman I give my greatest gifts and for whom I make my most costly sacrifices ... The body I live in now is marked by betrayals I've endured especially the ones I've inflicted on myself. But this body doesn't need to scream anymore to tell me what she likes or wants, what brings her pleasure. My life is listening (Autonomous, 2015, Living Amends Means Caring for My Future Self).

> If I have learned anything from the process of coming back to myself and accepting my female body as female, it is this: what we are is powerful beyond the measure and comprehension of men. The specific ways they target us can be read against the grain to reveal why they do these things to us (Autonomous, 2015, What Women Are).

One of the most memorable essays about the gendered life and the process of de-transitioning is called 'Women Transition' written by Crashchaoscats (2016). It reminds me of a triptych, defined as a work of art that is divided into three sections, or three carved panels that are hinged together and can be folded shut or displayed open.

In this triptych, de-transitioning courses through the trans traveler's life — three different phases hinged together by the glue of time: the natal sex one is born into; the transition undergone to conform to a masculine or feminine gender identity; and the de-transitioning movement.

Each paragraph at the beginning of the essay begins with the words, "Women transition." Repetition of this phrase is a refrain that takes the reader through the various high and lowlands that women inhabit during their de-transitioning process while living all the contradictions that these words — "women transition" — express.

> Women transition because we feel, see and experience ourselves as men, as genderqueer, as transmasculine ... as not female in some way ... because we look at pictures of transitioned FtMs and read about their experiences and feel desire for what they have ... as we watch their bodies change ... Women transition and take t [testosterone] for a year, four years, ten years before deciding to stop or start taking t and never stop ... Women transition and never pass ... Women transition and hear what men say amongst themselves, hear them talk about women like pieces of meat or discuss rape like it's no big deal ...Women transition and love how testosterone makes us feel psychologically ... more confident ... Women transition and ... argue for transitioning to be made more accessible ... Women transition and just want to be seen and treated like any other man.

At some midway point in the essay, the iteration changes to "Women stop transitioning."

> Women transition and then stop and go back to living as a woman ... because we transitioned so young and have never lived as an adult woman before ... and feel like we've ruined or mutilated our bodies ... Women stop transitioning and have to question a lot of what we used to believe in ... Women stop transitioning and become radical feminists ... Women stop transitioning ... and think transitioning is still helpful for the majority of people who pursue it ... until we start talking to other women who stopped transitioning, until we start comparing and contrasting our experiences and gradually come to see this as a social problem rooted in patriarchy ... and discuss

how trans ideology restricted our vision ... and finally say what we couldn't say when we were part of the trans community ... Women stop transitioning and talk amongst ourselves about our trauma, about the hardships we endure for being female in a society that hates females, about how this influenced our decision to transition ... Women stop transitioning and find our power in our Selves and in our bodies (Crashchaoscats, 2016).

For trans travelers like Crash, her travels took her to a dramatic turnaround — unfortunately a repudiation of much of what she had written in her evocative essays on de-transitioning.

Several years after she wrote her lyrical article on 'Women Transition', Crash gave an interview to *Slate's* pro-prostitution journalist Evan Urquhart about her recent disavowal of the de-transitioning movement that she had helped found. Using her original name of Ky Shevers, Ky/Crash recanted her former feminist position, saying that her retraction was prompted by the UK Keira Bell Court decision — a decision that she said deprived trans-identified persons of needed health care. "Trans people deserve access to support and it makes no sense to shut down peoples' health care" (in Urquhart, 2021).

But trans health care is neither 'care' nor healthy and calling it 'health care' ennobles it and covers up the medicalization of thousands of children who undergo extreme procedures such as lifelong hormone treatment and unnecessary surgery and then suffer its medically-induced consequences.

For a talented writer who appeared to understand the relationship between personal and political factors, and who lived the feminist refrain that the personal is political, Ky/Crash has resorted to a very individualistic apologia for her severance from the de-transitioning movement and her re-embracing of a transmasculine identity (but still using she/her pronouns). In the background of this personal decision are the resources of a gender industry that minimizes de-transitioning and supports recanting.

It's instructive that Ky/Crash's disavowal of her past has occurred in a political climate where several significant institutional events have been successful in rebuking the official purveyors of transgenderism. First came the UK government determination that the Gender Recognition Act of 2004, an Act of Parliament that allows people who have gender dysphoria to change their legal gender if they undergo certain medical requirements, would *not* be changed to include gender self-identification, a proposal that had been backed by transgender advocates and organizations. Feminist and other gender critics welcomed this decision that preserved women's rights: "The government has acknowledged women are stakeholders too and policies must fairly balance the conflicting rights of trans people and women" (Murphy and Brooks, 2020).

Next came de-transitioner Keira Bell's victory in the High Court of London's decision that Bell never should have been given puberty blockers and testosterone treatment, as well as a double mastectomy at the Tavistock Clinic. The Court ruled that it was "highly unlikely that a 13-year-old and doubtful that 14- and 15-year-olds are mature enough to consent to such procedures, and that doctors treating 16- and 17-year-olds may also need to consult a judge before starting" (*The Economist*, 2020).

In December 2020, following the High Court judgment in the Bell case, the Gender Identity Development Service (GIDS) at the Tavistock Clinic suspended all new referrals for hormone treatment. Within a period of three years, over 35 clinicians had resigned from the Clinic, with most being critical of the way in which children were being processed as through an assembly line, and given quick affirmation for puberty blockers and hormonal treatments. Numerous patients were very young children. Rather than continuing to participate in what they called the 'transgender lunacy' of chemical and surgical mutilations, these clinicians were "fed up with the number of children that are being over-diagnosed and over-medicalized as part of the societal blitz to turn everyone into some kind of trans-mutant ... more children than before are being approved for transgender therapy by a complicit medical system with no concern for their well-being" (Onyenucheya, 2020).

The gender identity movement in the UK has been dealt a strong rebuke. Trans activists and journalists like Evan Urquhart are keen to recruit high value sources for their articles, especially those like Ky/Crash who have recanted their past approbation of de-transitioning. Journalists like Urquhart play a role in trying to discredit these decisions by enlisting defectors like Ky/Crash to reassert trans orthodoxies that aim at confronting these defeats with personal testimony to the contrary.

Given the fact that there is now a legal basis for resisting dubious puberty blockers and hormones, the UK decisions may be the tip of the iceberg if they result in a cascade of lawsuits that could bring other aspects of the medicalization of gender dissatisfaction into question.

Ky/Crash is not the only woman of late who has recanted her past affiliation with the de-transitioning movement. Several sources conveyed to me that there is a backlash against feminists by some de-transitioners who have done a complete about-face in revisiting the LGBT+ and queer hangouts they formerly dissociated from and now blame feminist friends for gaslighting them into feminism. Articles like Urquhart's 'ex de-transitioner' piece exploit these tensions in the de-transitioning movement.

The Numbers Game: Research on De-transitioning.

Trans advocates and many clinicians minimize the prevalence of de-transitioning by arguing that journalists are creating a 'panic' about it. They support questionable studies that claim de-transitioning is rare.

UK de-transitioner Charlie Evans explains why there may be so few credible investigations focused on de-transitioning:

> There's a lack of interest in de-transitioner studies and outcomes and data, because it doesn't really suit the people who are pushing this ideology to know about the bad outcomes — even the doctors who are

following a protocol with their head in the sand … De-transitioners are the rejects … they're not the good examples from the production line of bodies that transition. In a sense, they're the damaged goods no one wants to acknowledge (in Walsh, 2019).

After Charlie Evans spoke on television about her experience of reversing her status, 300+ prospective de-transitioners contacted her, most born female. She has set up a non-profit service in the UK called the Detransition Advocacy Network to assist those who want to de-transition. Because the majority of de-transitioners are women who identify as men, they are viewed as traitors to the cause, which may be one reason why de-transitioning is being attacked by trans activists who are mostly men.

Those who pay attention to community-based research have found that there are hundreds of de-transitioners like Sinead, for example, who knows about "100 de-transitioned women" like herself. "I think we are the tip of the iceberg. There will be many of us to come" (in Dodsworth, 2020).

De-transitioners report they have been harassed by trans activists who claim that de-transitioning is a danger to trans rights. One de-transitioner stated that for her, "detransitioning has resulted in the most harassment she has ever faced in her life" (Pollock, 2018).

Dr Jacky Hewitt, a Monash University academic and pediatric endocrinologist who directed a 2012 study on 39 children and adolescents given hormone treatment between 2003–2011 at the Royal Children's Hospital in Melbourne (RCH), has stated:

> There is a need for both research and medical services for people who previously had gender dysphoria and hormonal/surgical intervention, who are now de-transitioning. This [need] is regardless of whether they represent a tiny minority, or a larger group than previously thought (in Lane, 2019a).

Dr Hewitt cautions that long-term outcomes of hormones and surgery are unknown. Critics of the current 'affirmation model' say that regret is being defined very 'narrowly' and does not take into account the fact that "de-transitioners often have no desire to report back to the gender clinics that encouraged their mistaken belief they could change sex" (Lane, 2019a).

In the UK, there was a 1,000 percent increase in the number of natal males seeking gender services from 2009–2019. But the numbers of natal females wanting to transition during the same period increased by 4,400 percent. The internet has played a large role in making transitioning information and trans communities available to young girls, and the LGBT+ circles that they move in. Similar increases have been reported in other western countries such as Australia (Lane, 2019a).

Clinical procedure suggests another reason why the numbers are increasing. Trans activists and organizations have pressed hard against medical and psychological 'gatekeeping' practices of the past, urging clinics to give way to the 'affirmation' model. Many de-transitioners have reported that they had undergone minimal evaluation of their self-perceptions. Affirmation treatment advocates promote immediate transitioning, which has become the standard in clinical situations where self-identification is the norm, and many children slide through the trans pipeline quickly.

As more young transitioners age and suffer medical and psychological problems, there will be more seeking help and health, and there will certainly be more legal blowback from those who will challenge the consequences of their affirmation treatment in court.

The frequency of de-transitioning is part of the fallout from aggressive trans advertising online that has swayed an outsize numbers of girls and young women, many now criticizing their transitions. As of 2018, a Reddit group for de-transitioners had 84,000 members and it estimates that about half are de-transitioners (Dockray, 2019).

A 2016 open-ended survey entitled *Female Detransition and Reidentification* publicized on Tumblr, Facebook groups, and the blog, 4thWaveNow, received 203 responses, a noteworthy total in a survey that was open for response only during a short two-week period. It was designed for any natal females who had formerly self-described as transgender and had subsequently de-transitioned, as well as those who still identify as nonbinary and gender fluid but "had desisted from medical or social transition" (Archive, 2016).

Most of the respondents (179) checked their current identity as female, and many specified that they did not 'identify' as female but 'are' female. Asked how stopping transition impacted their 'dysphoria', 129 responded they were better after stopping, and 22 answered the dysphoria was completely gone. By far, the most common reason for de-transitioning was "shifting political/ ideological beliefs" (63 percent) followed by 59 percent who stated they found "alternative coping mechanisms" (Archive, 2016). Participants could check multiple responses from a list of options that applied to them.

Of those who sought therapy, only 12 felt they had been given sufficient counseling and information about transitioning. Some were passed along a trans conveyor belt that ultimately ended with hormones and surgery after experiencing only one or several visits to a therapist. Trans advocates know that the longer the waiting period for treatment, the more time a person has to change her or his mind and to test the 'affirmative' process (Archive, 2016).

Counselors and clinicians are biased toward transitioning and trivialize de-transitioning. In an interview with writer Kate Herzog, Jackie thinks clinicians are part of the problem. "I didn't really feel like I could talk to my counselors about de-transitioning … because they have specific political views, and I felt like if I said I had these criticisms of the whole concept of transitioning, they would have thought I was being brainwashed by transphobic bigots" (in Herzog, 2017).

Instead of seeking out therapists, Jackie found online support that prompted her to start a resource center for de-transitioners at *Detransition Info* on Tumblr. Jackie reports that her online community is in the hundreds.

Those who minimize the number of de-transitioners deride de-transitioning as a 'panic' while other proponents disdain de-transitioners as not 'true' trans persons to begin with. For example, in Melbourne, Australia, The Royal Childrens' Hospital (RCH) clinic director Michelle Telfer dismisses media reports of de-transitioners, claiming most were not "true" cases and blaming "outside pressures, such as from family." And the RCH trans treatment guidelines make no mention of de-transitioning (in Lane, 2019b).

Likewise, psychologist Rachel Heath, co-author of a book on transgender health, said she believes the percent of de-transitioners is no more than one percent. Professionals like Heath believe advocates of de-transitioning are creating a 'panic', or they patronizingly argue that de-transitioners are "just temporarily confused or suffering from a misdiagnosed psychological disorder." Heath also thinks that de-transitioner campaigns are designed by "ignorant people" to "eliminate all trans people" (in Lane, 2019b).

Jack Turban, a psychiatric resident at Massachusetts General Hospital and specialist in trans youth research, asserts without any evidence to support his claim, that the "most prudent course of action," in general, is affirming a child's gender transition (in Marchiano, 2020). Prudent? What could be more reckless than to begin a course of puberty-blocking drugs and then encourage young girls and boys to continue with cross-sex hormones and surgery, especially when the evidence shows that the majority of young children who present as transgender eventually choose their natal sex if allowed to age without medical interventions?

Surveys that are often quoted and which estimate a low number of de-transitioners, do not account for those who disidentify as transgender. Lisa Marchiano, a respected clinical social worker and therapist, states that most of the women she counsels would never be tallied in the flawed professional studies that mainly interview those who still self-identify as trans. The women she sees in her practice identify as de-transitioners and have left the confines of trans communities. "Indeed, most of them are still likely counted by their transition doctors as examples of 'successful' transition stories, since they have simply stopped reporting for treatment" (Marchiano, 2020).

Marchiano states that transitioning failed to address her de-transitioners' problems and instead exacerbated them, often disrupting their educational or vocational goals during their time in trans culture. For most of them, declaring as transgender worsened their mental health and the drugs they took — drugs that initially may have enhanced their confidence and well-being — in the long run intensified vulnerabilities. Those who submitted to mastectomies or hysterectomies report nerve damage and, for some, lifelong dependence on controversial hormones that became a painful part of their lives (Marchiano, 2020).

Marchiano has been "overwhelmed" by the numbers of parents who phone her in the hope that she can help them with daughters who want to transition. When she explains that she doesn't set up parental appointments, they ask if she can recommend "any therapist who won't just affirm and greenlight their children for medical transition." Most of them are desperate, and clinicians who parents formerly consulted have dismissed their concerns. They express relief that their fears are recognized as real (Marchiano, 2017).

One young de-transitioner speaking at a Manchester UK panel said, "I regret it all." She and many in the audience view the professionals who treated them as "the post-modernist version of those who sought to turn gay people straight — only now they are seeking to fix bodies rather than sexual desires." Another panelist remarked, "Transition has been presented as so progressive, but the only thing I see is it reinforcing gender stereotypes" (in Joyce, 2020).

Not to be ignored is the destructive role of online subcultures where the transgender craze has gone viral. Before the internet, many gender dissatisfied persons were isolated from each other, whereas now they can find their trans online community and join the ones that suit them best. On the majority of these sites, de-transitioning is marginalized mostly as a myth, viewed not only as transphobic, but also as an incitement to trans suicides.

Two groups that are closely allied with the view that de-transitioners are few in number are the World Professional Association for Transgender Health (WPATH) and the US National Center for Gender Equality. Both conducted studies that conclude that de-transitioning is very rare, and point to a low incidence of de-transitioners. However, both these organizations promote transgenderism and accept its core ideology as a given.

The WPATH research estimated that in 2014, the numbers of de-transitioners ranged from one to five percent (Wikipedia, n.d.). WPATH was founded by the 'father' of transsexual surgery, Dr Harry Benjamin, and was formerly named after him. Its mission is devoted to the understanding and treatment of 'gender dysphoria', educating professionals who work in medicine, psychology, law, social work, counseling, sociology, and sexology — a veritable transgender empire.

In a 2015 survey of nearly 28,000 people conducted by the US-based National Center for Transgender Equality (NCTE), eight percent of respondents reported de-transitioning (Knox, 2019), a statistic that is larger than the WPATH study quotes. However, the numbers might well be much higher since the NCTE, which was founded in 2003 by transgender activists, conducted the 2015 Survey and is a leading policy advocacy organization devoted to transgender goals.

These two studies have been controversial because of their similar ideological positions that promote transitioning and frown on de-transitioning. Potential respondents who would be critical of their earlier trans-identifications might decide not to participate in these particular studies because of the organizations' affirmation policies and promotion of transgender ideology and practices.

Other studies are more credible. An earlier 2008 study found that 'gender dysphoric' adolescents desisted from their transgender identity before they reached the age of 29; and a 2013 study found 63 percent desisted before age 20 (Wikipedia, 'Detransition', Occurrence). A 2003 German study documented an increased demand for de-transitions, charging that "well-meaning but certainly not unproblematic clinicians who — contrary to international best practices — assumed that transitioning as quickly as possible should be the only course of action" (Wikipedia, 'Detransition', Occurrence).

Preliminary findings by Shute in 2017 revealed that growing numbers of young people, particularly women, regretted their transitions. A Belgrade doctor told Shute he had been asked to carry out an unprecedented number of reversals in 2014. Finding that little research had been conducted on de-transitioners, he sought out those willing to talk with him, but many said they were too traumatized to talk about it (Wikipedia, 'Detransition', Occurrence).

James Caspian and Lisa Littman are two academics who have undertaken evidence-based research on de-transitioning but whose work has been censored by their own academic institutions when they found that de-transitioning was on the rise among their interviewed respondents.

Caspian, a counselor who specializes in transgender therapy and who was pursuing a higher-level degree at Bath Spa University in the UK, had his research proposal revoked. He had proposed a project that focused on the reasons why former transitioners chose to reject their earlier transitions and were in the process of de-transitioning. Caspian's research would have added an important dimension to the academic literature that has been very opposed to studying de-transitioning and its prevalence in the transgender population. Caspian alleged that when attacked on social media, the university backed off because it was "a potentially political piece of research, [which] carries a risk to the university" (in Weale, 2017) and may be detrimental to its reputation.

On its website, Brown University in Providence, Rhode Island, initially featured a press release about Dr Lisa Littman's published study entitled 'Rapid-onset gender dysphoria in adolescents and young adults' (Littman, 2018). As a researcher and medical doctor at Brown, Littman's study appeared in the academic journal *PLOS One* where she wrote that it was mostly young women who initially were declaring themselves trans and that they were highly influenced by social media and peer pressure.

Transgender activists rushed to discredit Littman's research as transphobic and attacked the university and the journal in which her research was published. The university alleged it was concerned about her methodology — an easy cover to avoid controversy — and initially removed the press release from its website.

It is not the job of a university to suppress research that offends any group's 'opinions'. Rather, its mission is to foster critical research and open debate and not cave in to any faction that would violate its mission by trying to gag a faculty member or student's research and publication (see Chapter 6).

In August 2017, the Mazzoni Center in Philadelphia, Pennsylvania, held a trans health conference — an annual meeting of trans-identified people, transgender advocates and health providers. The conference cancelled two panels that focused on de-transitioning and alternate methods of working with 'gender dysphoria'. The organizers claimed that the topics were too controversial, and it was their duty to make sure the debate "does not get out of control" (Mazzoni Center, 2017). However, this was just one more occasion when a legitimate critical research spotlight was turned off by conference organizers. How can transgender advocates claim that de-transitioning is rare when they suppress any investigation that might prove otherwise?

Like trans activists who target their critics as transphobes, others treat de-transitioners as outcasts, freaks, failures and traitors to the cause of trans liberation. The vitriol has reached a point where many of those who are dissenters, critical of trans tactics and sympathetic to de-transitioners, are unwilling to go public with their disagreements lest they too become targets of trans wrath.

Trans vs. Trans

The transgender community is also at odds with itself and rife with conflict. Disagreements exist over who is a true transgendered person — individuals who are pre-operative, post-operative or those who simply self-identify as the opposite sex, many of whom shun hormones or surgery. And there are wide divisions between self-declared men and self-declared women.

As early as 2008, Cathryn Platine, a trans-identified woman, wrote about being punished for talking about "the dirty little secrets of the 'trans community' that ... is often not reality based and has a huge amount of both gynophobia and patriarchal thinking" (Platine, 2007). Platine describes the breach between those who identify as transsexuals and those who identify as transgender.

Transgender activists often view older post-operative trans-sexuals as the enemy, particularly if they dissent from more recent transgender orthodoxies. Platine describes the vitriol and shunning aimed at anyone with a transsexual history who even attempts to criticize any aspect of the newer trans ideology and is immediately branded a 'post op nazi', 'transsexual separatist', or 'gender essentialist'. A transgender opponent who disliked Platine's politics outed Platine at work, her first "decent post-transition job," which was followed by many death threats and being driven from trans e-mail lists (Platine, 2007).

Displays of hostility between self-declared women and self-declared men are rampant. Much of the antagonism centers on the alleged 'privilege' of access to women and women's events that natal women extend to self-declared men because of their dual experience of being both natal women and trans. Writer CJ Atkinson states that because of the "lazy assumption that being trans masculine is somehow 'easy', because of the belief that trans men can pass by unnoticed as men, our transmasculine stories are erased" (Atkinson, 2018).

Self-declared women (men) complain that self-declared men (women) are accepted as full members of spaces set aside for women. They say, "'Trans men' are welcomed as beautiful subversive heroes while we're left as monstrous unfuckable unwelcomes ... they're regularly listened to in radical spaces." They contend that, "everyone who is not a trans woman 'authors trans women's oppression'" (Fake cisgirl, n.d.). This same commentator wrote, "Pretty much nothing makes me feel worse than reading some of the hateful screeds levelled at 'trans men' by 'trans women' and posted on this website" (Fake cisgirl, n.d.).

T's story published in the collection, *You Told Me You Were Different*, speaks about her experiences in the trans community:

> It was considered acceptable for 'trans women' to say horrible things about 'trans men', including calling us transphobic and misogynistic slurs. And if any of us called out 'trans women' on it, or if we dared to talk about the abuse we faced at the hands of 'trans women', we were deemed transmisogynistic" (in Kitty Robinson, ed, 2021, p. 136).

As reported in Chapter Four on trans violence against women, this pattern of 'trans women's' behavior constantly violates women's boundaries, such as when women say "no, I'm not interested," or "no, I don't wish to meet up in person for a date," or "no, I won't have sex with you" (in Kitty Robinson, ed., 2021, p. 137).

Self-declared men (women) say it's infuriating to discover the jealousy of self-declared women (men) who lust after women's body parts such as breasts and wombs, and who constantly seek affirmation as women by eliciting assurances that they meet shallow standards of feminine clothing and makeup, and who don't view women as whole persons.

Another source of divisiveness is the 'true trans' debate. For example, Twitter troublemakers have told de-transitioner Sinead that she never was a true 'trans man', and that she is transphobic. Because they can't accept the growing numbers of de-transitioners, they turn their anger on those who do (in Dodsworth, 2020).

Likewise with de-transitioner Thomasin, "A lot of people have said to me I was never trans. Well, I was. I was seen by my GP, the gender identify clinic — people accepted it. I changed my passport, all my documentation" (in Dodsworth, 2010).

Heath Russell, one of the early women who began the hormonal process of transitioning to masculinity and then de-transitioned writes:

> While the trans community likes to say that we are special and unique snowflakes, they don't take into account that we have different experiences. If you stray from the trans narrative, you are condemned. I have had people tell me that I was never 'really' a trans person because

I de-transitioned. If I were to use my [breast] binder and go back on hormones, I would be told, 'You go, bro!' (in Vigo, 2013).

As for breast binders, a 2016 study entitled 'Health Impact of Chest Binding Among Transgender Adults: a Community-Engaged, Cross-Sectional Study' found that over 97 percent of respondents reported at least one of 28 negative outcomes attributed to binding including pain, overheating, and shortness of breath. A substantial percentage even reported rib fractures (in Peitzmeier et al, 2016).

Another harmful effect was back pain. The more frequent the binding, the more it was associated with negative outcomes. Breast binding involves compression of chest tissue, scarring, and dermatological problems caused by binders, elastic bandages and duct tape or plastic wrap (in Peitzmeier et al, 2016). Additional consequences of breast binding, reported by individuals not part of the study, are lower lung capacity and permanent shoulder 'dents'.

In spite of these risks, many of the respondents said they would continue binding because of the psychological relief it provided as well as enhanced ability to pass as men in public (in Peitzmeier et al, 2016).

Young women who are de-transitioning have been indelibly marked by their quest for manhood. They bear not only the mental scars but also the body wounds inflicted by long term cross-sex hormones, changes that deepen voices and cause receding hairlines. Then there are the effects of mastectomies, along with ovariectomies and womb removal that result in infertility.

Survivor and writer Max Robinson views transition as medical abuse embedded in a culture of woman and lesbian hating. "Experiences of FTM transition fit in alongside other female experiences of oppression" (Max Robinson, 2020, pers.com.). For Robinson, the solution was not in changing her body, having undergone long-term hormones and an eventual mastectomy. "It was engaging within a feminist context, where 'woman' meant something I was happy to be a part of" (Max Robinson, 2020, pers. com.).

Get the L Out of LGBT or Drop the T

The trans movement "has ridden the coattails of the lesbian/gay political movements. We opened the doors, they walk through them. We set the stage, they take over and turn the discussion to themselves. They had no original movement of their own, but have bent our arguments to their own purposes" (Noanodyne, 2013).

Well-meaning liberals have supported the LGBT movement not understanding that many lesbian and gay male activists reject this flawed coalition. As feminist and lesbian writings and blogs have led the resistance to this forced group marriage, LGBT solidarity is beginning to crack.

In 2018, lesbians marching in the London Pride parade led the procession with banners stating 'Transactivism Erases Lesbians'. Their action was called 'Get the L Out of LGBT'. The banner, and especially the placing of the lesbian contingent at the front of the line, caused quite a stir, but proved to be a central spot in getting across the message that lesbians have been erased by transgender demands. The group protested the non-consensual enrolling of lesbians in the LBGT movement.

In Britain, Europe's biggest LGBT organization called Stonewall was accused of favoring transgender rights and becoming increasingly devoted to replacing sex with gender by redirecting its staff to prioritize fundraising for transgender projects. In a *Quillette* article entitled 'It's Time for 'LGB' and 'T' to Go Their Separate Ways', opinion editor Brad Polumbo wrote:

> We've been forced to watch the simple moral logic of non-discrimination be transformed into a self-parodic alphabet soup of invented identities ... The increasingly ridiculous conceit that all of 'alphabet people' are happy fellow travelers ... have been revealed to be unnatural bedfellows (Polumbo, 2019).

Gay activist Ronald Gold, who died in 2017, was one of the first US gay men to recognize the fallacy of transgender and say no to the notion of transgender. Gold rejected "... as just plain silly the idea that some cosmic accident just turned these people into changelings"

(Gold, 2009). His advice to parents of gender-non-conforming children was prescient:

> As for adults struggling with what to do about their [children's] feelings, I'd tell them to stay away from the psychiatrists — those prime reinforcers of sex-role stereotypes — and remind them that whatever they're feeling, or feel like doing, it's perfectly possible with the bodies they've got (Gold, 2009).

You won't find such an analysis coming from any corporate-style mainstream gay or lesbian group today.

In 2015, a now-defunct US group of lesbians and gay men publicly asserted that transgender organizations should dissociate from the LGBT+ coalition because of different goals. These critics launched a petition on Change.org asserting transgender ideology to be completely different than that promoted by the LGB community. Drop the T was also very concerned about the increased promotion of gender identity clinics that diagnose children as transgender.

The Drop the T movement maintained that transgender activists displace same-sex attraction by redefining it as same-gender attraction. Drop the T argued that not only is transgender ideology a threat to lesbians, but also to all women because it erases the singular experience of what it means to be a woman in a patriarchal society that dismisses women's history and life knowledge.

The Drop the T movement asserted that ideologically, whereas feminists, lesbians and gay men want to challenge the concept of gender, "the trans movement is regressive, insisting upon re-asserting and codifying classic gender concepts of what is masculine and what is feminine" (Drop the T, 2015). Gay and lesbian organizations even changed their names and mission statement headings, for example the Human Rights Campaign went from "Working for lesbian and gay equal rights" to "Working for lesbian, gay, bisexual and transgender equal rights" (Drop the T, 2015).

The result of this forced merging of LGBT+ is that ordinary people link all these separate concerns and campaigns, not realizing that some of the groups that are lumped together have very distinct agendas and that some of these agendas are detrimental to others. For example, when trans activists hassle gender-non-conforming girls to accept self-declared women (men) as sexual partners insisting that their penises are actually 'lady sticks', this constitutes bullying and sexual harassment.

Self-declared trans lesbians do *not* speak for lesbians, but the US National Gay and Lesbian Task Force acts as if they do. If judged by its budget allocations, the Task Force seems to be more interested in trans priorities than in fighting for its lesbian and gay members. The Human Rights Campaign has also been outspokenly focused on transgender concerns, as has a string of other gay and lesbian organizations such as the Astrea Lesbian Foundation for Justice and The National Center for Lesbian Rights. These groups have, in effect, capitulated to the trans activists.

UK Stonewall is the British counterpart of these US organizations that appear to have minimized their original lesbian constituency. The lion's share of its 2017 budget of £7 million funding "seems not to fund any lesbian only groups or activities" (Bindel, 2018b).

Critics have speculated that these mainstream LGBT organizations have learned a devil's lesson and want to avoid the deluge of cyber bullying that happens to organizations that are targeted as transphobic. Some have alleged that the 'T' was also added to increase funding (Noanodyne, 2013). With fewer subsidies going to gay and lesbian groups, especially after gay marriage was passed in the United States and other western countries, mainstream gay and lesbian organizations lost much of their funding, and transgenderism was recognized as the issue that would bring back more funding. The cost of this forced merging was subservience to trans priorities.

CHAPTER FOUR

The Trans Culture of Violence Against Women

Punching TERFs is the same as punching Nazis. Fascism must be smashed with the greatest violence to ensure our collective liberation from it.

—Edinburgh Action for Trans Health

Transgender activists, many of whom are self-declared women (men), have invented a new equation i.e. violence = the misgendering or mispronouning of any trans-identifed person. As one trans activist tweeted, "intentional misgendering is violence and should be met with violence."

In this view, violence is not mainly physical aggression or assault but rather words that trans activists find objectionable. Conflating misgendering and mispronouning with actual physical violence diminishes the meaning of battering, rape, and other forms of physical harm and frees its perpetrators from any accountability. Actual violence loses its meaning.

When actions such as misgendering and mispronouning become your definition of violence, the real male violence against 'trans men' that results in trans injury and death goes unrecognized and unpunished. In the long run it also harms trans-identified persons. And it allows trans activists to accuse women, especially radical feminists, of committing violence against trans persons.

Not one natal woman has physically injured any self-declared woman (man). Not one natal woman has killed any man or woman who identifies as trans, but plenty of natal men have assaulted 'trans women'. It is men who commit actual violence against self-declared women (men). Why aren't self-declared women and their allies targeting the men who commit these acts of actual violence? Differences of opinion and dissenting from transgender orthodoxies should not be conflated with violence.

If anyone questions any tenet of transgender ideology, it is called violence against trans-identified persons; if parents question the prescribing of dangerous puberty blockers and cross-sex hormones given to their children as young as eight, that is called violence against trans children who are being denied 'needed medical care'; if lesbians or other gender critical women refuse the sexual overtures of natal men who claim to be lesbians, that is called violence against 'trans lesbians' who wield their 'lady sticks'.

A self-declared woman (man) can engage in the worst kind of threats and violence against feminist critics, but no woman can dare to speak out against trans dogmas without being accused of hate speech. Any questioning of trans truths invites threats and violence against so-called TERFs.

At the core of trans ideology is the insistence that self-declared women (men) are women. But self-declared women are not women historically, experientially, or biologically and certainly not by reason of a simple declaration that they expect everyone to accept because they say it is so. "I feel it, thus it is real." The feeling may be real, but the facts are otherwise. If critics don't cooperate in this fantasy, they are labelled 'violent TERFs'. Any dissent from trans dogma is considered a mortal sin, even when male biology and masculinist behavior are graphically on display. In translandia, any disagreement with trans dogmas is treated as disputing trans existence or, in trans speak, as "killing us."

There is an undercurrent of actual violence in the mob rule of trans activists that harass, bully and threaten especially radical feminists and lesbians and makes cowards of many bystanders.

As more of these gender posses are allowed to wreak their 'narcissistic rage' on natal women who disagree that men can be women, male entitlement is solidified and misogyny spreads like the plague. Gender critical women can't expect solidarity from groups like the Human Rights Campaign or the American Civil Liberties Union (ACLU), but women should be able to expect support from organizations that promote women's human rights, especially those who campaign against violence against women. Unfortunately, this is not the case.

And how about male allies? It's so much easier for men to assert that they stand with women when the 'women' are biological men. Male bonding prevails when the feminist opposition is divided and even feminists give trans-identified men their support. As journalist Tom Farr has asked:

> Where are all the fucking men? Why are men not recognising this for what it is and raising their voices. When women who want to organize or plan a women-only meeting without being threatened with violence, why isn't this enough to mobilize ... Many men on the left constantly, and unbearably, stumble over themselves to show how 'Woke' they are, whether it be through supporting a woman's right to be trafficked and abused, or by graciously deciding to choke them during sex (Farr, 2019).

I would add that many men are cowards, especially when it comes to making themselves and other men accountable for their misogynist actions. Leftist men are often the least likely to challenge violence against women, particularly when self-declared women (men) are perpetrating the violence. "Want to call a woman a cunt but scared of sounding like a misogynist? Don't worry, call her a TERF instead!" (Farr, 2019).

When trans activists crash women's events in mobs, they heighten the threat risk. Threats of violence power large segments of the transgender community where self-declared women and their allies encourage violence against women on a constant basis. If there is a women-only event, trans activists will arrive in numbers and cause trouble.

The trans-invented term of TERF invites violence against radical feminists and other women who won't get with the transgender program. Their branding of women as TERFs is a form of trans hate speech that attempts to shame radical women and provoke compliance with trans activists' demands.

Social Media Threats of Violence Against Women

The ever present threat of violence is perpetrated by trans activists who have become experts in the classic art of reversal i.e. the act of changing or making something change to its opposite. For example, in the trans world, women become perpetrators, not victims of male violence. *Reversal is a strategy trans activists have perfected.*

TERF is a slur, and its use has enabled enormous levels of bullying, abuse and violence against women especially in trans tweets that appear on social media. Two of the most frequent trans refrains are "Kill all Terfs" and "Punch Terfs" as if punching and killing are games in which one player tries to surpass the other in viciousness.

The following small sampling of screenshots documents the utter depravity of trans abuse, harassment and misogyny, which pervade sites like Twitter and other social media (Terf Is a Slur, n.d.). Hundreds of tweets and re-tweets are incitements to violence used by perpetrators who employ bullying and intimidation as their weapons and who oppose open discussion and civil discourse. This sample of tweets is only a fraction of those online.

"shoot a TERF today."

"All TERFs deserve to be shot in the head."

"somebody slap this TERF cunt across the face."

"trans women aren't real women, ya know what'll be unreal? ur pain when my fist meets ur face."

"All TERFs need to cease existing. All of them. Gone. Wipe them from the Earth. They are a plague to be purged."

"pop quiz: if you kill a terf, is it a crime? Answer: it is not. They are not considered lifeforms."

"Enjoy my lady stick in your mouth."

"why can't we just throw every TERF into the volcano and watch them burn."

"I wanna direct a snuff film where multiple TERFs get shot in the head but don't die, they just suffer in agony."

"my feelings on gun control are rather complex but there's one group who I'd have no problem with openly carrying assault rifles. Arm trans women."

Some of these threats of violence are aimed at specific women and even children:

"murder Germaine Greer."

"hope someone slits Germaine Greer's saggy fucking throat."

"@sarahditum@TerrorizerMir suck my girlcock cunts."

"I'd pay to watch someone violently tip her ovaries from her abdomen."

"I want to set every single TERF kid on fire"

"I can't believe these dumb bitches [a handful of trans women who counsel moderation] who are like, 'Don't threaten TERFs with violence, violence is wrong.' Beat TERFs. Lynch TERFs. Especially get TERFs fired from their jobs. This is a war between them and us for our very existence. Bowing out = losing."

Trans violence against women on social media mirrors the wider cyber-misogyny that pervades woman-hating sites. Even when actual violence is threatened, social media companies do not take seriously the posts that target women, such as "I kill bitches like you." Instead, the posts are passed off as 'controversial humor' rather than as incitements to violence against women.

Companies like Facebook, Twitter and YouTube host such harassment claiming they are not the arbiters of people's free speech.

Yet they forcefully intervene when feminists post online to expose and counter the misogyny of trans activists, by censoring and cancelling gender-critics' accounts.

It is outrageous that this online preoccupation with killing radical feminists is ignored and treated as insignificant, and instead Twitter has closed down the accounts of feminist critics such as Meghan Murphy, the editor of *Feminist Current*. Twitter permanently shuttered Murphy's account in November 2018, after she referred to a self-declared woman as "him."

Many will justify this kind of menacing behavior as less than actual violence, or simply excuse it as the blather of vocal trans activists online. This kind of intentional unawareness encourages those who should know better, and the public-at-large, from condemning these venomous tweets. Those who plead ignorance can hide behind the smokescreen of free speech and not speak up when trans activists threaten women, or they dismiss trans Twitter harassment as acceptable because it is 'only' empty threats.

When women are the targets of venomous trans tweets, women don't experience this misogyny as an empty threat. As Andrea Dworkin has written, "most women have experienced enough dominance from men — control, violence, insult, contempt — that no threat seems empty" (Dworkin, 1987, p. 70).

When the bullying and incitement to violence comes from those who claim to be women (men), many will minimize it because self-declared women are considered a victimized class. Appeasers will claim that trans violence against natal women is a small part of the trans activist community. But this claim is belied by the actual numbers of trans activists who reveal their true hatred of women, blatantly displayed on social media. Even if one assumes only a small segment of the trans movement acts out this hatred of women, we are still left with a vocal number of men who target women online and are applauded and inspired to escalate their abuse. Those who would attack and censor feminist critics are not just outliers in the trans community.

Trans activists are playing a thug's game online. The tactics mirror Donald Trump's words when he advocated that his supporters "knock the hell" out of hecklers. Especially on social media, trans activists are guilty of provoking violence towards women. Like Trump apologists who say that his pugnacious words are "just how the president talks," it appears that many are prepared to ignore the violence in the fighting words of trans activists.

Violence Against Lesbians

"Attn cis lesbian TERFs. You ugly fucks deserve to be buried alive ..."

In addition to the cyber threats, harassment and bullying of feminists is the actual physical violence that self-declared women (men) have committed and continue to commit against lesbians.

In 2018, a group of lesbian activists organized a peaceful action at the Pride March in London. They marched at the front of the parade carrying banners and distributing leaflets with the slogan, "Get the L out" of the LGBT acronym. A "Get the L Out" spokeswoman said: "We protested to protect our rights and on behalf of all the lesbians intimidated, threatened and silenced by the GBT (Gay, Bisexual and Trans) community everywhere."

The backlash after the Pride action included threats and demonization of the lesbian feminist activists who organized the action. The official march statement that followed called lesbian protesters "disgusting, bigoted and transphobic." Manchester UK pride organizer Tony Cooper went outrageously further in his remarks asserting that the London Pride protesters should have been "dragged out [of the march] by their saggy tits." This is the kind of hate-mongering that lesbians have to put up with.

The 'cotton ceiling' is a term frequently used by trans porn star Drew De Veaux. It takes its reference from the glass ceiling, a term that feminists invented to explain why women in the workplace could only advance so far before they met a glass ceiling barrier that held them back from getting paramount positions. Self-declared trans lesbians (men), with penises intact, whine that they must break through the 'cotton ceiling', a reference to the cotton underwear lesbians wear that has become a metaphor for lesbians who won't have sex with men.

If indeed self-declared trans lesbians (men) truly believe that they are real lesbians, perhaps they should be having sex with other self-declared trans lesbians (men). This would help them overcome their own internal transphobia — as well as homophobia — and conquer their exclusionary sexual practices. In overcoming their reluctance to sexually embrace each other, they could be reveling in the pleasures and possibilities of self-declared trans lesbian sex thereby creating 'a beloved community' of dedicated sex partners!

LGBT Affinity Groups and Culture Are Dangerous for Lesbians

Outright misogyny, especially the hatred of lesbians in LGBT+ culture, drives the sexual violence and exploitation that is now happening to women whose social circles are dominated by trans and queer ideology.

Many young lesbians socialize in LGBT+ groups but have never been exposed to lesbian feminism. Their transgender friends and acquaintances, including numerous self-declared women (men), pressure them for sex, intimidating them into saying yes, "resulting in them having non-consensual sex under pressure" (Wild, 2019).

What these young women learn from mingling with the LGBT+ crowd is never to use the word lesbian — never mind feminist — to describe themselves, lest they also be branded as TERFs. Self-declared lesbians with their 'lady sticks' relentlessly hassle them into believing it is discriminatory to set sexual boundaries.

When Max Robinson, a young detransitioned lesbian, mixed in the queer community, she began to question the lies and manipulations of self-declared women who asserted they were lesbians. After several of her friends were raped or beaten by these men, she began to recognize that trans and queer ideologies impair women's ability to "name what is happening" and to disregard their own sexual abuse (Wild, 2019).

As Robinson stated in an interview with Julie Bindel (2019c):

> There's no way to be lesbians in that scene. If you're a lesbian, you have to fuck trans women and if you don't want to fuck trans women then you're evil … they will come right after you. The sexual harassment and explicit sexual violence was rampant and perpetrated by trans women. And it wasn't just a few — there were a lot of trans women acting that way.

The *Lesbians at Ground Zero* report by Angela Wild has been instrumental in exposing the LGBT+ quagmire by naming trans violence and sexual exploitation for what it is. Designed as a "research survey of 30 questions relating to lesbian experience in LGBT groups and on lesbian dating sites … [T]he survey was sent to women-only and lesbian-only groups on social media and to individual lesbians" in the author's network. It makes no claim to be a representative sample of the lesbian community. Rather, a major value of the study was to survey women who had been silenced up to that point, with 80 women responding (Wild, 2019).

Some of the findings are: 66 percent of responders reported being intimidated or receiving threats in their LGBT group[s]; 50 percent reported being excluded from their LGBT groups[s] when they questioned trans doctrines and afterwards were targeted as transphobic; 48 percent reported visiting lesbian dating sites where they were accosted by 'trans women'. One woman added, "There are so many men that appear as 'women' on dating sites. It makes me paranoid that someone I match with could be a man." And 56 percent of the respondents said they were pressured or coerced to accept a 'trans woman' as a sexual partner. "Many of the experiences … classify as rape although were not named as such." The survey confirmed that lesbians have been subjected to a wide variety of sexual violence by men who identify as 'trans women' (Wild, 2019).

The testimonies that follow make palpable the findings of the *Lesbians at Ground Zero* report.

"You Told Me You Were Different"

Writers Max Robinson and her partner Kitty Robinson started a blog about de-transitioning, which became very popular. Soon after, the cyber threats and abuse piled on from transgender activists. "Hundreds of people were saying we're scum and shit. We had loads of detailed rape threats on line" (Max Robinson, 2020, pers. com).

The threats prompted the two activists to ask women in their social circles if they could give a personal example about whether and how they had experienced harm while being part of LGBT communities. Many young lesbians responded sharing multiple examples of abuse, from online sexual harassment to sexual exploitation and rape. So the two organizers decided to form online discussion groups using the feminist practice of consciousness raising to tell their stories and then to share them on blogs and social media and take action.

In trans culture, the naming of men's behavior as male violence and sexual assault is taboo. Thus, it was a relief for women to be able to speak candidly about their sexual abuse and, in some cases, to out their predators. Those who spoke openly were accused of lying, reproached for misgendering and not using other prescribed language, and told they were guilty of hate crimes against self-declared women (men).

From the online testimonies of violence against lesbians, Kitty Robinson decided to collect them in an anthology entitled *You Told Me You Were Different* now published as a book. "The topic was the harmful ways that male people who identify as trans treat female people within the queer and/or trans community" (Kitty Robinson, 2021).

The title captures the belief that these men, most of whom identified as women or non-binary, purported to be 'different' rather than the very models of male sexual entitlement and abuse which they turned out to be. Also, the title is meant to convey the unique context in which this harm was perpetrated and the whitewashing of rape and other sexual violence that victims of male violence documented.

Female victims of male violence in LGBT culture — whether they identified as lesbians, 'trans men' or gender non-binary — write about the ways in which they were lured by men's claims of being distinctly different from abusive straight men, and about the harms victims experienced in past relationships. Men who perpetrated the violence identified as 'trans women', as 'trans lesbians' or as gender non-conforming. All claimed to be 'different', but committed the same violence against women in the same ways that other men do. "We traced the patterns together. We talked about what we had experienced, what we had witnessed, what had been done to us" (Kitty Robinson, 2021).

The excerpts that follow are taken from selected stories in the *You Told Me You Were Different* anthology. They are appalling testimonies of harm.

A Letter to My Therapist by Eli W.
Pressure, control, manipulation, threats, lies, a hand raised, then lowered, raised again. Screaming at my flinching. Telling me he wished I dressed like a real girl so he could borrow my clothes. Inebriated rages, then sober ones. Ignoring my no. Forcing my legs open.

I Don't Care by Evona Woods
I don't care that you're genderqueer … [Y]ou still raped her … I don't care that you wear pride pins or colorful hair. I don't care that you like wearing skirts and makeup. I don't care that you 'don't trust cis men'. I don't care that you think you're different. I don't care what flavor of dysphoria you have on any given day … I don't care that you're genderqueer — I know what you really are.

The Snare by Anonymous
It has been nearly a year since the last time I saw you. The last time you slapped me across the face, because it aroused you. The last time you choked me in the most dangerous way you knew how, because it aroused you. The last time you engaged in unprotected sex with me,

because it aroused you that the idea of pregnancy made me dysphoric. The last time you told me how you had masturbated to the idea of raping me … [W]hat an ideal victim I must have been! A young woman with years' worth of sexual trauma, I have found myself and reclaimed my lesbian sexuality. I have made peace with my body and stopped hating myself for not being born male. I have found a community of women that support and love me. I am the happiest I have ever been in my entire life.

My beautiful son by m

The last time we talked on the phone, he told me he thought he was non-binary. And a while after that, he came out as a woman … [H]e started doing some work with other men at his university about porn and porn addiction … he was taking steps to be a better man … [T]hen, the second he found out that there was activist cred in talking about his experiences as a 'gender minority', all the feminist ally work stopped … [T]he fucker suddenly more oppressed than the fuckee. I saw him at his most vile, most male.

An Organizer's Story

It was one of those open secrets that often go unconfronted in the LGBT community. Whispers of rape and sexual assault, particularly of minors and trans-identified females. …We first collected testimonies from individuals who had been victimized by him… [W]e then found the email addresses of all the higher ups at the various non-profits he claimed to be employed at and sent them all the same email with the testimonies attached imploring them to remove him from their staff …

First of all, one of the trans-identified females we emailed was all too ready to defend one multiply accused male from the anonymous accusations of countless females … [S]o much for LGBT groups being above the kinds of victimization that other activist circles are so often rife with … [W]e just asked that B no longer have access to vulnerable LGBT kids … we found out that several days later, B's name was gone from the Pride website … we were proud to have gotten one abuser taken out of a leadership position, but unfortunately countless others are still out there using their trans identity as a means to gain access to young, impressionable females. … Where serial rapists are concerned, it takes a village to bring them down.

L'inferno or: the Burning Rage I feel When I Think of You by Virgil
(Accompanied by graphics in the original piece)
See, the thing is this: You told me you were different. I could see the pain and guilt on your face as you told me about it. You only spilled it because I probed you … [Your] HIStory of abusing trans men? Of treating us like SEX OBJECTS for you to STICK your broken dick into.

After I said I couldn't handle sex anymore … [Y]ou just fucking left. … You wanted another inexperienced trans guy to take advantage of … I have so many regrets. … I pray to God you stop preying on trans men. … Because Hell has a special place for men like you.

Jordan's Story
You didn't tell me you were different. You told me I was different [saying] 'You're so special. You're the only one who understands me. The only one who likes me. The only one I can count on. No one loves me but you. I need you. Please don't leave. I can't do it without you.'

I was fifteen, and I wasn't the only one … [A] twenty-year-old man never wants to be friends with a fifteen-year-old girl. A twenty-year-old man wants a girl. A little girl. A good girl. A special girl …

You're a child, and he asks you about your body … You only wanted a friend … Your friends know it isn't okay. You know it isn't okay … You tell him you thought he would be different. He's not. You're guilty. You're wrong. He's wrong. He isn't lonely. He doesn't need you. You do not need him … He was never different.

∞

It is ironic that these young women, many who declared themselves 'trans men', came to these LGBT+ circles with all the baggage of female vulnerabilities. In spite of their male and gender non-conforming identities, all were treated as women to exploit, whereas the male abusers who were self-declared women or non-binary behaved with all the oppressive behavior of predatory men who seek to confuse and abuse women. And of course, the exploitation was enhanced by the progressive claim that they were 'different' from the male lowlives who regard women as sexual objects to be fucked.

As Max Robinson confirmed, "There is a male violence problem in the LGBT+ community. There are these patterns of sexual entitlement and harassment, and out and out assault, and domestic violence going completely undiscussed. We were just threatened and told to shut up" (Robinson cited in Bindel, 2019a).

If anyone speaks out against 'trans women's' sexually abusive behavior, the threat of suicide is a silencing tactic used by trans activists to muzzle criticism. Even if a woman has experienced this abuse herself, and the person who harmed her is known as a predator, victims are told, "even if it's true … you shouldn't say it." The message is, "you are contributing to their deaths," or "killing transwomen" or propping up the "myth of the predatory transwoman" (Kitty Robinson, 2021). These threats silence women who have been raped and sexually assaulted by men who identify as women and as lesbians.

In the *Lesbians at Ground Zero* report where 66 percent of respondents said they had been intimidated or had received threats in their LGBT group, these threats included verbal abuse, rape and death threats, threats of physical or sexual violence, threats to kill family members, and online 'doxing' that exposed their names, pictures, and home addresses. Young women in the 18–24 year old age group were the most vulnerable to coercive sexual overtures to sleep with self-declared women to prove they were not TERFs (Wild, 2019).

Male Ancestors of the 'Different Men' of the Trans and LGBT+ Communities

The *You Said You Were Different* stories told by so many violated women is a throwback to the sexual revolution culture of the 1960s, or the sixties as I call them, where young women idealized men who said they were 'different'. In her illuminating work, *Right-Wing Women*, Andrea Dworkin exposes the misogyny of the flower power boys of the era:

Juxtaposed with the warmongering men who defended the Vietnam war ... [A] bunch of boys who liked flowers were making love and refusing to make war ... [T]hey wanted peace ... [T]hey grew their hair long and painted their faces and wore colorful clothes and risked being treated *like* girls ... No wonder the girls of the sixties thought that these boys were their special friends, their special allies (Dworkin, 1983, pp. 88–100; all following quotes are from Dworkin, 1983).

The girls had idealized these boys because they believed in peace and freedom. The boys told women they were a 'different' breed of men. Sexual liberation, what was also called sexual radicalism, was the alleged antidote to the restricted lives of many of the girls' mothers — lives that the girls renounced. But they found themselves just as constrained by a sexuality defined in male terms such as group sex, frequency of sex, and pressure to eagerly engage in unwanted sex.

For girls, the special attraction was "the lessening of gender polarity that kept the girls entranced, even after the fuck had revealed the boys to be men after all ... the dream for the girls at base was a dream of a sexual and social empathy that negated the strictures of gender, a dream of sexual equality" (Dworkin, 1983, p. 90).

In trying to erode the boundaries of gender through a sexual radicalism that purported to be a roadmap to women's liberation, women regressed to an environment that made them more sexually accessible to men who became more aggressively dominant. Sexual liberation left women more available for men to use without the protection of any bourgeois constraints.

The sexual revolution ideology was that fucking was good, and that girls and young women should be pleased and ready to be fucked by men who claimed to be different. But the peace and freedom boys were not different. Forced sex happened often at events like Woodstock. When rape occurred, "it was an event that occurred outside the political discourse of the generation in question and therefore it did not exist" (Dworkin, 1983, p. 92).

Lesbianism was viewed as a misfortune, a deficit of men in women's lives, but mostly as a pornographic prop for men to get it up.

A major obstacle to the sixties/sexties countercultural idealizing of fucking was women's fear of pregnancy, which held sex somewhat in check because it gave women a reason for rejecting it. Knowing that abortion must be available to women on demand, so that sex would be available to men on demand, men chose a feminist issue to support/exploit for their own purposes.

The sixties/sexties counterculture has passed into history, but its standard of sex on demand resonates with a more ominous male mandate for women's sexual attention. Today, self-declared women (men) who try to compel sex with lesbians echo the creed of the male incel movement of discontented men who feel they are owed sex with women by any means possible. Incel's philosophy and tactics are based on a notion called 'involuntary celibacy' (thus incel).

The movement of self-declared women (men), many who identify as trans lesbians and who are now demanding their 'right' to have sex with lesbians, is filled with threats of violence. Like the incels who feel scorned by women, self-declared lesbians believe their rejection is a crime punishable by "torture for the rest of their slutty lives" and that "women need to suffer" (Beauchamp, 2019). Incel misogyny is fueled by online clusters of men who share experiences and bond over not getting the sex they want, and then blame women for their sorry state.

Just as incels intentionally work to convince other incels that raping women is a justified response to sexual rejection, so too do the men who claim their penises are 'lady sticks'. Just as dissatisfied men adhere to the incel creed of beliefs, self-declared lesbians (men) insist that women owe them sex, and that there is something wrong with a world in which women have the power of rejection.

There is an incelian feel to the gangs of self-declared women (men) who identify as trans lesbians and moan about lesbians who reject their sexual advances. Trans activist campaigners, particularly the contingent of self-declared women who are trying to pressure lesbians to have sex with them, are engaging in real violence against real women.

By supporting the rights of men who identify as lesbians over the rights of lesbians to choose their sexual partners, men who identify as lesbians are in fact enforcing heterosexuality on lesbians.

Real Violence Against Real Women

Deep Green Resistance

In 2013, attacks on the feminist environmental group called Deep Green Resistance (DGR) foreshadowed future destructive trans tactics. At a Portland Oregon conference, ironically called Law and Disorder, DGR had set up a table to hand out literature and sell the organization's publications. A band of trans and queer activists approached the table, began shouting at the women using threatening and aggressive language, and then grabbed and vandalized their materials. When one of the women at the table tried to protect the materials, an aggressive intruder marked her hand and arm.

The following day, these trans extremists returned, escalating their actions by throwing trash and food at a male DGR member. After the conference, queer and trans activists threatened DGR members with arson, rape and murder and called for their mass beheading.

Organizers of the conference did not intervene to stop the assault but instead issued a statement insinuating the attack was deserved because of DGR's alleged transphobia. One organizer excused the attack. "Speaking personally as a white male, it is not my place to dictate how anyone who feels unsafe or oppressed by DGR's transphobia should respond to it." DGR countered, "So safe space does not in any way mean physical safety, as in freedom from aggression and assault. It means *freedom to be aggressive and assaultive* if you feel oppressed" (Keith and Jensen, 2013, italics mine).

DGR captured the idealizing of trans aggression and assault. "What's most disturbing is the public response. Men who have assaulted women are held up as heroes; the angry mood is celebrated. There is a war on women on the left as well as the right. If you don't believe us, speak up and see for yourself" (Keith and Jensen, 2013).

The San Francisco Library Exhibit

Justifications of trans violence against women were shockingly on display at the San Francisco Public Library (SFPL) where a trans group exhibited blood-stained t-shirts encouraging viewers to 'punch' feminists. Launched in 2018, the exhibit also featured installations of deadly weapons and baseball bats covered in barbed wire and axes, all designed with the expressed intention of killing feminists and lesbians.

The Library was responsible for approving and funding this horror show of paraphernalia including the actual weapons used to incite violence against women. The show was created by a group called The Degenderettes led by Scout Tran Caffee, the founder of Trans Dykes: The Anti-Lesbian Antifa that proudly declares its identity and specifically targets lesbians because they reject the sexual overtures of self-declared trans lesbians. A former Antifa organizer told an interviewer: "The idea in Antifa is that we go … to cause conflict, to shut them [opponents] down where they are, because we don't believe that Nazis or fascists of any stripe should have a mouthpiece" (Suerth, 2020). In the eyes of Antifa, radical feminists are comparable to Nazis and other fascists.

A Change.org petition called on the library to remove the display and warned, "The exhibit openly and unapologetically advocates violence against feminists, many of whom are lesbian and/or gender abolitionist, and as such should be removed" (Change.org. 2018). However, only one of the blood splattered t-shirts was removed from the exhibit after feminists objected that the cache of weapons legitimated violence against women, and the exhibit remained open.

A small group of California Bay Area-based activists led by women called on women to participate in an action protesting the exhibit. On their Facebook page, the organizers state:

It seems highly improbable that the SFPL or any other publicly funded institution would partner with an organization that has called for violence against black people, Jewish people, disabled people, or any other oppressed population. Therefore, their willingness to partner with an organization that calls for violence against women comes across as blatant sexism (San Francisco Public Library, 2018).

The fact that a major US city library would even countenance such an exhibit tells us that not only are groups like Trans Dykes and the anti-lesbian Antifa becoming more blatantly violent, but also that public institutions are joining their cause, dressing up violence against women as 'art'. As Julian Vigo has written, "The bigotry of old has taken on a strangely progressive turn … where the most regressive ideology is seen as progressive" (Vigo, 2018). The exhibit at the San Francisco Public Library shows how much the word TERF has become a slippery slope and an easy gateway to violence against women, and how public institutions are ready to accommodate and empower its perpetrators.

The Vancouver Rape Relief and Women's Shelter (VRRWS)

In Canada, trans activists vandalized and promoted the defunding of a women's shelter that provides needed services to female victims of male violence. In 2019, staff at the Vancouver Rape Relief and Women's Shelter (VRRWS) arrived at work to find violent messages scrawled across their windows: "Kill TERFs, Fuck TERFs, Trans women are women." A dead rat was nailed to the front door. One woman coming to the shelter and experiencing the scene said, "Haven't we suffered enough?" (in Kearns, 2019b).

The women who use the shelter's services are women who have experienced rape, battering, prostitution and other forms of male violence. They have been physically and mentally harmed. They have experienced real violence, not the fake violence that trans activists conjure up when they claim that misgendering or using the 'wrong' pronouns is violence.

How insidious and hateful that the goal of trans activists is to close down a venerable feminist organization that has been a mainstay of protection and assistance to women for almost a half century. Instead of supporting such an organization, these trans activists work to undermine VRRWS by starving its funding because the shelter has stayed true to its mission of providing services to natal women. After pressure from trans activists, VRRWS lost a $30,000 grant that would have been used for public education and outreach services regardless of gender identity.

This was not the first time that VRRWS has been targeted by trans activists. In 1995, transsexual Kimberly Nixon filed a human rights complaint against the Shelter for refusing to take Nixon on as a volunteer peer counselor for female victims of male violence. They offered him other positions but held to the Shelter's mission to provide woman-to-woman counseling to victims of male violence when he claimed discrimination. Nixon insisted on putting vulnerable women who had just been battered by men in the position of being counseled by a person (himself) who is biologically male.

Nixon sued, and VRRWS lost its case initially at the Human Rights Tribunal, which later overturned its decision in favor of the Shelter. Nixon then appealed to the British Columbia Court of Appeals where he lost, and the decision was unanimously decided in VRRWS's favor. In 2007, the Supreme Court of Canada dismissed Nixon's request to appeal the decision and charged him with covering the Shelter's legal costs. This allowed the Shelter to adhere to its women-only policy and affirmed its legitimate interest in preserving this kind of service.

That was in 2007. That battle took 12 years, years that put the VRRWS in jeopardy and stressed the organization's mission and finances. But today is a different battle in which VRRWS is fighting for its life, and the courts cannot be counted on to recognize trans misogyny. In spite of its latest setback, the remarkable tenacity and courage of the VRRWS women continues to be inspired by its feminist philosophy that women are an oppressed class and are therefore entitled to be helped by other women — not by men who declare themselves women and have no history of oppression as women.

Women's Prisons and Male Criminality

Trans activists have argued that 'trans women' should be billeted in women's prisons for protection from dangerous male inmates, which is the same reason why many women are arguing that trans-identified women (men) should *not* be housed in women's prisons i.e. for protection from dangerous male inmates.

Trans activists have branded feminists who argue for this necessary protection as transphobic, accusing us of encouraging the 'myth of the predatory transwoman', asserting there is no evidence that confirms trans-identified women are a danger to women prisoners.

On the contrary, there is such evidence.

In 2017, a comprehensive report published by the UK group Fair Play for Women provided an analysis of individual prison inspection reports for all English and Wales prisons. The report confirmed that 60 of the 125 transgender prisoners in English and Welsh prisons are convicted sex offenders or have committed dangerous category A offenses such as attempted murder, rape and indecent assault, numbers later confirmed by the Ministry of Justice (MoJ). The fact that half of all transgender prisoners in these two countries are sex offenders is an astounding revelation.

The numbers in the *Fair Play for Women Report* suggest that "sex offending rates among trans prisoners is at least comparable to [natal] male rates" (2017). This makes sense because self-declared women are men. What is clear from the study is that men who identify as women (called TIMs, or trans identifying men in the report), despite identifying and dressing as women, "do not exhibit a pattern of criminality in any way similar to that of women. If they did, we would expect to see virtually no sex offending by the TIM inmates" (Fair Play for Women, 2017).

In England and Wales, only five percent of all those incarcerated are natal women. If self-declared women prisoners (men) are transferred to women's prisons, any minor increases would present a large and serious risk of violence to the extremely small number of women housed there, given the fact that half of the self-declared women (men) are sex offenders with functional penises. "It is estimated that 80–95 percent of trans-identifying people have not undergone genital reconstruction surgery" and retain their biology (Fair Play for Women, 2017).

The 2004 UK Gender Recognition Act (GRA) formerly required a prisoner to have been issued a gender recognition certificate attesting to a diagnosis of gender dysphoria and living two years 'in the role'. Recently, the GRA has rejected self-declaration as a criterion for changing sex, meaning that a man cannot now use it in order to be transferred to a women's prison (Murphy and Brooks, 2020).

Dismissal of self-declaration is a welcome step and will help in avoiding violence against women such as that perpetrated by prisoner Karen White. White, a self-declared woman, committed several rapes and other sexual offences against women prisoners after being transferred from a UK men's to a women's prison. White also admitted to a rape *before* being sent to prison, a prior offence that should have triggered an appraisal of White's previous offending history. However, the Ministry of Justice admitted that authorities did not carry out this assessment.

Looking at the gender prison debate in the United States, over 300 inmates in California prisons — self-declared women — have requested transfers to facilities congruent with their gender identity. Requests followed after the passage of a 2020 law gives the right of incarcerated self-declared women (men) to be housed in women's prisons. Under the new law, trans, intersex, and non-binary inmates in the California prison system have the right to choose whether they will be housed in a 'male' or 'female' prison.

California's law is similar to those recently passed in Connecticut and Massachusetts. The federal Prison Rape Elimination Act (PREA) states that decisions about housing a biological male inmate cannot be based solely on genitalia and requires that a petitioner's views on their own personal safety must be seriously considered (Miller, 2021).

In the state of Washington, the American Civil Liberties Union (ACLU) has sued a private citizen, and members of the media, for trying to access public records that identify the number of male prisoners currently in women's prisons there. The Washington Public Records Act guarantees that citizens have the right to access these records. Shamefully, the ACLU, which has been the historical avatar of wresting public records out of withholding government agencies, is attempting to block this citizen from obtaining information that would document the number of male inmates who identify as transgender women in women's facilities in the state.

The female citizen has asked not to be named because of safety concerns, but the ACLU is identifying her in their lawsuit to prevent the public records from being released. "In a twist of irony, the citizen tells us she used resources provided on the ACLU's website to draft the public records request which they are now seeking to squash" (WoLF, 2021c, April 14).

The Women's Liberation Front (WoLF) is representing the citizen in her response to this hypocritical lawsuit that betrays the ACLU's own basic principles. Known for its success in using the Freedom of Information Act (FOIA), the ACLU has gained access for its clients to many public records. But in the Washington state case, the ACLU appears to betray its original mission.

The judge gave a 'both hands' ruling. On the one hand, he ruled in favor of the ACLU. Still, on the other hand, the ruling revealed that a serial rapist is housed in the Washington Correctional Center for Women. It confirmed that a number of inmates have been transferred from a men's facility to a women's and that the number of those transferred is three and the total number of males "who identify as female, non-binary or any other gender identity" is seven (WoLF, 2021e, May 19). The judge's ruling also granted "an injunction against the public release of these documents" including infraction records of several men housed in the state's women's prisons today, along with 309 pages documenting violations committed by one particular male inmate (WoLF, 2021e May 19).

Unfortunately, the judge decided that none of these documents could be released to the public, concluding that it would be a breach of the federal Prison Rape Elimination Act (PREA). What an irony — that a law that aims to eliminate rape can't protect women in prisons when the rapists are men who declare themselves women and are now increasingly being accommodated!

Continuing the saga of California's women's prison disaster, conditions there have been described as "a nightmare's worst nightmare" with the recent announcement in July 2021 that contraceptive resources would be distributed to female prisoners, "a tacit admission by officials that women should expect to be raped" (WoLF, 2021g, July 15) when male prisoners who self declare as women will be allowed to request a transfer to move into women's prisons.

In women's prisons across the state, similar provisions had gone into effect in January 2021 following the initiation of SB 132 after which the numbers of male requests for transfer reached 300. Many of the requests came from criminal sex offenders who, it seems, are taking advantage of this invitation into a rape paradise for further indulging their criminal misogynist behavior. Thus far, 20 transfers have been processed, and no requests have been denied.

Adding insult to injury, the California Department of Corrections and Rehabilitation has devised the 'security measure' of mandating that all men who have requested transfer to a women's prison must take a course in how to deal with *their fears about living with women* (WoLF, 2021g, July 15), a blatant reversal of reality! There are some ideas so absurd and dangerous that only male bureaucrats could conceive them.

Simply from a public health perspective, you don't endanger the lives of many women to oblige fewer men who claim they will benefit by transferring to women's prisons. SB 132 will hurt the thousands of women who reside in women's prisons throughout California, based on the belief that accommodating the 300 men who are requesting transfers is more important that the rights and safety of the state's 5,849 female prisoners, 25.9% of whom are African American (Public Policy Institute of California, PPIC, 2019).

One woman housed in a California women's prison has stated:

> When we reach out for help we get nothing ... There has been an assault on a woman and we still are silenced ... Does anyone care that we are being forced to house with 6'2, 250+ lbs men with penises that are here for brutally raping women ... If we say we are in fear, we are the ones locked up (WoLF, 2021g, July 15).

Another woman added, "You might as well declare the prison is co-ed and ship us off to Pelican Bay!' (WoLF2021g, July 15). (Pelican Bay is the supermax prison in the state of California.)

SB 132 is the consequence of the prevailing trans ideology that men can be women. This cannot stand.

Another serious consequence when men are counted as women and allowed a transfer to a women's prison is that the collecting of accurate evidence and data on all kinds of male violence against women — rape, domestic violence and other crimes primarily perpetrated against women and girls — becomes distorted. This data is necessary to fund violence against women programs that provide assistance to women in need. Mary Lou Singleton, a US midwife and nurse practitioner, has warned that US crime statistics are changing. "Men who identify as women rape women with their penises, and these crimes are being recorded as committed by women" (in Hedges, 2017).

The London Attack on Maria MacLachlan

There has been no shortage of trans activists who have transformed violent threats into actual physical violence against women. Helen Lewis wrote in the *New Statesman*, "You would have thought that a feminist getting punched in the face would be reasonably large news — particularly if her attacker earlier had boasted online of wanting to 'fuck up some feminists', comparing them to fascists" (Lewis, 2018).

In October 2017, Tara Wolf, a self-declared woman, attacked 60-year-old Maria MacLachlan, hitting her in the face for being an alleged TERF. When the punch happened, MacLachlan was filming a group of women who had assembled at a London meeting spot called Speakers Corner to discuss proposed changes to the UK Gender Identify Act. Wolf threw his punch during a counter protest. The attack ended up in court where Wolf was charged with one count of assault. Wolf's supporters defended the violence stating, "… acts of physical violence against those who are systemically violent are self-defence" (Turner, 2020).

Even more unsettling are the opinions expressed by some feminist and leftist groups. Sister Uncut, a group that has protested the closure of UK domestic violence services, tweeted that Wolf was the real victim and called a protest outside the court to support Wolf whom they alleged is "… a transwoman targeted … and harassed by TERFs, transmisogynists and cops … Attacks on trans lives will not be tolerated" (Lewis, 2018). Rightly, the judge didn't buy this reasoning and rejected Wolf's defense ordering Wolf to pay several fines amounting to £430.

In her *New Statesman* article, Lewis captured this kind of craven anti-feminist attitude:

> The … imperceptible pause of both the left and right to see if it's the 'right' sort of perpetrator, and whether the story therefore fits their particular narrative … [M]any so-called progressives were dismissive of MacLachlan's account of the incident because it was inconvenient to their narrative. She was lucky that video footage existed showing the assault (Lewis, 2018).

Lewis depicts a hierarchy of leftist 'self-righteousness' that dictates progressives' responses to blatant trans violence against women. She writes that excuses escalate from: "some feminists have a different conception of gender to me" climbing to "some feminists talk about me in ways that I find offensive" and ultimately, "some feminists are basically Hitler, trying to eradicate people like me." The final opinion becomes a self-justification for slapping a woman or worse (Lewis, 2018).

The day after MacLachlan's attack, the Edinburgh organization, Action for Trans Health, tweeted, "Punching TERFs is the same as punching Nazis. Fascism must be smashed with the greatest violence to ensure our collective liberation from it." Beyond the realm of tweets, the Edinburgh group is actively promoting violence against women, not just expressing dissent with those they differ but also extolling "the right to punch women with whom they disagree" (Lewis, 2018).

Leftist and selective women's groups act as if tweets exalting violence against women don't really matter because they are words and not actions. But the distance between tweets that incite violence and actual physical violence against women is very short. As we saw in the MacLachlan incident and the other assaults listed in this chapter, threatening tweets can move easily into physical violence, become a defense for it, and eat away at women's safety. And the stew of threats against feminists that boils on social media helps normalize violence against women, poisoning discourse with words and ideas that were once unspeakable.

The Attack on Julie Bindel in Edinburgh

In September 2019, after the Maria MacLachlan assault, journalist Julie Bindel was attacked in Edinburgh. Newspapers such as *The Scotsman* published articles about the confrontation, and Bindel herself has written about it in several media including in *The Sunday Times* of London (Bindel, 2019b).

Bindel was speaking at Edinburgh University about male violence when the violence against her took place. As she was walking to her taxi after a very successful event — despite efforts to cancel her appearance, attempts by trans activists to set off stink bombs in the hall and a security presence around her — "a man wearing a long skirt and with lots of dark stubble, started screaming and shouting at me, calling me a Nazi and Terf scum." It was obvious that he was waiting for Bindel near a couple of trans-identified women (men) who held the usual signs displaying, "No Terfs on our turf" and "Die cis scum," epithets especially aimed at prominent gender critics like Bindel.

The man who attempted to punch Bindel, who goes by the Twitter handle of Town Tattle, lunged at her trying to land the blow on her face. Bindel said,

> He was shouting and ranting and raving, 'you're a fucking cunt, you're a fucking bitch, a fucking terf' and the rest of it, when the security guards pulled him away. I have been beaten up by men in the past but not for a long time, and I knew precisely what was coming when I saw the rage on his face, and I am just so sick of this (in Davidson, 2019).

Attacks are nothing new for radical feminists who clearly acknowledge that men are not women. At a conference in Copenhagen over a decade ago at which Julie Bindel and I were both speakers, trans activists formed a gauntlet of hate that we were forced to run through, as we exited the building with police protection. Although some academics, journalists, and therapists have been condemned for their gender-critical work, radical feminists remain the primary targets of trans activists.

In an *Open Letter to the British Media: You are Complicit in Male Violence Against Women*, journalist Dan Fisher accused British media outlets of responding "shamefully" to the attack on Julie Bindel. He particularly condemned articles covering the attack that were filled with repeating the claims of trans activists and downplaying the assault; and argued their prolific use of the term TERF to describe radical feminists helped to justify the attack instead of condemning the violence. Fisher reproached the kind of journalism that, when confronted with contentious issues, follows the cowardly path of least resistance. "We must stand up to the attempted manipulation of language and definitions or else be complicit in their proliferation" (Fisher, 2019).

Trans Violence in Argentina

In Buenos Aires, a group of radical feminist women was scheduled to speak at a feminist event called Ni Una Menos (Not One More Woman), in keeping with the advent of International Women's Day. Their designated speaker, Ana Marcocavallo, a member of FRIA/ Feministas Radicales Independientes Argentina (Independent Radical Feminists of Argentina) was attacked by a self-declared woman (man) activist. When Ana went to take the microphone and was identified as a radical feminist, the crowd began chanting, "Kick her out! Kick her out!" (in Rosario Sanchez, 2019).

The assailant was a tall man who emerged from the crowd dressed in a mini-skirt and charged at Ana with a defiant fighting pose. Ana was there to speak about the organization's abolitionist position on sexual exploitation until the man began to threaten her, shouting and fisting in the air as he stopped her from talking.

The attacker grabbed Ana by her t-shirt at the same time that he was trying to snatch the microphone. From a video that recorded the attack, it appeared that he was trying to punch her when another woman pulled him off. At this point, he began to throw punches at that woman, which fortunately did not land. Other persons in the crowd wrestled him to the ground. But the disheartening moment was when the crowd started shouting support for the trans activist, and other women tried to prevent Ana and FRIA members from speaking — what Ana called "a hard emotional punch" (in Rosario Sanchez, 2019).

Before the attack, a left-wing Argentinian newspaper had published a threatening article by a trans activist that condemned radical feminists for their alleged transphobia. "There will come a time when we will be offered equality, sovereignty and autonomy. And when that time comes, we will put you [radical feminists] on trial, just like we did with Nazi genocides, and wherever you are, we will seek you out" (in Rosario Sanchez, 2019).

Other feminist organizations such as Feministas Radicales de Argentina (Radical Feminists of Argentina) or RADAR no longer felt safe to speak. "We believe that this censorship of our ideas was rooted in a backlash from sex industry advocates who want to foment infighting against the movement to abolish prostitution" (Rosario Sanchez, 2019).

After the attack, Ana was interviewed about what had happened. She stated that prior to the violence, many threats were directed at her group, threats that included setting feminists on fire or breaking their teeth. She noted that social media encourages this kind of chatter but that she had never expected the threats would be carried out in direct physical violence, as happened at the event.

Ana said that FRIA received very little support from abolitionist organizations in Argentina, and even a dollop of solidarity was mixed with a larger dose of reluctance. They rejected the violence, but they made clear they didn't support transphobia. Ana interpreted this as a ratification of the claim that radical feminists are transphobic. Other feminist organizations showed no solidarity, and some even supported the attack. "The Ni Una Menos collective apologized, not for the violence against women, but for the fact that we were even allowed to speak."

As they put it: "We received more support from radical feminists abroad than from feminists in our own country. After what happened, we feel devalued and are concerned about the way we are being defamed and abused … to the point that we fear for our safety" (in Rosario Sanchez, 2019).

Magical Thinking

It seems that the mere claim of men who self-declare as women is sufficient to convince many that males who appropriate a female gender identity are indeed women. Years of living as men with male privilege, and indulging in toxic masculinity, do not disappear with a man's self-declaration as female.

When we examine how self-declared women (men) behave towards natal women who challenge their right to usurp a woman's identity, it is clear that such men are indulging in the privileged behavior that we recognize as male entitlement. The most telling proof that self-declared women are still men is their misogynist conduct.

It is magical thinking to believe that men socialized as male could simply transform themselves and their masculinist behavior when they put on a skirt. In fact, self-declared women have more in common with natal men because by the time many of them declare their new gender identity, they have often spent more of their lives living as males than as self-declared females.

One Swedish long-term study of "transsexual persons under-going sex reassignment" found that regarding any crime, including violent crime, "male-to-females had a significantly increased risk for crime" (Dhejne et al, 2011). Self-declared women can and do pose the same kind of risk to natal women, as do natal men. If men are misogynistic before transitioning, undergoing transsexual treatment or self-declaration as a woman does not automatically produce any major behavioral transformations that mitigate their socialized abusive behavior.

This is not to argue that men cannot change their masculinist behavior, but rather to say that declaring yourself a woman doesn't result in a behavioral transformation. To disarm male privilege and male dominant behavior entails a lot of self-reflection and hard work (see Jensen, 2017). In spite of all assertions that a gender identity change eliminates the risk of male violence to women, e.g. when men are billeted in women's prisons, self-declared female identification does not outdo years of male socialization to violence or abuse.

If the threats, bullying and harassment perpetrated by trans activists are not yet inciting mass physical violence, these threats are definitely normalizing violent behavior, whipping up mob tactics, and encouraging 'lone-wolf' violence.

Unfortunately, many people want to 'see no evil, hear no evil'. There is a deafening code of silence about the misogyny of trans activists and a painful lack of responses, especially from progressive men and women, to challenge rampant trans tyranny at women's events and on social media. Too many bystanders are looking the other way and are allowing trans violence against women to spread, whether in words or in deeds.

Equality for women cannot exist with the fiction that men can be women or with the threats, the bullying, and the harassment that undermines women who bravely reject men's self-declaration as women.

CHAPTER FIVE

Gender Identity Trumps Sex in Women's Sports and Children's Education

*The more incredible a woman is, the more barriers she busts
through, the more gender non-conforming she is deemed to be ...
the more amazing a woman is, the less she counts as a woman.*

—Abigail Shrier

In 2004, men who identified as women were allowed to participate in women's Olympic sports events only if they had undergone transition surgery. The surgical requirement has since been dropped, and the standard of measurement that now rules the Olympics is focused on hormone levels, specifically testosterone. According to the new rules, men who identify as women must declare their gender identity as female, keep that identity for four years, and lower their hormone levels.

The women's sports debate publicly exploded when tennis champion Martina Navratilova wrote a robust opinion piece in the UK *Sunday Times* stating her view that "Letting men compete as women simply if they change their name and take hormones is unfair — no matter how those athletes may throw their weight around ... The rules on trans athletes reward cheats and punish the innocent ... It's insane and it's cheating" (in Allen, 2019). Unfortunately, Navratilova later walked back some of these words when she was interviewed by the BBC and said, "but for now I think we need to include as many transgender athletes as possible within elite sports while keeping as level a playing field as possible" (BBC, 2019a).

Retribution was fast in coming. Athletes Ally, an organization that promotes LGBT+ (mostly T) inclusion in sports, demanded that Navratilova be removed from its board, and, as is the usual insult aimed at those who dispute any facet of transgenderism, she was denounced as transphobic. The organization declared, "First of all, trans women are women, period ... There is no evidence at all that the average trans woman is any bigger, stronger, or faster than the average cisgender woman" (in Allen, 2019). Not so. There is mounting evidence to the contrary, as referenced below.

It's Not All about Hormones

For years, Olympic emphasis on hormone levels has dominated the decisions made by various sports committees governing national and international competitions. Debates raged over women runners whose higher hormone levels did not meet official standards. In the Olympic doping scandals of the late 1990s, female athletes from Russia and the eastern bloc countries were reputed, many without evidence, to have been treated with testosterone, giving them an unfair advantage over their sister competitors. The games pitted women against other women on the basis of their hormone levels, and some were disqualified. Now, women are pitted against trans-identified women (men) and their higher hormone levels.

Since 2004, certain track and field events have allowed men who identify as trans women to compete with natal women if they comply with the reductions set for their hormone levels. Despite the fact that these male-bodied women must reduce their testosterone, they are allowed to participate with much higher levels of the hormone than natal women athletes possess. For example, in order to compete in women's Olympic track events, male-bodied women must reduce their testosterone levels to 5 nanomoles per liter (nmol/L), a level still decidedly higher than natal women who have lower testosterone levels averaging 2.6 nmol/L. In other words, although the Olympic Committee has set a maximum level of testosterone for men who identify as women, it's still not anywhere near the lower natural testosterone levels that disadvantage natal women if they must compete against self-declared women.

In contrast to the lenient levels mandated for men who identify as women, the Olympic Committee has historically been much more discriminatory about monitoring women's hormone levels to the point of requiring drug tests. This bias was acknowledged in 1998 when the Chairman of the Olympic Committee's medical commission admitted that Florence Griffith (Flo-Jo) Joyner was singled out for intense drug testing in the 1984 and 1988 Olympic games. Joyner is an African American track champion and the fastest runner in the world with times in the 100m and 200m dashes that remain a world record to this day. The Chairman concluded, "We performed all possible and imaginable analyses on her. We never found anything. There should not be the slightest suspicion" (Yang, 2020). It is discriminatory that historically only women, not men, were ever subjected to gender verification tests.

Ana Paula Henkel, the Brazilian volleyball player, reminds us that for 24 years she and other women were submitted to rigorous anti-doping tests that measured their testosterone levels in order to prove that they were women. And those measurements kept various women from competing. "This level of rigour has been completely abandoned to accommodate transsexuals who, not long ago, identified as men" (Henkel, 2018).

More recently, the hormone gauge was used in another pernicious way against Caster Semenya of South Africa, an Olympic multiple medal-winner with a genetic variant whose natural hormone levels were outside the expected female range. In her final petition to the Olympic Court of Arbitration for Sport (CAS), the Court denied her appeal to compete in the 2021 Tokyo Olympics 800m race. The Court discriminated against Semenya, it admitted, "in order to guarantee fair competition" in certain track and field events and, as a prerequisite to competing, instructed that she undergo hormone therapy to reduce her hormone levels" (in Longman, 2020). Otherwise, the Court suggested she could compete against men rather than women and enter (non-existing) intersex athletic competitions.

Bravely, Semenya has refused to comply, arguing that the potential harm of the hormone reduction requirement is unethical and not based on medical need. She has intimated that instead she may run in the 200m race that is not hindered by hormone restrictions.

However, it's not all about hormones. The hormone test has never made much sense because the male physiological advantage is due not simply to testosterone but to other biological differences between men and women that favor men — including higher oxygen-carrying capacity, longer and larger bones, stronger ligaments and a higher ratio of muscle mass to body weight. All these physiological advantages have made men stronger and faster.

Women are more competitive in sports that require endurance, such as ultra long-distance running where they have defeated men. In these ultra long sports events, women have the advantage of being able to convert glycogen more easily into energy that is necessary when glucose levels drop. Like the history of a woman's life, endurance is the sine qua non, the essential condition of a woman athlete's existence.

In 2019, British doctor Katie Wright beat 40 men and six women to win an ultra-marathon in New Zealand, running almost non-stop for 30 hours. "Women are actually going out there and beating the men. We're going to see it much more often. They're finding their feet with ultra-events and you will see many more women rising to the top" (in Williams, 2019). But that prognosis has not yet materialized in other sports. For example, swimmer Allison Schmitt set the 200m world record at 1:53.61 minutes, a major victory in women's swimming. But Michael Phelps' time in the 200m men's event was 1:42.96 minutes.

There is no scientific evidence that simply decreasing male hormonal levels is sufficient to eliminate the male competitive advantage and can smooth men's way into women's sports. Given the male physiological advantage in most sports, and as more men who self-identify as women demand access to competing against women, the category of women's sports becomes a charade of justice. If the Olympic standards are based on fairness, as Semenya's court decision maintained, why are men who identify as women — with their physiological advantage — allowed to compete in women's sports?

One dubious supporter of preserving women's sports is Caitlin Jenner who rejects 'biological boys' competing in female events. Now a Republican candidate for governor in California, Jenner has stated, "It just isn't fair and we have to protect girls' sports." Given Jenner's past acknowledgment that young trans athletes should be "given the chance to play sports as who they really are," blowback from activists was quick in arriving, calling him no LGBT friend and "a cog in the GOP machine" and asserting he should return all his trans hero awards (in Marr, 2021).

Paula Henkel has been one of the few Olympians who has spoken out in an open letter to the International Olympics Committee (IOC) — an eloquent and heartfelt rejection of men playing in women's sports. "If someone has to go public and pay a price in the name of truth, common sense and fact, I'm willing to bear the consequences. The space, won with integrity by women in sport is at play." Also, women's volleyball coaches in Brazil and Italy are revealing that sports agents are 'selling' places on women's volleyball teams to male-bodied women who are usurping women's places (Henkel, 2018).

Henkel observes that if there were no male competitive advantage, why the need to set the men's volleyball net height at 2.43m and the women's at 2.24m? She attributes the march of males entering women's sports to a "political militancy that condenses and reduces thinking to ideological soundbites that deny reality;" to sporting entities who "blind themselves to human biology in an attempt to hoodwink science in the name of politico-ideological agendas;" and to the "complicity of sports authorities around the world" who engage in a "supreme form of misogyny. ... It represses, embarrasses, humiliates and excludes women" (Henkel, 2018).

And a majority of Americans agree with her. A March 2021 poll conducted by *Politico* and *Morning Consult* found that 53 percent of those in the survey "support a ban on transgender athletes competing in women's sports." The extremist proposal to impose biological males into women's sports is not mainstream (Justice, 2021).

On the US Legislative Front

The States

There are at least 50 different bills pending in US state legislatures across the country that protect women's single sex rights in sports. It is disappointing that these bills are primarily being launched in conservative states like Mississippi, Georgia, South Dakota, Oklahoma, and Texas, mostly states with conservative legislative majorities when more liberal Democratic majority states are doing the opposite and instead are protecting the 'rights' of men.

The impact of US legislation is key to the hopes of young women and girls who compete in high schools, colleges, state and national sports. The story of Linnea Saltz brings this legislation home and represents the expectations of many girls and women who excel in competitive sports and whose future in sport is crushed when physiologically-advantaged boys or men who identify as girls or women capture the best times and awards. As a star runner in her senior year at Southern Utah University, Saltz had won the US Outdoor Big Sky Conference championship in the 800m race and hoped to win it again so that she could advance and then compete for the All-American title.

Saltz discovered that her competition would include a male-bodied 'woman' whose personal best time in the 800m was ten seconds faster than her own record and who had broken world records in the 1500m race. These were numbers that exceed all

Division 1 records for women, the highest level of intercollegiate athletics.

Troubled that the gender identity model abolishes fairness in women's sports, Saltz said, "It is discouraging for girls and women everywhere to think that they may have to compete against an individual that has a biological advantage over them." She felt that fairness in women's sports was disappearing before her eyes. "Taking away our opportunities will run us out of the sports world, which we already had to fight so hard to be a part of " (in Romboy, 2021).

Saltz didn't leave it at discouragement but decided to testify before Utah lawmakers who had launched House Bill 302 called *Preserving Sports for Female Students.* If passed, it would establish that sex, not gender identity, would govern K-12 and college sports in the state. Trans advocates organized to oppose the bill and as of this writing, it looks like it will not be passed.

The Women's Liberation Front (WoLF), which monitors this legislation, has publicized a list of specific examples of boys and men who identify as female and who have sidelined young women athletes. The list was originally written to explain some of the reasons for submitting a federal *Protection of Women and Girls in Sports Act,* initiated by Republican Senator Mike Lee of Utah.

- In track and field, male high school runner CeCe Telfer won three titles in the Northeast-10 Championships for women's track, and received the Most Outstanding Track Athlete award.
- In softball, male player Pat (Patrick) Cordova-Goff took one of 15 spots on his California high school women's varsity softball team.
- In basketball, a 50-year-old, 6-foot-8-inch, 230-pound man, Robert (Gabrielle) Ludwig, led the Mission College women's basketball team to a national championship with the most rebounds.
- In Connecticut's state track and field championships, two male high school runners, Andraya Yearwood and Terry Miller, took first and second place in multiple events, beating out top

high school girls from across the state. Yearwood was named Connecticut (CT) Athlete of the Year (WoLF, 2021, 5 February).

The elite girl athletes now called the Connecticut Three who lost to these two boys — Selina Soule, Chelsea Mitchell and Alanna Smith and their families — filed a legal suit against the Connecticut Athletic Conference and several state boards of education to challenge Connecticut's policy of allowing self-declared girls to compete in girls' sports. At the end of April 2021, a federal judge dismissed the young women's case. Not letting this legal setback rule, they plan to appeal the dismissal (WoLF, 2021d, 26 April).

The Feds

Whether the appeals court will treat the Connecticut sports policy as a violation of Title IX is not a cause for optimism in the Biden era. Title IX reads: "No person in the United States shall, on the basis of sex, be excluded from participation in, be denied the benefits of, or be subjected to discrimination under any education program or activity receiving federal financial assistance."

Obviously, the original drafters saw no need to define sex in the text. However, since its passage, different administrations and rulings have relied on diverse definitions of sex, and whether or not sex includes gender identity. The ambiguity surrounding the definition of sex that now exists in life and law has undermined women's sports and threatened the remarkable results of the Title IX revolution that accelerated women's and girls' participation in sports.

The Trump administration's Office of Civil Rights (OCR) in the Department of Education (DOE) stated that Title IX regulations allow single-sex spaces and sports. But the Biden administration's new Secretary of Education, Dr Michael Cardona, has over-ridden that policy, saying he will not enforce Title IX and will allow boys and men who identify as female to play in female sports (WoLF, 2021b, 9 April). How this will affect state laws is not clear.

WoLF submitted a Petition for Rulemaking to "protect the Title IX rights of women and girls." The petition responds to President

Biden's executive order on 'gender identity' that directs federal agencies to interpret 'sex' to include 'gender identity' and create new regulations that conform to this interpretation. WoLF's petition requested the agency to affirm that Title IX be enforced on the ground of sex, referenced the former OCR's emphasis on single-sex spaces and sports, and also affirmed that 'sex', under Title IX, refers to biological sex (WoLF, 2021b, April 9). The DOE rejected the petition but invited WoLF's participation in a public hearing organized by OCR. After the hearing and a comprehensive review, OCR will publish a notice of proposed rulemaking that may or may not amend the current OCR interpretation that sex includes gender identity.

In June 2021, the Department of Education invited Title IX complaints that are based on sexual orientation or gender identity. Although this is not yet a regulation or a law, it is a pronouncement of how the Education Department intends to proceed with its self-declaration policy before a law, if passed by Congress, can be put into place (WoLF, 2021f, June 17).

When Congress passed the Title IX bill back in 1972, they ordered the Department of Education to allow for female-only sports and sex-separated spaces, with the understanding that single-sex spaces are necessary for women and girls. The newly announced Biden policy in 2021 states that male athletes, if they declare they are female, cannot be excluded from women's sports.

No one knows yet if this new policy will be encoded in a new rule or administrative directive, but for now the document serves as a "clarification of the Department's position and has invited students especially to begin submitting complaints." The Department of Housing and Urban Development has already opened up university single-sex dorms and showers to men who self-identify as women (WoLF, 2021f, June 17).

On his first day in office in 2021, President Biden signed an *Executive Order on Preventing and Combating Discrimination on the Basis of Gender Identity or Sexual Orientation.* According to the White House, "The order mandates that all students, including transgender students, be able to learn without facing sex discrimination, and as part of that, transgender women should compete on female teams" (Sadeghi, 2021). An executive order is not a law, but rather a policy that remains active during the administration of the president who enacts it.

Opponents of Biden's executive order have warned that it endangers not only women's sports but also the women and girls themselves who risk physical injury. In mixed martial arts, for example, male fighter Fallon Fox smashed female fighter Tamikka Brents' eye socket and gave her a concussion. Brents said she "never felt so overpowered in her life" (in BJJ World, 2018).

When girls and women are compelled to compete against boys and men who identify as female, it undermines Title IX's expansion of opportunities for girls and women — particularly in school athletics — that have advanced US women's sports for almost five decades. Instead, Biden's executive order shrinks girls' opportunities.

Fifty years ago, women and girls worked diligently to pass Title IX legislation that helped level the playing field by promoting and funding women's sports.

> Since the enactment of Title IX, women's participation in sports has grown exponentially. In high school, the number of girl athletes has increased from just 295,000 in 1972 to more than 2.6 million. In college, the number has grown from 30,000 to more than 150,000. In addition, Title IX is credited with decreasing the dropout rate of girls from high schools and increasing the number of women who pursue higher education and complete college degrees (History.com, 2020).

Biden has urged Congress to pass *The Equality Act*, a new law that is, in fact, a frontal attack on females who participate in a range of sports. If passed by both the House and Senate, this law will be difficult to change, going beyond any policy or executive order that any administration has launched.

Just within the last decade, male-bodied competitors have outperformed elite female athletes, forcing them to settle for third or fourth places, setting records that are out of girls' reach, filling the available spots that disqualify girls from races they had formerly run, and forcing girls to become onlookers of their own sport as they watch their male-bodied opponents capture the best times and awards. A whole generation of young female athletes is being betrayed.

Biased Press Coverage

In the usual coverage of transgender issues published in *The New York Times*, there has been a spate of articles addressing boys' entrance into female sports — that is, boys who identify as girls. Like much coverage of trans issues in *The Times*, the articles consider this issue a civil rights battle, and they highlight the rights of male-bodied girls to compete in female sports.

This defense of boys' and men's rights to compete in female sports reprises familiar ground and has been highlighted in several *Times* articles. The articles repeat hackneyed themes such as: boys who identify as girls *are* girls; male-bodied girls have the right to compete in girls' sports; opposing their rights is discrimination against trans athletes; and social conservatives are leading the campaign for state laws opposing male-bodied girls' participation in girls' sports. The feminist opposition to these bills is ignored or represented as transphobic, and anyone who supports these bills is called bigoted.

More recently, the *Times* defense of male-bodied women's rights to compete in female sports, appeared in an article entitled 'Transgender Girls in Sports: G.O.P. Pushes New Front in Culture War'. The journalist contended that these bills emerged from a culture clash that appears to "come out of nowhere," evidently missing the many years of controversy over male-bodied athletes' entrance into female sports on the local, national and international fronts of the last few decades (Peter, 2021).

The *Times* article was tilted to floodlight opposition to these bills as only coming from right-leaning groups with no mention of feminist organizations, such as the well-known Women's Liberation Front (WoLF). WoLF has supported bills in different states based on feminist principles with a focus on fairness to women. Instead, the article only focused on social conservatives and claimed they "breathe new life into the issue" and "are creating a false and misplaced perception of victimization … that often reduces the nuanced issue of gender identity to a punchline about political correctness" (Peter, 2021).

Echoing the *Times* position, journalist Masha Gessen has concluded that the goal of the campaign for fairness in girls' sports "is not to protect cis-girl athletes as much as it is to make trans athletes disappear." She uses old tropes to delegitimize this campaign for fairness calling it a 'panic' and the result of a fatuous 'gender ideology' that in her rendering is called "a favorite bugaboo of the global far-right movement." She too is seemingly ignorant of the feminist campaign against gender ideology (Gessen, 2021).

The Hopes of Young Female Athletes Shattered

The impact of US legislation is key to the hopes of young women and girls who compete in high schools, colleges, state and national sports events. In one of his first executive orders in 2021, US President Joe Biden has devastated those hopes and the careers of many young female athletes who must now compete with young men or boys who identify as women or girls. The Executive Order that Biden signed on his first day in office, and *The Equality Act* that Biden has urged Congress to pass, provide no equality at all for women athletes.

The ultimate tragedy of the gender identity dogma now governing female sports is the shattering of young women's hopes for a future in sports that would guarantee genuine fairness, not the lip service of the national and international sports organizations that support male incursion into women's sports. Alanna Smith, one of the valiant Connecticut Three challenging the Connecticut decision, struck the downbeat felt by competitive girls when she said mentally and physically they know the outcome of the race at the starting line. "Biological unfairness doesn't go away because of what someone believes about gender identify" (WoLF, 2021d, 26 April). Worse, young women like the Connecticut Three "are being bullied and called 'sore losers' or 'transphobic' for simply seeking fairness in sports" (Stanescu, 2020) and losing out on sports scholarships to college.

Selina Soule is among the best athletes in the State of Connecticut. She started to compete in track and field as a young girl and amassed titles and awards, always moving from level to level and setting new records. Her proud mother has stated, "There's no question that competing for her school team has been the primary highlight of her high school experience" (in Stanescu, 2020). These girls are training with all their youthful might and want to win, not spend their energy in resisting the boys who identify as girls and who are disrupting many young women's sports events.

If those who think that opposing trans-identified girls (boys) is discrimination, consider these words of Selina's mother:

> Boys with mediocre times can compete in the boys' category and then completely dominate girls' events just a few weeks later. I've already seen this happening in Connecticut. After a series of unremarkable finishes as a boy in the 2018 indoor season, the same athlete began competing — and winning — as a girl in the outdoor season that started just weeks later (in Stanescu, 2020).

What is truly troubling is the pandering of elite American women athletes like tennis great Billie Jean King, soccer star Megan Rapinoe and basketball sharpshooter Candace Parker, who all joined an amicus brief supporting the rights of male-bodied women and girls to participate in female sports in Idaho (Avery, 2021).

Another group of women's sports leaders, including tennis legend Martina Navratilova, several Olympic gold medalists and five former presidents of the Women's Sports Foundation, is asking Congress and the Biden administration to limit the participation of trans-identified girls and women post puberty — the scientific line for separating the sexes in sport. Trans athletes, they stated, could be accommodated in other ways. "Options could include separate heats, additional events or divisions and/or the handicapping of results" (Brennan, 2021).

Another member of this group is Nancy Hogshead-Makar, a Title IX attorney and one of the leaders of the Women's Sports Policy Working Group, who has stated:

> Competitive sports ... require a science-based approach to trans inclusion ... The details of President Biden's executive order remain fuzzy ... asking women — no, requiring them — to give up their hard-won rights to compete and be recognized in elite sport, with equal opportunities, scholarships, prize money, publicity, honor and respect ... [this] does the cause of transgender inclusion no favors ... It engenders justifiable resentment, setting back the cause of equality throughout society (Brennan, 2021).

As the summer Olympics in Tokyo got underway, more athletes were predicted to oppose the forced entrance of male-bodied men in women's events. One of the more recent protests came from female weightlifters, including New Zealand athlete Tracey Lambrechs, who has said that admitting male-bodied Laurel Hubbard to take part would be "unfair to other women" and who points out that a female-bodied athlete has lost her spot. "We're all about equality for women in sport but right now that equality is being taken away from us." Lambrechs has disclosed that female weightlifters are "being told to be quiet when they complain that a woman will lose out" (in Mitchell et al, 2021).

Weightlifters and coaches had earlier protested Hubbard's inclusion in the sport, and scientists have questioned the recently updated guidelines that allow men into women's sports. Scientists have confirmed that the IOC guidelines, revised as they are, will do little to lessen male competitive advantage. But the New Zealand Olympics Committee (NZOC) has held out for a number of male-bodied athletes to compete in the Tokyo games. The IOC stated that it was currently reviewing its guidelines to examine the "perceived tensions between fairness, safety, inclusion and non discrimination" (in Mitchell et al, 2021).

Hubbard's gold medal victories at the 2019 Pacific Games in Samoa, beating the Games champion Feagaiga Stowers, sparked outrage on the island. Since 2017, Hubbard has competed in seven tournaments and has accumulated six gold medals and one silver. However, Hubbard failed in his 2021 Olympic competition and couldn't complete a single lift (Doyle, 2021). Despite the fact that he lost, he gained enormous media attention and, of course, one more woman was deprived of her spot in the competition.

As Charlotte Allen has written:

> For decades feminists have castigated heterosexual men for trying to 'erase' women — from history, from society, from political life. But the real erasure of women these days is coming from their fellow progressives. They are being denied their distinctive female sports, their distinctive female bodies, and, ultimately, their distinctive female identities (Allen, 2019).

∞

Learning to Become Transgender

Most parents have no idea that many school systems are now citadels of transgender education. Journalist Abigail Shrier has published the go-to book on what is happening in US schools that teach gender identity. Having interviewed many parents, Shrier states that the problem goes far beyond political boundaries of liberal and conservative. She found that many parents, but especially progressives, are in distress about their children's declarations of transgender, most often coming from their daughters.

Across the political spectrum, most of these parents are worried that their children are being confused about the gender identity 'education' students are receiving in schools (Shrier, 2020). K-12 educational institutions (primary through secondary schools) have been captured by transgenderism.

States with Transgender Mandates

The majority of schools in 15 states and DC offer 'LGBTQ-inclusive sex-ed' (Stratford, 2019), but certain states stand out from the pack. California, New Jersey, Colorado, and Illinois have passed laws requiring LGBT+ history to be taught in schools. Shrier points out how history is being re-written in social studies and other courses to accommodate interpretation of historical figures as non-binary, genderqueer, or trans — a "baptism of the dead" as she calls it (Shrier, 2020, p. 63), i.e. a historical person's submersion into a new-born role, typically accompanied by a new name. Joan of Arc, Catherine the Great, George Eliot, George Sand, Sally Ride — all reemerge as pivotal in trans history. "But none of these women thought she was really a man" (Shrier, 2020, pp. 62–63).

Shrier calls out the identity politics that is marching "through the front door" of education, a "large-scale robbery ... the theft of women's achievements. The more incredible a woman is, the more barriers she busts through, the more gender non-conforming she is deemed to be ... the more amazing a woman is, the less she counts as a woman" (Shrier, 2020, p. 63).

California has the most extensive gender identity program, "statutorily mandatory for all students enrolled in grades K-12," and it explicitly bars parental opt-out. The claim is that such instruction is essential to "prevent discrimination, harassment, and bullying" (Shrier, 2020, p. 61) and to do so, it's necessary that all children be taught about this fiction called transgender.

As the largest gender identity clinic is located in Los Angeles (LA) so too is LA the home of the second largest school district in the United States with over 600,000 students attending 1,200 schools. The array of services that are supported by California public schools is astounding, from reading, writing and arithmetic, to three meals a day, backpacks with which to carry school materials, and topped off by free medical and dental services on site. As Abigail Shrier comments, the latest addition to these services is social justice initiatives mainly focused on gender identity education.

Judy Chiasson, the program coordinator for human relations, diversity, and equity for the LA School District confirms that the district has expanded its educational mission with new roles and responsibilities, including teaching on gender identity. "Our role continues to expand. The outreach now is profound" (Shrier, 2020, p. 61). And the outreach is a welcome mat to trans activists and organizations that are now helping to shape the curricula and are lecturing in classrooms.

It is unlikely that feminism is a large part of the curriculum developed specifically for grades K-12. Are feminists being invited to lecture students and to write a feminist curriculum? And what about the prevalence of racial justice programs and whether they receive the same outreach and resources as gender identity programs?

In both public and private schools across the country, gender identity education is teaching a far more all-encompassing view of gender than most parents realize. For example, Shrier cites the case of a kindergarten class in California where teachers told five- and six-year-old students that their sex was randomly declared at birth and that their mission is now to explore what their real gender is — and that anyone who questions this search is abusing them (in Shuster, 2020).

The high school version of gender education could pass as educational pornography, "so raunchy, explicit and radical" that it was difficult to determine whether teachers were trying to incite orgasm or turn students off sex. "Anal sex is promoted so often that one would assume they had invented it. Fisting and anal stimulation by mouth are discussed … leaving nothing to the imagination. No orifice is left behind" (Shrier, 2020, p. 68).

Parental Erasure

In all levels of schooling, Shrier finds a pattern of parental marginalization. Kids are taught that the home is not always a safe place for them. Parents are often the last to know that their children are declaring they are trans. A fifth grade teacher stated: "It's not the school's obligation to call up and 'out' a kid to a parent … You're sending them home to somewhere that's going to be very unsafe and a lot of misinformation … and it's just not going to be a safe place for that kid" (Shrier, 2020, p. 68).

In June 2019, the California Teachers Association voted to support a proposal to allow students to leave school to receive cross-sex hormone treatments without parental consent. School planning for gender identity education has kept parents so thoroughly out of the loop that teachers have had to sneak this information out of the teacher meetings to warn parents. California, New York and New Jersey have a policy that allows children to leave school during school hours for hormone treatments, without parental permission (Shuster, 2020).

Due to such policies, parents are often the last to know about their child's transgender identity. Parents are viewed as a problem, and teachers often treat parental questioning as a cardinal sin, especially when parents don't approve of hormone treatments or question any aspect of transgender ideology. Parents are often placed in the role of 'enemies' of their child's assuming of a trans identity when in reality they are fulfilling their duty of care to question and make decisions. As if parents don't have enough to contend with, they now must assume an additional burden — that of challenging the schools when the teachers fail to acknowledge that the gender identity curricula they are teaching is not backed up by any science that proves boys can be girls and girls can be boys.

Who Develops the Gender Identify Curriculum?

Positive Prevention PLUS is among the most used curricula in schools that promote gender identify education. One of the lessons asks students, "Are you entirely female? Are you sure?" It is as if two-sex biology is passé to be rejected as a relic of a more repressive era. When a child 'chooses' a trans identity, peers who have gone through aspects of the transgendering process celebrate the initiate.

LGBT+ organizations and gender activists are invited into the schools to give 'lessons' in gender identify. In the United States, the ACLU and the Human Rights Campaign (HRC) are two organizations that supply curricula materials. For example, the Human Rights Campaign in its 'welcoming schools' program playbook states: "Educators should support students on their gender journey even if they do not have affirming family ... Identify a safe person or people on staff for a student to talk to who will check with them weekly while at school" (Human Rights Campaign, 2020).

HRC advertises its services on its website: "HRC Foundation's Welcoming Schools program has expert trainers across the country ready to work with your school or district to improve school climate with gender and LGBTQ inclusive trainings" (Human Rights Campaign, 2020b).

The ACLU touts a resource called *Changing the Game: The GLSEN Sports Project*. "This project gives ideas for students and parents to take steps within their own schools to make school sports a more inclusive, safe space for LGBTQ students, including resources on Title IX as they relate to the protection of transgender athletes" (ACLU, n. d.).

"This is how gender ideology is taught in the schools: with the materials, curricula, speakers, and teacher trainings supplied by trans activists: LGBT activists are brought into schools to teach students about transgender" (Shrier, 2020, p. 64). It has become almost an irreversible truth that family will fail these students.

The Minnesota Department of Education (MDE) launched a student survey of ninth to eleventh graders throughout the state asking them to specify if they are 'trangender', 'gender queer', 'non-binary', 'gender fluid', 'pansexual', 'trans male' or 'trans female', or 'questioning'. In 2017, MDE approved a 'transgender tool kit' that was distributed in all public schools in the state. "The tool kit instructs schools to treat 'transgender and gender nonconforming students' as the gender they identify with for bathroom and locker room use, sports team participation, overnight accommodations on school trips, dress codes, pronoun use and school records" (Kersten, 2019).

If schools don't comply with this program, they could face legal consequences. And the MDE program kit implies that if parents of 'gender dysphoric' youth are judged to be 'insufficiently supportive', the student support team should follow their protocol for reporting child neglect or harm (Kersten, 2019). This is reminiscent of Stalin's dissidents being sent off to the gulag, or Mao's Cultural Revolution, a sociopolitical purge of dissenters accused of a repressive ideology that required re-education.

Like the Tavistock clinicians who dissented from the gender identity program at the clinic and subsequently resigned, one dissenter said, "it felt as if we were part of something that people would look back on in the future, and ask, what were we thinking?" (Kersten, 2019).

This kind of education should be kept out of the classroom. The way in which gender identity knowledge contradicts biological sex and teaches students that they may appropriate a male or female sex, or both, has no place in schools where, hopefully, they may be learning in biology classes that only two sexes exist. Are biology instructors the next to be told what to teach?

Anti-Bullying Education?

If students question tenets of transgenderism, it is branded as bullying. Anti-bullying education seems to need a transgenderist curriculum. According to the California Board of Education, gender non-conformity often invites many forms of bullying. The Board contends that as students learn to accept differences, they also learn how to avoid bullying. However, as the gender identity curriculum gains momentum and becomes an expansive part of classroom learning, it appears that the primary 'difference' students are learning about is that of transgenderism.

Does it require an entire curriculum on gender identity to prevent bullying? Does the California Board of Education also offer new curricula on racism to solve bullying of African Americans in the schools? Does an anti-bullying curriculum teach not to slur female students as TERFs (trans exclusionary radical feminists) and 'front holes'?

"'Bullying' is used as an excuse for a thorough indoctrination in gender ideology and the insistence that transgender students must be 'affirmed' or suffer a steep psychological toll ... the anti-bullying effort is only a pretext for gender identity education." In order to protect children, schools are indoctrinating "the entire student population in gender confusion" (Shrier, 2020, pp. 74, 75). The attention given to transgender education is totally disproportionate to that of any other program in the social justice curriculum.

Angus Fox explains how exploitation of anti-bullying education was at work in the case of a boy who was subjected to peers calling him 'sissy' and 'girly'. "The easiest way for him to process the insult was the most literal way, as a genuine assessment of deficient masculinity" (Fox, 2021). He was unable to recognize his bullies' cruelty for what it was, the bullying of boys who learn toxic masculinity in their teenage years. To the boy, "the most logical explanation was that he was female in a male body" reinforced by a school curriculum that gave him the same message, and an internet-scripted culture that also confirmed this prognosis and provided him with a tribe (Fox, 2021).

There is no doubt that gender non-conformers of all stripes are victims of bullying, but the antidote to bullying does not lie in the development of a major curriculum on gender identity. It requires, however, that school authorities make student bullies accountable for their actions and that bullying be outlawed.

The Marriage of Gender Identity and Sexual Orientation

'Sexual Orientation' is another difference that transgenderism exploits. The rise of transgenderism was built on a forced marriage with the gay and lesbian movements. It is unfortunate that sexual orientation and gender identity are bedfellows in the proposed US *Equality Act*, for example, where they are joined together as wedded partners in being exploited. The transgender juggernaut latched onto the success of the lesbian and gay rights movements to carve out a room of their own and then built a marriage and a mansion of multiple rooms in which the T has the largest rooms and the LGB rooms are the smallest. The LGBT marriage sends the message that the two are indelibly linked, but they are not.

In New Zealand, when a Select Committee was considering a petition to outlaw homosexual conversion therapy, proponents of transgenderism latched on to the process urging the committee to include transgender counseling "that would have prevented counselors and others from exploring the reasons why children and young people take on a transgender identity" (Rivers and Abigail, 2020). This has been the *modus operandi* of transgender advocacy from its early inception. Tag onto gay and lesbian initiatives and legislation and stay married to their issues.

When Miranda's 14-year-old son Seth came out as gay, it was no surprise to both parents. "We love you no matter who you are," she told her son. For a while, things were fine, but then Miranda started to observe worrisome behavior. Seth told her he thought he was born in the wrong body and was adamant about having hormones and surgery, refusing to discuss it any further. Miranda mentioned gay men of her own generation who say that if they were growing up today, they might have been designated as trans. Seth rejected this comparison and avowed he was a straight girl, not gay (Fox, 2021).

Miranda discovered that Seth was seeing a school counselor, sometimes multiple times a day, without her knowledge. She met with the counselor who was impervious to Miranda's concerns and instead taught Seth about Jazz Jennings, the young American male who declared as female when he was five years old and became a trans icon with a widely viewed television program, and whom the counselor presented as a role model to Seth (Fox, 2021).

Transgender educators are supporting a program that directs large numbers of vulnerable gay children into becoming transgender instead. At the same time, they are ignoring studies which conclude that left to their own devices, gender questioning children will not undergo transgender treatments and instead many will grow up to be gay or lesbian. But once the hormone treatments begin, it is unlikely that these children will follow their earlier inclinations.

In 2019, former staff at the UK Tavistock clinic publicly expressed concern about the erasure of gay and lesbian identities in the treatment of youth.

> So many potentially gay children were being sent down the pathway to change gender ... there was a dark joke among staff that 'there were no gay people left' ... Young lesbians considered at the bottom of the heap suddenly found themselves really popular when they said they were trans ... For some families, it was easier to say this is a medical problem, 'here's my child, please fix them!' than dealing with a young gay kid (Rivers and Abigail, 2020).

An increasing number of gay men are speaking out about the erasure of homosexuality calling it 'transing the gay away'. Because of this forced marriage, gender identity and sexual orientation are mistakenly lumped together in the public eye, when these two movements do not share the same goals. There is no demand for pronoun or body changes to become gay or lesbian. Sexual orientation requires no puberty blockers or cross-sex hormones. And sexual orientation is about same-sex desire and intimacy and has nothing to do with the kind of trans surgery that many consider genital mutilation. Adhering to the dogmas of transgenderism does the lesbian and gay movements no good.

Academic and author Angus Fox has written:

> Just six years after the United States Supreme Court ensured that gay men and women in all 50 states have the right to marry one another, a new form of homophobia this one masked as progressive gender ideology, is being used to instil doubt in the hearts of vulnerable gay teens (Fox, 2021).

Gender identity legislation that now exists in states like California and New Jersey has been introduced at the federal level by the proposed *Equality Act*. The United Nations is also pushing for 'comprehensive sexuality education' that really means comprehensive gender identity education.

Gender Identity Education in School Systems Internationally

Britain

The United States is not alone in promoting gender identity education in the schools. In 2020, all British high schools were directed to begin teaching "LGBTQ inclusive sex education." British teenagers will learn about lesbian, gay, bisexual, transgender and queer sexual health and positive relationships (Kuhr, 2020). At the primary level, all schools must teach about different relationships and family types, which includes LGBT families. At the secondary level, all schools must teach about sexual orientation and gender identity. The announcement of the curriculum does not seem as raunchy as in US high schools, and the British sex education program is restricted to high school students.

Josh Bradlow, policy manager at the organization Stonewall, has applauded the move but is concerned that teachers have not received enough training. That translates into the suggestion that educational institutions should hire more LGBT+ organizations as consultants. As in the United States, Stonewall, a gay and pro-trans organization, is hoping to expand its influence in developing school curricula. Bradlow has stated that Stonewall has already helped 1500 schools across England, and it will start offering virtual lessons that will aid more teachers develop the materials and lesson plans based on Stonewall's guidance (Kuhr, 2020).

But it looks like the walls may be falling around the organization with a founding member of the charity accusing it of giving incorrect advice on equality law and also arguing that Stonewall had assumed an 'extremist stance' on the issue of transgender. The former founder stated that Stonewall should stick to its original mission of promoting LGB rights and separate itself from the trans (T) issue. News that a cabinet minister may be on the brink of advising that all government departments should withdraw from Stonewall's Diversity Champions Program followed the decision of the Equality and Human Rights Commission (EHRC) that quit the Program in May of 2021 (Siddique, 2021a).

A number of these withdrawals and potential separations from the organization appear to be based on dissociating from Stonewall's extremist position on trans rights and its policy of shutting down debate. Although its most recent CEO, Nancy Kelly, had earlier told the *Observer* that "the organization would no longer seek to persuade its critics to accept its views on gender" (Siddique, 2021a), that promise has not been fulfilled. Instead, Stonewall has doubled down on its portrayal of trans critics as Nazis, white supremacists and anti-semitic, and continues to denigrate women and lesbians.

New Zealand

In New Zealand, the Labour government has signed on to a whole range of transgender initiatives — affirmative treatment for kids, teaching gender in schools, self-id, the inclusion of gender in hate speech legislation, and outlawing any attempt to change a person's declared gender identity — what is now called their version of conversion therapy — when it actually may be intelligent questioning of tenets of transgenderism (Rivers, 2021).

The prior 2012 guidelines, which cautioned that most young people with gender issues would desist if allowed to proceed without treatment, have been replaced with the more recent 2018/2019 government policy. Just as more countries like Britain and Sweden have recently rejected puberty blockers and cross-sex hormones for children, New Zealand is promoting these blockers, further hormonal treatments for youth, and surgical options for adults. The guidelines reinforce the fake science that puberty blockers are fully reversible, a statement with no scientific verification.

New Zealand guidelines govern school education policy and practice, advocating "early social transition socially and in school, with new names, new pronouns and 'gender appropriate' dress … The education system has recently reissued guidelines that bind teachers to teaching gender ideology" (Rivers, 2021). The New Zealand Education Council's teaching standards mandate teachers to "cater classroom practice not only to students' different abilities and needs, backgrounds … languages and cultures, but also their different 'genders'" (Gerlich, 2018).

As in other countries, non-governmental organizations (NGOs) are working with the schools to shape the curricula. Advocacy bodies such as Rainbow Youth and Inside Out are proselytizing both individuals and entire classes that a child can be born in the 'wrong body'. "Children are being presented with ideological beliefs taught as facts" (Rivers and Abigail, 2020).

Writer Renee Gerlich was among the first in New Zealand to recognize the harm of transgenderism and the inappropriateness of these two major government-funded registered 'queer' organizations working so ideologically close with schools offering classroom resources. She also discovered that Rainbow Youth uses its drop-in center to distribute breast binders for girls who want to fit in as male. These groups also provide other resources for teachers that advise "principals, boards of trustees, and teachers to 'affirm gender identities'" (Gerlich, 2018).

Gender diversity includes "takatāpui, lesbian, gay, bisexual, transgender, gender fluid (non-binary) agender, and intersex." School standards require teachers to tailor classroom practice to students' different 'genders'. At Kapaei College, an 18-year-old student identifying as male to female, Te Awarangi (Awa), began using the girls' bathrooms. "The Kapiti College principal expressed relief at not having to make an official decision about which bathroom Awa should use, saying, 'It was the girls who invited Awa in. It all sort of disappeared as an issue, nicely, without being an issue." This was the same year that a student at Marlborough Girls College named Laura expressed, "As a girl, I feel uncomfortable with a guy being in the same toilets." Liberal news site, *The Spinoff,* labelled Laura's concerns 'vitriolic barf' (Gerlich, 2018).

Gerlich believes that

> New Zealand women have been betrayed by the HRC (Human Rights Commission), the government, the media, universities, and our own women's organizations … We need to work harder to honestly examine the impacts of believing that anyone can be 'born in the wrong body'. Ultimately, we need to turn these misogynist, homophobic and medically reckless trends around (Gerlich, 2018).

Denmark, Sweden and the Netherlands have all implemented a "comprehensive curriculum that covers sexual diversity," but Sweden changed its policy to end all use of puberty blockers and cross-sex hormones for children in May 2021 (SEGM, 2021).

∞

There is no scientific reason to teach students that boys can become girls or girls can become boys. This is perverting science. As Andrew Sullivan has written,

> It takes the experience of less than one percent of humanity and tries to make it explain the 99 percent of their peers. It's nuts; and it will confuse children, particularly gay children (Sullivan, 2021).

When your country's education policy states that students have the right to be addressed by the names and pronouns that they desire, and that if teachers and school officials refuse to use the right name and pronouns, they may be breaking the law (US Department of Education, 2021), this is a government gag rule. When the institutions of government, medicine, education, sports and others are fighting trans critics all the way and threatening disciplinary action or loss of jobs, it is only the bravehearted who are willing to challenge this doublethink and censorship.

CHAPTER SIX

The Trans Gag Rules: Erasing Women, Pronoun Tyranny and Censoring Critics

There is a long list of the censored. The acceptable range of opinion is so narrow it is almost nonexistent.

—Chris Hedges

And if all others accepted the lie, which the Party imposed — if all records told the same tale — then the lie passed into history and became truth.

—George Orwell

Men in the guise of women are now deciding who counts as a woman. Women are not only being censored but also attacked for words that make trans activists uncomfortable, starting with the very word woman. Instead of woman we are hammered with demeaning terms such as cis-women, menstruators, front holes and TERFs. Given the fact that women worldwide have traditionally been denigrated by words not of our own making such as slut, cunt, and whore — misogynistic slurs that have belittled us for centuries — we are now being called upon to accept further offense by trans activists who find the actual word 'woman' blasphemous.

In using terms that trans activists invent, people say they want to be non-exclusionary, sensitive to trans-identified persons, and call people by what name they want to be called. But trans activists don't show the same sensitivity by asking women what we want to be called. The rarefied discourse of transgenderism — a discourse that is woman-hating at its core — is an attempt to impose their terms and then cry 'transphobic' if some resist.

To outsiders, much of the language we are being commandeered to use is ridiculously self-righteous and so confusing that it stifles communication. As Chrissie Daz has written, there are "blow-ups over the most silly and insignificant things" (Daz, 2013). Words that dominate transgender vocabulary often emanate from an exclusive and excluding alliance that mainly includes trans activists, academics, liberals and leftists — not from a wider population that does not use such words.

British-American writer and commentator Andrew Sullivan has noted that the trans movement has an "elaborate and neurotic fixation on language," such as using the word *transgender* rather than *transgendered*, as if this distinction would reveal one's 'inner bigot'. There is an obsession with policing the language, and UK police have even arrested a woman for the violation of 'misgendering' and kept her in a cell for seven hours (Kearns, 2019a). Yet when trans activists are guilty of *mis-sexing*, using gender to substitute for biological sex, there is little outcry.

The trans gag rule prohibits any reference to a trans-identified person's pre-transgender life. That would be 'deadnaming'. And you can't use transgender or transsexual as a noun but using them as adjectives is OK, as in a 'transgender event'. And you have to state what your pronouns are and whether you identify as he, she, they, or ze before you can communicate with a trans-identified person or activist. In fact, people are now encouraged to list their choice of pronouns in email signatures and other documents. Even the Biden White House, in revamping its digital platform, whitehouse.gov, has changed the contact form to include an optional category of pronouns if persons emailing the site wish to stipulate their preference from a menu of 'she/her', 'he/him', 'they/them', 'other' and 'prefer not to share'.

Transgenderdom is the rabbit hole of *Alice in Wonderland* where we are transported into a troubling surreal situation — where Alice is the metaphorical radical feminist and Humpty Dumpty is the transgender fabulist — a fable of words exemplified in the actual back and forth conversation between the two. First, Humpty Dumpty states with a full dose of masculinist certitude: "When *I* use a word, it means just what I choose it to mean — neither more nor less!" To which Alice responds, "The question is whether you *can* make words mean so many different things." To which Humpty Dumpty admits: "The question is which is to be master, that's all." And men, whether they wear skirts or not, are still trying to be the masters of women.

Hate Speech

Trans activists often accuse radical feminists of hate speech. For many, what qualifies as hate speech today includes behavior that simply disturbs a person. In degrading the meaning of 'hate speech' and 'violence' to 'misgendering' (using the 'wrong' pronouns) and 'deadnaming' (identifying one's pre-transition status), trans activists have corrupted free speech into hate speech demonizing critics as bigots.

The glue that binds trans activists together is the smothering of dissent. At the heart of trans censorship is a discrediting of feminists, lesbians, academics who are gender-critical, therapists and medical personnel who won't prescribe puberty blockers for children, and journalists who publish any mild criticism of transgender ideology and practices.

In 2015, the respected *Intelligence Report* of the Southern Poverty Law Center (SPLC) featured a cover article entitled 'In the Crosshairs. Transgender People, Especially Women of Color, May Be America's Most Victimized Minority'. The editor, Mark Potok, set the stage in his introductory editorial where he called out feminists for 'despising' trans women and for saying that men are not women (in Terry, 2015). In the context of the SPLC's mission to expose and root out hate groups, this statement seems to acknowledge that the Center consigns women who are critical of trans dogmas to the category of a hate group.

As a subscriber to the *Intelligence Report*, I wrote this letter to the editor, excerpted below, which was never acknowledged nor published:

> It is disturbing that your *Intelligence Report* — once the leading organization for spotlighting the actions of violent extremists and white supremacists — now associates radical feminist dissent about transgender orthodoxies with discrimination against transgender people ... equating the dissenting 'words' of feminists with hate speech and conveying the idea that a radical feminist viewpoint at odds with the ideology of transgender fuels transphobia. This brand of misrepresentation silences debate and constitutes its own form of propaganda ...
>
> Threats, online vitriol, intimidation and no-platforming of critics of transgenderism are all being used as weapons to suppress feminist dissent, under the pretext of opposing hate speech.
>
> Much of this online rancor about radical feminists is powered by misogyny, the misogyny of men who if they did not represent themselves as trans women would have little credence ... feminists who hold critical views have not advocated or engaged in violence against any group of people ... We call on you to correct this implication and to target the real extremists (Raymond, 2015).

Most open-minded people oppose discrimination against those who are trans-identified as they would oppose discrimination against anyone. But what now passes for discrimination is not discrimination but rather pronoun tyranny and the alleged crime of misnaming those who self-declare as women. *Disagreement* is renamed *discrimination* aimed at critics, rather than at those who are actively discriminating by perpetrating violence and harm against trans-identified persons. And the real prejudice, hate speech and violence are allowed to thrive. Bogus accusations of hate speech are in fact another type of hate speech.

In 2017, trans activists mounted a staged attack on feminists and feminist literature at the opening of a new women's library in Vancouver, Canada. In an exposé of what took place during the attack, Meaghan Murphy, the editor of *Feminist Current*, reminded her readers that during the second wave of feminism,

> [T]here was a bona fide feminist bookstore movement. Women's spaces, presses, writing, and events were seen as integral to feminism … women's bookstores were valued, not only as ways to make women's writing and work accessible, but as physical spaces within which women could gather … At one time, there were over 150 women's bookstores across North America … two decades later, almost every single one has closed down.

Women of all ages and backgrounds came to celebrate the opening but were met by protesters who harassed and attempted to prevent them physically from entering the library. One woman shouted, "No SWERFs, no TERFs," and another accused the library founders of 'violence'. The protesters poured red wine on the books and shelves, seized alcohol and pulled the fire alarm, resulting in substantial expense to the group of volunteers who staff the library (Murphy, 2017).

Any book associated with second wave feminism was put on the trans index of forbidden books. Authors critical of male violence and sexual exploitation were targeted, among them Andrea Dworkin's *Pornography: Men Possessing Women; Not a Choice, Not a Job: Exposing the Myths about Prostitution and the Global Sex Trade* by Janice Raymond; and Kathleen Barry's *Female Sexual Slavery*.

Fortunately, this protest and these demands of censorship had no influence on the opening of the library. Rebuking the attack, supporters and multiple donations poured in (Murphy, 2017).

Trans activists used another tool of 'book burning' enacted before the digital age. Stealing books from libraries and destroying them was a useful tool of censoring any material that the thief opposed. Over a period of several decades, I was frequently notified that many libraries that listed *The Transsexual Empire* in their card catalogues were without the book. When searchers sought to retrieve the book from its shelf location, the book had disappeared. Upon further questioning, they learned from the librarian that the book had been 'missing' for a long period of time. It appeared that *The Transsexual Empire* had been stolen from many libraries and not returned. Numerous searchers asked if I had any ideas about where they could find it, but by that time, the rights had reverted to me, and I placed a digital version of the book on my website that anyone can now download and read.

Higher Education: Lower Standards

Universities historically have aspired to be places where discussion could happen without worrying about 'trigger warnings' — alerts used to describe something that might upset students and make them feel bad — and demand for 'safe spaces'. If there were student protests, which were many at the university where I taught for 28 years, it was usually about political issues — not about affronted students who believed their emotional well-being was in jeopardy when faced with classroom debate and disagreement. These political protests usually generated a wider agenda that would be argued and advanced. In contrast today, individual students and faculty risk being censored for even organizing a discussion that one student might find offensive.

A substantial number of students on college campuses have sought protection from what they call 'microaggressions' — any words that students allege causes discomfort — and they take umbrage, for example, when anyone refers to a self-declared woman as 'he'. Teachers or schools are expected to issue 'trigger warnings' when students target academic content that may cause alleged trauma. Because transgenderism is now seen as a prohibited topic not open to debate or dissent, discussion of transgender has been subject to classroom censorship.

There have been movements of 'political correctness' before, but these were usually accompanied by accounts that met a standard of rationality that could be explained and argued, not stifled. The more recent trans 'woke' movement largely depends on personal claims that one's emotional well-being is 'assaulted' by debate and discussion and prompts the need for a therapeutic response.

We all have our 'triggers' that disturb us. Part of the growing up process is learning how to deal with persons who make us uncomfortable and that helps 'trigger' the tools with which we respond. The 'therapeutization' of the US university has been in effect for years, most recently in student demand for 'safe spaces'. But student interpretation of 'safe space' no longer means physical safety, i.e. protection from assault and violence, but rather protection from difference and disagreement.

Many such attacks on feminists who are glibly characterized as TERFs now take place on social media. Social media has positive uses, but it also creates a democracy of vitriol that encourages inbred communities of self-righteousness and outrage. Relying mainly upon subjective feelings to measure the offensive quotient of a comment by a professor or another student, and whether it constitutes grounds for a disciplinary action, is unreliable. Emotional reactions are not evidence and not always a trustworthy signpost of the truth, or an indication that someone has done a wrong deed.

Kathleen Stock, a professor at Sussex University in the UK, has stated: "It is a failure of our education system that it produces young people who think superficially about these issues; who think it is all about emotion, and who can't tolerate different points of view from theirs" (Fazackerley, 2018).

> A claim that someone's words are 'offensive' is not just an expression of one's own subjective feeling of offendedness. It is, rather, a public charge that the speaker has done something seriously wrong. It is a demand that the speaker apologize or be punished by some authority for committing an offense (Lukianoff and Haidt, 2015).

This climate of being offended is becoming institutionalized in academia, especially in gender studies programs, and affecting academic research projects that increasingly must conform to trans ideology.

The institutional ramifications of this culture of educational muzzling have been more critically analyzed in Britain than in the United States. Dr Heather Brunskell-Evans, an author of several books on the ravages of child gender transitioning, has cautioned that some universities are becoming authoritarian (Brunskell-Evans, 2018).

> Universities project themselves as places of open debate, while at the same time they are very worried about being seen to fall foul of the consensus … They are now prioritizing the risk of reputational damage over their duty to uphold freedom of inquiry.

During her academic history, Brunskell-Evans experienced pushback when researching the harms of prostitution. There were attempts to shut down any critical analysis that might offend advocates who support legalization of prostitution (in Grey, 2018).

Dr Werner Kierski, a psychotherapist who has taught at Anglia Ruskin and Middlesex Universities has warned:

> They [ethics committees in universities] have become hysterical. If it's not blocking research, it's putting limits on what researchers can do. In one case, I had an ethics committee force my researchers to text me before and after interviewing people … It's completely unnecessary and deeply patronising.

Kierski is worried that other countries will find UK research "insignificant," because researchers are so constrained by these requirements misnamed as ethical (in Grey, 2018).

As is the case when a university caves in to a climate of censorship, it creates an environment where dissenting voices are silenced. Students may censor themselves from asking questions. Professors may fear student opinion that might evaluate them and their research as transphobic. Trans activists behave as if there's never a time for discussion and debate because both question trans persons' existences. And they are devoting enormous amounts of energy attempting to no-platform speakers who remain critical of trans ideology.

Censorship of Academics, Researchers and Invited Lecturers

Germaine Greer

For years, Germaine Greer has been boycotted from university speaking events, accused of expressing transphobic views. During a 2015 lecture at Cardiff University, Greer stated unequivocally, "I don't believe a woman is a man without a cock ... You can beat me over the head with a baseball bat. It still won't make me change my mind" (Morris, 2015).

When someone mentioned that trans-identified people were being killed in the United States because of their gender, Greer replied, "We have two women a week being murdered in England by their partners. They are not my fault and the transsexuals in America aren't my fault either ... I don't accept postoperative males as females" (Morris, 2015).

Although Greer had been invited to lecture on the topic of women in political and social life, this fact didn't sway the more than 3,000 people who signed a petition that Greer not be allowed to speak because her views on trans-identified people were offensive. Uniformed police provided security outside the speaking venue but only a dozen protesters showed up. Tickets for Greer's lecture went quickly, and the lecture was well-received.

Maya Forstater

In 2019, researcher Maya Forstater lost her job at a British think tank in London because of her 'gender critical' views, which she expressed on Twitter. What was deemed offensive? Among her tweets she had written, "it is impossible to change sex." Forstater then filed a lawsuit against her employer alleging discrimination based on a person's beliefs, but an employment tribunal ruled against her stating that her views were "not a philosophical belief" that was protected in British law, "nor were they worthy of respect in a democratic society" (BBC, 2019).

Employment tribunal rulings are not binding legal precedents, but they can serve as a deterrent for others who share gender critical views and may feel inhibited from launching such future cases. Fortunately, Forstater challenged the decision and in 2021 the Employment Appeal Tribunal (EAT) ruled in her favor, finding that the "Tribunal Failed to remain neutral" and confirmed her belief that persons cannot change their sex as "worthy of respect in a democratic society" (Siddique, 2021b, June 10).

Selina Todd

The threats to Oxford University's Professor Selina Todd, who teaches courses on the history of women and the working class, were ominous enough to require the presence of security guards at her class lectures. Several concerned students had approached her and said they were worried about threats that had appeared on familiar social networks.

For her involvement in women's rights advocacy, trans activists had labelled her a 'transphobe'. Her offense? Saying people cannot change sex via surgery or self-identification.

Like many feminists who are treated as fascists and branded as transphobes, Todd said, "It is quite a strange situation to work somewhere where people make it clear that they loathe you." Given this situation where the threat level had been raised in her classroom with students who became "quite antagonistic" and "quite confrontational," Todd said, "we decided not to wait and see if I'd get hit in the face" before security was put in place (Slater, 2020).

Todd has been no-platformed from conferences and other events where she was invited to speak, some of them organized by groups who identify as feminist. Due to appear at the Oxford International Women's Festival, Todd not only received pushback from trans activists but also from the collective ironically called Feminist Fightback, and ultimately was excluded from the program.

Raquel Rosario Sanchez

One of the more disgraceful examples of a university's abdication of responsibility for protecting its students from harassment and threats of violence occurred at the UK University of Bristol. Raquel Rosario Sanchez, an immigrant student from the Dominican Republic studying violence against women, was thrust into living much of what she was researching. For over three years, Rosario Sanchez endured recurring bullying, abuse and intimidation from students at the University for speaking her feminist principles.

"When I came from the Dominican Republic, on a scholarship, to be at the Centre for Gender and Violence Research, my life felt like a dream come true." This dream became a nightmare. "I've read that I should be punched and terfed out of England. Trans activists have called for my deportation … targeting every feminist event I've participated in" (Rosario Sanchez, 2020). Rosario Sanchez was also subjected to increased online abuse during this period — much of it from Bristol's student bullies.

When she sought help from the University of Bristol, its first response was to interrogate her, never mind that her attackers' abusive behavior was violating university principles and policies. Initially, the university took disciplinary procedures against one student bully, but when he obtained legal representation, the process dragged on for over a year. Three other disciplinary hearings were closed before they began, based on security concerns when students showed up to protest the hearings. Trans activist students distributed flyers that said, "You're a shit and you know you are" (Rosario Sanchez, 2020).

The university took no action against the student bully but instead, with the bully present, allowed his lawyer to cross-examine Rosario Sanchez about her feminist ideas. She has been the only student called to answer any questions about the bullying and harassment. The university dismissed her complaint in February

2019, denying that bullying took place. Since then, she has continued to be browbeaten "by throngs of privileged British students who were making a sport out of bullying an immigrant … The impact of this both on my health and my academic performance was severe" (Rosario Sanchez, 2020).

After Rosario Sanchez spoke publicly about what had happened to her, and her story was featured on the BBC and in other UK major media, the University of Bristol pressured her to suspend her studies saying she was not making sufficient academic progress. The Dominican Ministry of Higher Education, Science and Technology, however, decided to fund her for another year. The Bristol University Centre for Gender and Violence Research has also supported her, issuing a public statement condemning the university's handling of the process. However, students continued to target her in attempts to close down feminist meetings that she had organized at the university.

Rosario Sanchez has launched a legal case against the university accusing them of sex discrimination and failure to apply their policy of no bullying to protect her as a student. The online funding platform of *Crowd Justice* has set up an account for people to donate to her legal expenses.

Rosario Sanchez sent an update on her legal case in April 2021 to all those who contributed and are interested in her case. It is particularly upsetting for her that the university has tried to move the timetable for her trial, originally set for early 2022, to begin later in 2022 "when they know full well, that as things stand today my British Residence Permit expires in April 2022."

> The University of Bristol which to this day has a duty of care to me, wants me to pack my bags, be at the final stages of a legal case and maybe finish a PhD all at the same time. Additionally, they wanted to ensure that I would not be present in the UK so that I could attend my own trial and have my day in court. The fact that they would treat any student this way, but particularly an international student given the added vulnerabilities we face being isolated from our homes, is beyond my comprehension. It is hard for me to put into words how repulsive

I find the actions of the lowlife people involved in my case (including the bullies). Just when I thought they could not sink any lower, they find a new comportment (Rosario Sanchez, 2021).

In June 2021, Rosario sent out another message about her legal case stating that the university was still playing the game of delaying the trial by withholding information that was ordered to be handed over to her legal team.

By far, the University of Bristol is one of the most craven of any academic institutions that I know of. It is shameful that this goliath of a university would inflict this punitive treatment on any student, but especially on an international student. If its intention has been to delay and isolate Raquel, it has made a huge mistake. Raquel is one articulately brave woman who should make any woman proud.

Julie Bindel and The UK National Union of Students (NUS)

For many years, the UK National Union of Students (NUS) has pursued the no-platforming of Julie Bindel. In 2011, the NUS Gay, Lesbian, Bisexual, Transgender (GLBT) conference voted to no-platform Bindel in a motion that attacked her very person stating, "This conference believes that Julie Bindel is vile." As journalist Sarah Ditum points out in her incisive *New Statesman* article about no-platforming, at the same time that the NUS was targeting Julie, "various tyrants and dictators have been hosted by NUS venues" (Ditum, 2014).

"Why, in the new economy of outrage, have people like Bindel … attracted the opprobrium that was formerly reserved for hypermasculine, anti-semitic white power movements?" (Ditum, 2014). The only way that censors like the NUS can defend their no-platforming position, which is overwhelmingly deployed against radical feminists, is by reinventing the definition of violence. In this view, violence is anything that causes offence, which then becomes branded as 'hate speech'.

In 2013, the NUS explained its position. "We refuse to allow fascists an opportunity to act like normal political parties … which sometimes includes physically denying them the freedom to operate" (Ditum, 2014). Since then, the no-platform policy of the NUS and other groups appears not to target hate groups who issue blatant fascist messages, often accompanied by threats of violence, but rather they attack feminists whose message is that men are not women.

One of the rare published protests made against the silencing of transgender critics was a 2015 statement signed by over 100 people, most of them academics in the UK. Published in *The Guardian*, the statement pointed to a pattern of intimidation and censorship of those deemed 'transphobic' or 'whorephobic'. Most of those censored were feminists who had written critically about the sex and the transgender industries and never advocated or perpetrated any kind of violence against any group. The statement concluded, "Universities have a particular responsibility to resist this kind of bullying. We call on universities and other organisations to stand up to attempts at intimidation and affirm their support for the basic principles of democratic political exchange" (Campbell, 2015).

Kathleen Stock, Rosa Freedman and the Dishonorable Natacha Kennedy

In 2018, Natacha Kennedy, a UK researcher at Goldsmiths University in London, instigated a smear campaign aimed at academics deemed to be transphobic, 'dangerous' and guilty of 'hate crimes'. Their alleged wrongdoing was disagreement with current gender theories dominant in many academic circles. All of those targeted were women, many of them feminists and lesbians who had publicly stated in various ways that men could not be women.

Kennedy invited thousands who were part of a closed Facebook group to develop a list of offending UK academics and circulate it to discredit and blacklist these women, ultimately plotting to get them removed from their jobs. Universities such as Reading, Sussex, Bristol, Warwick and Oxford, were branded as 'unsafe' because they employed faculty and staff who disputed that men could become women and who argued that transgenderism was disenfranchising women and women's rights.

Kennedy coached list members in the correct language to use in filing charges against 'unsafe' professors such as Kathleen Stock. They accused Professor Stock of creating an 'unsafe environment' by arguing against the trans dogma that men could self-identify as women and/or lesbians. Kennedy advised list members to file a hate crime report against her, and then proceeded to badger departmental chairpersons. "Drag them over the fucking coals," Kennedy declared (Bannerman, 2018).

Professor Stock had been publicly branded as 'transphobic' by the Sussex students' union, followed by student protests against her on campus. Faulted for her views on transgender, the union statement read: "We will not tolerate hate on campus, and we will do everything in our power to protect our students" (Talk, 2018). The union has sent emails to senior officials asking them to condemn Stock's views.

More recently, in a letter entitled 'Open Letter Concerning Transphobia in Philosophy', 600 of Stock's peers from academic institutions in several countries criticized the decision to award her an OBE (Order of the British Empire), because of her alleged 'harmful rhetoric' and 'transphobic views'. Not to be dissuaded, Stock responded with a courageous rebuttal and vowed not to be silenced in continuing to advocate that men are not women and should not have access to women's private spaces:

> When I accepted my OBE I did so in full knowledge there would be backlash from academic philosophers in my discipline, and here it is. The letter contains some basic errors about my view — but that's to be expected as their aim is not truth.
>
> I won't bother correcting errors, as I've made my written position clear many times before. We aren't dealing here with an ordinary philosophical dispute, but rather a pathological desire to roleplay an ethical stance for public applause. But their stance isn't ethical … (in Greep, 2021).

Rosa Freedman, a law professor at the University of Reading, had challenged trans activists in stating that self-declared women should not be admitted to women's refuges. She received abusive messages with penis pictures that said, "suck my girl cock." Professor Freedman called this "straight-up, aggressive, anti-woman misogyny ... The idea that writing about women's rights automatically becomes a hate crime in some people's eyes is ludicrous" (Bannerman, 2018).

Professor Freedman focused on the UK Gender Recognition Act (GRA). "I am deeply concerned by how the conflation of sex and gender is leading to subjugation of women and is undermining the specific protections guaranteed to women under international and national human rights law," she warned (Fazackerley, 2018). The efforts of Freedman and other feminists led to the British government's 2020 announcement that it will not change the GRA to recognize self-declaration of sex. Both Professors Freedman and Stock praised the support they received from their academic institutions.

In the meantime, questions about Natacha Kennedy had surfaced. Kennedy had appeared *twice* in the Goldsmiths College staff directory, once as Natacha Kennedy and once under the heading of Mark Hellen. Employed to teach a course on 'gender confusion in children', Kennedy/Hellen appears confused herself/himself about whether he/she is one or two persons. Goldsmiths College has confirmed Natacha Kennedy was an employee but wouldn't or couldn't explain why Kennedy appeared twice in their staff directory as two different persons.

To create more mystery surrounding her/his identity, an academic paper published in 2010 cited both Natacha Kennedy and Mark Hellen as the co-authors. Neither Kennedy nor Goldsmiths would confirm whether two individuals or the same person wrote the paper! Kennedy/Hellen has registered LinkedIn pages under both names, and 'they' present there as two different people. In addition to assaulting the academic freedom of those smeared on the list of 'unsafe' academics, Kennedy may have committed academic fraud by misrepresenting her/his status as two different persons.

Heather Brunskell-Evans

Dr Heather Brunskell-Evans, an expert on the transgendering of children has also written on the subjects of pornography, prostitution and the sexualization of young women. Many who do critical research in these areas also engage in serious study of transgender.

While working at the University of Leicester, Brunskell-Evans had prepared a critical analysis of *Vanity Fair's* cheerleading cover and coverage of Bruce Jenner's surgical conversion to Caitlyn Jenner. Her piece was pulled after complaints were made, but when the university's lawyers were consulted, her analysis was republished.

When Dr Brunskell-Evans spoke on a UK radio show, she questioned whether parents should confirm every child's wish for a medical remedy for being born in the 'wrong body'.

As one of the founders of the UK Women's Equality Party and their spokeswoman on violence against women, one might assume that Brunskell-Evans would have had the support of Party members who would show solidarity. After she expressed her views about the medical transitioning of children on BBC's Moral Maze and on Twitter, trans activists conducted a campaign of harassment against her. Party members showed no solidarity and instead dismissed her as its spokeswoman. It took only one transgender member of the Women's Party to lodge a complaint accusing her of promoting prejudice.

Brunskell-Evans has succinctly characterized this environment as "a cold wind of authoritarianism that is blowing through our allegedly progressive, liberal-democratic society. When telling the truth becomes hate speech, when oppression becomes ethics, when non-facts become Truth, we all better look out" (Brunskell-Evans, 2018, see also 2020).

Sheila Jeffreys

Professor Sheila Jeffreys, author of many influential books on women's and lesbian history, retired political scientist at the University of Melbourne, and survivor of many trans activist attacks directed at radical feminists has said:

> The work done by myself and others would not happen today. University now is about only speaking views which attract funding … I was offered the job in Melbourne because they wanted someone specifically to teach this stuff. It would have been difficult to get back [into a British university]. I suspect that even if I wanted to take up a fellowship I would struggle (Jeffreys, 2021).

In 2001, transgender activists submitted the first complaint against Jeffreys to the University of Melbourne where she was teaching, and also to the Equal Opportunities Tribunals in Victoria and New South Wales alleging that she taught 'hate speech'. Her 'crime' was in affirming that transgender is socially constructed. The activists sent out a clarion call for others to bombard the university's vice-chancellor with complaints. In 2001, the university supported Jeffreys' teaching and research but in following years, transgender mobs would bully other students and the faculty and learn how to make their attacks on dissenters felt (Jeffreys, 2020/2021).

Trans activists would later find a footing at the university, and Jeffreys would become their punching bag. Jeffreys' head of school was instructed by the school's equal opportunities committee to require her to write to two complainants stating she would "never speak in such an offensive way again." Of course, Jeffreys refused and although her head did not agree to this censorship, she was concerned that the attempt to discipline her, at the whim of two men, underscored the influence of transgenderism and mob rule that were able to mount such campaigns and browbeat university officials (Jeffreys, 2020/2021).

At the end of the semester, trans activists joined by pro-prostitution supporters began to crash Jeffreys' lectures where they tried to disrupt her teaching and for the rest of the year, security guards were placed in her classes. This was followed by online threats and viciousness that made it harder for Jeffreys to speak in public; and she was advised to take the nameplate off her door to make it more difficult for troublemakers to find her office, to use care in walking home, and to remove her phone number from the staff webpage (Jeffreys, 2020/2021).

Lisa Littman

The censoring and research condemnation that gender-critical academics experience resonates with the previous Trump administration's scorn for science. At Ivy League Brown University in Providence, Rhode Island, what happened to professor and medical doctor, Lisa Littman, is common to many researchers in an anti-scientific climate where scientists are warned not to stray from politically approved topics and conclusions.

Dr Littman published a peer-reviewed article in the online journal, *PLOS One*, reporting on some of the reasons why there has been a huge increase in adolescents, mainly girls, who are seeking cross-sex hormones and surgery. Littman's study concluded that 'social contagiousness' through circles of friends and social media was an influential factor promoting what experts call 'rapid-onset-gender-dysphoria' (ROGD) (Littman, 2018).

Initially, Brown had placed a favorable news release of Littman's study on the university website. But the university succumbed to mob rule from trans activists and promptly backpedaled by deleting the release. Littman's Dean of the School of Public Health replaced the release with an explanation claiming that there might be methodological problems with the study, and that Dr Littman's work could be harmful to members of the trans community.

For transgender activists, the study obviously was not a popular narrative since it implied that gender identity is a social construction, not fixed in any kind of biological essence. Activists also attacked Littman for engaging in hate speech and using 'transphobic dog whistles' — a coded message communicated through words or phrases commonly understood by a particular group of peoples, but not by others.

Four thousand academics and researchers signed a Change. org petition in protest of Littman's censorship after which Brown and *PLOS One* said they would both review the study design. The upshot of this six-month review resulted in the journal publishing a revised version of the article that added context and more cautionary language, but the original findings and conclusions remain unchanged. Littman has said that she is "happy with the final product" (in Bartlett, 2019) and will keep studying the subject of rapid-onset gender dysphoria.

The fact remains, as former dean of the Harvard School of Public Health Jeffrey Flier argued, that the ability to conduct research must be protected, "whether or not the methods and conclusions provoke controversy" (in Bartlett, 2019). Yet many universities are not standing up for the integrity of their own faculty's research.

Donna M. Hughes

The founder of Rhode Island (RI) might turn in his grave at the recent betrayal of principles on which the state was founded. Roger Williams, banished from the Massachusetts Bay Colony for his radical views, believed in religious freedom, tolerance and the separation between church and state. Unfortunately, Rhode Island is now known for its attempts to censor academic free speech and tolerance at its two primary universities.

Professor Donna Hughes, a scientist and Women's Studies scholar, who holds an endowed chair at the University of Rhode Island (URI) wrote an article comparing the extremist right-wing political beliefs of a US group called QAnon with the false and extremist trans-sex beliefs of the political left. As a result of writing this trenchant essay, Hughes was denounced by students, faculty and administrators who called for her firing from a tenured position at the university. Hughes observed that no attention was paid to her criticism of right-wing beliefs (Hughes, 2021, April 28).

Professor Hughes is a respected scholar on sex trafficking and the sexual exploitation of women and children. She is also a scientist who supports scientific knowledge, not the fatuous untruths of right or left-wing proponents. She founded the academic open-access journal, *Dignity: A Journal of Sexual Exploitation and Violence*. In 2017, the university even recognized her work by presenting her with its Annual Research Award. She is obviously both a renowned scholar and professor. So what changed? She dared to dispute transgender ideology and practices, thereby giving the usual student mobs cause to descend on her, and freeing the so-called 'adults in the room' to bend over backwards in appeasing the youthful protesters.

Youngsters led the fight and the adults capitulated. Hughes was branded a transphobe, monster, and other hateful names. Students and others launched three online petitions denouncing her and agitating for her to be fired or not allowed to teach her courses. They threatened to denounce her department if it would not condemn Professor Hughes. Her head of department, Dr Rosaria Pisa, rapidly affirmed student demands and released a statement denouncing her to other faculty members with lies about her entire research career. This is an academic who admitted to Professor Hughes that she really didn't understand being transgender and know what 'It' is (Hughes, 2021, April 28).

Then followed the official pile-on where the authorities expressed their views in a statement of university compliance with student demand, the first by Dr Jeannette Riley, the Dean of the College of Arts and Sciences, which was released by the URI news bureau. University Provost, Dr Donald DeHays, supported the statement.

Due to the fast intervention of her attorney and her insistence that Professor Hughes have all the rights of free speech, the university has taken no action against her. The university's lawyer has affirmed that Hughes has the right of free speech both on and off campus and can't be retaliated against for speaking her views nor subjected to investigation or penalties by a URI 'diversity and inclusion' committee. And over 2,300 signers on a Change.org petition entitled 'The Univ. of Rhode Island Must Support Professor Donna Hughes' Right to Free Speech" agree (Change.org, 2021).

Donna Hughes has learned many lessons from this ordeal. First, 'Stand firm. Do not apologize. Do not try to explain.' Second, 'Retain an attorney early in the process.' Third, 'Expect your colleagues and students whom you have supported and provided with recommendations to turn against you just as eagerly as the others.' "It is possible to survive a cancel culture" (Hughes, 2021, April 28).

Kathleen Lowrey

Professor Kathleen Lowrey, associate professor at the University of Alberta in Canada, was asked to resign from her administrative position as associate chair of undergraduate studies in the department of anthropology. Anonymous students said her views caused them 'harm', but Lowrey questions whether these students were actually taking her course. Her teaching evaluations revealed that Lowrey is an 'awesome' professor, and she receives consistently good reviews.

Lowrey refused to resign from the committee, insisting that the University should explain in writing its reasons. In a letter to Lowrey, Lesley Cormack, the Dean of the Faculty of Arts, gave no substantive reasons other than the tepid response that Lowrey "was no longer effective in your administrative role" and "it is not in the best interests of the students or the university for you to carry on" (Labine, 2020). No specifics were given about why Professor Lowrey was "no longer effective" in her role, but Lowrey believes that the dismissal was based on her gender critical views. When she met with Cormack and her department chair, they merely told her that students felt 'uncomfortable' (Labine, 2020).

Lowrey has gone to great lengths to be explicit about her teaching, even informing prospective students that she would be using gender-critical materials in her class. On the first day of semester, she notified students that they would be reading critical feminist works "that are currently out of fashion in academia," and added that students need not agree with her. "Since this is a university, I think it's important literature they should be aware of" (Labine, 2020).

Although most of the censorship has targeted women who conscientiously dissent from transgender orthodoxies, a small number of male academics, researchers, journalists and clinicians have also been attacked. Journalist Robert Jensen, a retired professor of journalism at the University of Texas, Austin, has been censored for his views on transgender, which credit the work of radical feminists.

When Jensen submitted an article entitled 'Feminism Unheeded' to a website that had earlier published his work, he cautioned the piece was controversial and might be subjected to objections. Sure enough, "a reader denounced me as transphobic, and the editors of the site, who had originally thought the piece raised important questions, took it down within a few hours (it was posted later on a different site)" (Jensen, 2016).

Social Media Citadels of Censorship

Wikipedia and the Silencing of Radical Feminist Critics

The Wikipedia editing squad deletes any criticism of transgenderism and inserts their personal opinions into Wikipedia pages not their own. For example, my page has been constantly edited to spotlight accusations such as: "Her statements on transsexuality have been criticized by many in the LGBT and feminist communities as transphobic."

Since the beginning of Wikipedia, radical feminist entries have been purged of any criticism of transgenderism. Every time my technical assistant tried to re-do what was censored from my Wikipedia entry, her changes were deleted again and again and again. Wikipedia is one of the most regressive sites on the internet that erases radical feminist views on transgender, employing a cadre of pro-trans editors who use their editing power to alter any posts containing even mild criticism of transgenderism.

Wikipedia user TaylanUB has exposed how an eternal string of edits of his own posts provides documentation of bias against radical feminist pages and their views, giving a full exposé of every 'edit and undo' of what he published there. TaylanUB is an impressive critic of transgenderism, painstakingly detailing the editing of his own content and the struggle with pro-trans editors whose behavior is biased against feminist views.

For example, pro-trans editors claimed that citing the radical feminist website *Feminist Current* as a source for authenticating bias on Wikipedia was not a 'reliable or notable' reference, and therefore they deleted information based on this source. TaylanUB refuted Wikipedia's actions by pointing out that *Feminist Current* is not only Canada's biggest radical feminist website but its "biggest feminist website in general … This can be verified through Alexa [a site that ranks blogs and websites], Google ranking, and social media follower counts." He attributes the absence of any radical feminist representation on Wikipedia to the general male bias that permeates the site. He asks the pertinent question, "What kind of sources/DO these editors consider reliable/notable?" (TaylanUB, 2017).

When TaylanUB mentioned the attack at Speakers' Corner where Maria MacLachlan was assaulted by a trans activist (see pp. 147–149 this book), and also the trans activists' vandalization of the Vancouver Women's Library (see p. 187 this book), this content was deleted from his page, without his consent. An anonymous editor changed mention of the attack on MacLachlan at Speakers' Corner and claimed the incident was an 'altercation' rather that Taylan's wording of 'assault' (TaylanUB, 2017).

Forced censorship of content is rampant on Wikipedia, and the back and forth of principles involved in the undoing of radical feminist gender-critical content is based on clear bias. The sheer volume of edits made to gender critical content is dizzying.

Twitter

Like the amending of content on Wikipedia but going further, Twitter has joined the chorus of censors. Its updated terms of service announced in 2018–2019 are the product of trans activists' lobbying and trans staff that pushed internally for the change.

Tucked into Twitter's 'Hateful Conduct' policy is the banning of "Repeated and/or non-consensual slurs, epithets, racist and sexist tropes, or other content that degrades someone." The policy specifies:

> We prohibit targeting individuals with repeated slurs, tropes or other content that intends to dehumanize, degrade or reinforce negative or harmful stereotypes about a protected category. *The specifics of the policy target misgendering or deadnaming of transgender individuals* (Twitter Help Center, 2019, italics mine).

This defense of delusions is thought control.

In its protected categories, the policy mentions groups that are "disproportionately targeted with abuse online. This includes: *women*, people of color, lesbian, gay, bisexual, transgender, queer, intersex, asexual individuals, marginalized and historically underrepresented communities" (Twitter Help Center, 2019, italics mine). Unfortunately, Twitter has not enforced its policy against those who perpetrate the massive number of rape and death threats aimed at gender critics, mostly women.

Since women are listed as a protected category in the policy, we need evidence that the policy will be put into practice on behalf of women, especially when enforcement conflicts with trans activists who are the ones engaging in the most misogynist tweets. But it appears that Twitter does not enforce its protected category policy against users who consistently attack women on the site. Is this *because* enforcement would mean banning multiple trans activists from Twitter?

Instead, Twitter has chosen an easy mark of banning women. Who was quickly censored after the 'hateful conduct' policy went into effect? That would be Meghan Murphy, the editor of the largest feminist website in Canada. Murphy's alleged offense — billed a hate crime — was for saying "men are not women." Yet multiple men on Twitter, such as conservative political commentator Ben Shapiro, have made the same kind of statement, and their Twitter accounts were not closed. Twitter is applying a double standard when the trans critic is a radical feminist woman.

Twitter's refusal to target misogynist and threatening tweets, especially when coming from trans activists, is far more offensive than banning persons for 'misgendering or deadnaming'. Misnaming or misgendering are not threats but rather are invented words to target feminists who don't accept that men can be women. Trans activists want to eliminate the word woman and substitute words like TERFs, ciswomen and menstruators that insult groups of women, and which women have rejected. But Twitter has not included these words in their hateful conduct policy.

It appears that Twitter has no plans to shut down the misogynist tweets of trans activists, in spite of having added 'sexism' to its hateful conduct policy. Their policy pretense of including women is window dressing if Twitter continues to ignore its own standard for closing down multiple Twitter accounts that promote sexism and threats of violence against women.

Twitter also tolerates a mass blocking tool, @Blockterfs, used by trans activists to encourage Twitter users to label those who are radical feminist critics of transgender ideology and practices as transphobic (Bindel, 2018b). The Internet Society has recommended that policymakers and others "think twice when considering the use of Internet blocking tools to solve public policy issues. If they do and choose to pursue alternative approaches, this will be an important win for a global, open, interoperable and trusted Internet" (Internet Society, 2017).

It is likely that the large presence of self-declared women (men) in the tech industry, many onsite at Twitter, was instrumental in drafting their policy. In the earlier days of the internet, trans-identified women were very involved in its development. In fact, writer and trans-identified woman Cathryn Platine contends that the transgender community is a product of the internet. "Insular transgender online communities feed on their own versions of reality" amounting to what Platine labels a 'group psychosis'. "Silencing the dissenters becomes a virtue ... The internet was transformed from a tool to reach other isolated individuals to one that actually fosters avoidance of reality" (Platine, 2007).

Writing in *Medium*, trans-critical author Kitty Robinson has asked, "… am I supposed to believe that the many trans women rubbing elbows in the tech industry didn't come together for this policy change?" She writes about what the Twitter policy conveys to women who are survivors of male violence perpetrated by self-declared women.

> This policy is horrifying to me … if I wanted to go on Twitter and tell the story of how a male trans person who I trusted pulled my underwear down while I was sleeping and began penetrating me vaginally without using a condom, ignored my frightened efforts to pull away when awoken, and then ejaculated viable sperm into me without my consent resulting in an unwanted pregnancy and subsequent miscarriage [by Twitter's standards] I would need to call this person 'she'" (Kitty Robinson, 2019).

With powerful clarity, Kitty Robinson goes to the heart of the matter. She targets the web of entanglement that women sexually violated by self-declared women (men) experience and how submersion in the queer/trans communities gaslights their ability to recognize they were raped and to name their victimizers 'he' instead of 'she'. Robinson observes (2019):

> I would have to say 'she' ejaculated in me, I would have to say 'she' listened in silence on the phone when I called 'her' up hysterical and bleeding … I'd have to say 'sleep sex' (porn in which sleeping/passed out women are raped) was one of 'her' favorite porn categories.

The insularity of the trans/queer community drives cult-like behavior, depriving victims of male violence of the language to name their experience as *male violence*. In fact, if a woman expressed doubt about men calling themselves women, she was told that this skepticism contributed to hate crimes against self-declared women, allegedly the 'most vulnerable population on earth' (see Chapter Four for more details). Naming the violence from self-declared women as male violence is one of the greatest taboos in the LGBT+ community. And publicly 'deadnaming' them as men would probably get most disbelievers kicked off Twitter.

We have come a long way from viewing the internet only as a force of progress. Instead, in the 21st century we are confronted with online extremist views, cyber militias who stalk dissidents online and are adept at organizing campaigns that use scorched-earth tactics to censor those who are trans-critical from speaking at public events. Brutishness dominates these sites, and radical feminists have become the number one enemy, not the men who commit violent acts against trans-identified women.

Government Involved Censorship

Several UK police interventions have investigated trans complaints against women, at least one that resulted in jailing the alleged offender.

Kate Scottow

Hertfordshire (UK) police became shamefully intrusive with the arrest and detention of Kate Scottow. Treated as a common criminal, Scottow was transported to police headquarters, where they fingerprinted her, took her mugshot and detained her in a jail cell for seven hours. The police also seized her mobile phone and laptop computer.

The police arrested Scottow on charges of harassment and "malicious communications" after she 'misgendered' Stephanie Hayden online, addressing the self-declared woman as 'he' and 'him'. Scottow was also accused of calling Hayden a 'racist', following his tweet in response to a black man who challenged him on gender identity ideology. She also described Hayden as a "pig in a wig."

While the trial was pending, Scottow was subject to a court order forbidding her to refer to Hayden as a man, but she declared that she holds a "genuine and reasonable belief" that a human "cannot practically speaking change sex."

A Magistrates' Court judge found her actions to be "unkind and abusive," and convicted her of persistently making use of a public communications network to cause annoyance, inconvenience, and anxiety to Hayden. Scottow was fined £1,000 and subjected to a two-year conditional jail discharge. Her supporters protested the verdict outside the court, chanting "pig in a wig" and "he's a man — go on prosecute me" (Shaw, 2020).

Scottow appealed the verdict, and, in December 2020, won her case to overturn her conviction. "I have no idea why the conviction was quashed. Once reasons are available, I will comment further," she said (in Odling, 2020).

Caroline Farrow

Journalist Caroline Farrow was informed by the police that she was under investigation for misgendering Jackie Green. Farrow had claimed on a TV program that Jackie, billed as Britain's youngest transsexual, had undergone penile inversion surgery. Farrow argued that this was "mutilation, castration and child abuse" prompting Jackie's mother, the Mermaids charity founder Susie Green, to shriek on Twitter that in writing these words, Farrow had misgendered her son, now a self-declared woman. Susie Green complained to the police who subsequently opened an investigation into these claims (Hill, 2019).

In defending herself, Caroline Farrow declared, "I have pointed out to police that I am a Catholic journalist/commentator and it is my religious belief that a person cannot change sex." She added that she would "happily do jail time" for her "right to say that people cannot change sex" (Hill, 2019).

Under the UK *Malicious Communications Act*, it is a crime to send messages that are indecent or grossly offensive, threatening, or contain information, which is false or believed to be false, if the purpose for sending it is to cause distress or anxiety:

> If a person is found guilty of an offence under this 1988 legislation, they may be sentenced to a prison sentence of up to 12 months or a fine or both, following a conviction in the Magistrates' Court, or a prison sentence of up to two years or a fine or both on conviction in the Crown Court" (JMW Solicitors, n.d.).

The investigation was one-sided, since the police did not investigate when Farrow received a blitz of intimidating online abuse filled with threats, which they didn't seem to consider an incitement to violence and a hate crime!

Ultimately, Green withdrew her complaint but not before the police investigation was underway to decide whether Farrow had committed a criminal offense by misgendering Green's 'daughter'. Farrow stated that the police decision to investigate her was an 'outrage'. What business is it of the police to prevent people from offending each other?

Margaret Nelson

After referring to a self-declared woman as a man, 74-year-old Margaret Nelson received a phone call from a Suffolk police officer who was investigating gender-critical statements Nelson had placed on her Twitter account and blog. Nelson had also asserted on Twitter that "Gender's fashionable nonsense. Sex is real ... Gender is BS. Pass it on."

The officer told Nelson that some of her statements could "upset or offend" transgender people, and the officer suggested that she stop writing such statements in the future and remove the offending tweets. However, Nelson indicated that she would not be deleting the posts and would continue to write and exercise her free speech. The officer did not claim her statements were illegal and gave no legitimate reason for the call. So Nelson phoned the Suffolk police for an explanation. The police responded they had received a number of online comments and complaints about her.

When an officer of the law interrogates an independent plainspoken woman and asks her to muzzle her gender-critical comments, one wonders why this is a police matter at all. Offending people on social media is not a crime. But others less steadfast than Nelson might be intimidated into silencing themselves if they received a police request.

Suffolk police later apologized to Nelson for the intrusion. "We accept we made a misjudgement ... As a result, we will be reviewing our procedures for dealing with such matters." This is fine, but as James Kirkup has written, "why on earth did anyone ever think that this was the right thing to do?" (Kirkup, 2019a). Only in translandia would personal offenses be considered a cause for police involvement.

In a period when trans activists have joined large public protests against police powers and interventionism, it is hypocritical to be advocating that police use their powers of enforcement to investigate trans critics and criminalize dissenting speech. You can't be working for criminal justice reform at the same time you are merchants of censorship and calling on police powers to indict those who are trans-critical.

Unfortunately, trans activists are promoting legislation in several countries in which gender-critical speech becomes a legal offense that would mandate police involvement. We have seen critics targeted as lawbreakers and dragged into jail or court for 'crimes' of simply offending transpersons. At a time when the actions of the police and their behavior is being interrogated, making the police agents of censorship does them no favors and gains them no public approval, except from trans activists.

Janice G. Raymond

My own experience of government censorship took place in Oslo, Norway in 2013. After inviting me to speak on a panel, the Norwegian governmental Ombuds Office, ironically an anti-discrimination unit, disinvited me to speak on the subject of prostitution and the Norwegian law against the purchasing of sexual activities. The day I arrived in Oslo, the Ombuds Office informed me that I had been excluded from the panel of speakers because of my views on transsexualism.

In a letter to *Dagbladat*, a prominent Norwegian language newspaper, four signatories represented my writings as 'transphobic'. The Ombuds director took as truth what was actually a misrepresentation of my views without ever asking me if their letter to the editor was a valid account of my work. Furthermore, I was invited to speak on prostitution, not transsexualism.

A more distorted and defamatory letter authored by Synnøve Økland Jahnsen, a researcher at the University of Bergen purporting to quote my work, was printed in *Klassekampen*, a daily left-wing newspaper. Using quotation marks, this second letter stated that I believed "transsexuals should be eradicated on moral grounds." The quotation of course was false, intellectually irresponsible, and what appeared to be a deliberate misquoting of my actual words written in the appendix to my book, *The Transsexual Empire*.

Klassekampen printed my response to Jahnsen's distortion of my words. Nowhere had I written that "transsexuals should be eradicated on moral grounds." I responded that Jahnsen's quote had overtones of ethnic cleansing and made it sound like I want to eradicate trans-identified persons from the face of the earth. I wrote, "Jahnsen also objects to my views on prostitution. Given the way in which she has misconstrued my words about transsexualism, she would possibly accuse me of wanting to eradicate women in prostitution because I want to eradicate prostitution!"

I ended my rejoinder by adding I can only believe that either Jahnsen is a very uninformed researcher who has never really read my book, or that she has deliberately twisted my words to discredit my views on prostitution and the sex industry.

> I cannot believe the University of Bergen is well-served by such academic incompetence and/or intellectual dishonesty when a basic premise of academic research is to ensure that a researcher quotes her or his sources faithfully. I would hope that the university has an academic standards committee that would review Jahnsen's research to ensure that such distortions of any scholar's words do not happen in the future (Raymond, 2013).

The Liberal Left and Transgenderism

Founder of the Vancouver Rape Relief and Crisis Center, Lee Lakeman, attributes the political left's failure to protect women to its loss of values. "The problem with the left is it is afraid of words like 'morality'. The left does not know how to distinguish between right and wrong." Lakeman continues, "The left is full of … feckless liberals … [who] think physical abuse of a woman is abhorrent if it occurs in a sweatshop but somehow is acceptable in a rented room, an alley, a brothel, a massage parlor or a car" (in Hedges, 2015).

The same leftist activists that define prostitution as a 'choice' are many of the same individuals who are members of organizations that are now defending transgender as a human right. The left has always been wary of women's actual liberation and instead has chosen to put its mouth and money into those women's rights that benefit men. Simply speaking, the moral bankruptcy of the left does not recognize women as a political class, nor that misogyny is real, excusing leftist men of taking responsibility for their own abuse of women. As Rebecca West wrote of the leftwing "carriage trade, they want to be right, not to do right."

Transgenderism offers leftist and liberal organizations a way to avoid supporting radical feminist views and campaigns, for example, on pornography and prostitution, because these issues come too close to divesting men of their sexual privilege. Supporting the transgender program allows leftist men and organizations to publicly inject men's rights into their campaigns and claim they are upholding women's rights, that is, the rights of men who declare themselves women. These are the same organizations that allege prostitution is a 'choice', pornography empowers women, and women are not a victimized class.

Prostitution, pornography, surrogacy, and transgenderism are now being defended as women's rights and are powered by foundations that pour money into sustaining organizations that champion these abuses. "We have never stopped having to deal with misogyny among activists," Lakeman argues. "Globalization and neoliberalism have accelerated a process in which women are being sold wholesale, as if it is OK to prostitute Asian women in brothels because they are sending money home to poor families" (in Hedges, 2015). Efforts to decriminalize prostitution, which claim to serve the interests of prostituted women by endorsing sex buyers and pimps, have the full backing of the sex industry and, unfortunately, the support of many women's and human rights activists.

Leftist organizations such as Stonewall in the UK, are acting like a transgender 'revolutionary vanguard' by back-stabbing feminists. Many leftist organizations tolerate threats, bullying and violence against women, even encouraging the purges of so-called TERFs. No credible revolution would brook such retrograde thinking and action.

Australian academic and writer, Caroline Norma, has called transgenderism "the latest anti-feminist wedge issue of the left" (2015). A wedge issue can be defined as a political or social concern, often of a controversial or divisive nature, which divides a particular group. It can also be used to defend a position that might be indefensible if discussed upfront yet carried out through covert means.

For example, leftist groups are using transgenderism as a wedge issue to deflect attention from their historic silence about violence against women by pointing to their politically correct credentials in defending trans-identified women (men) as legitimate women. When issues such as pornography, prostitution, surrogacy and now transgender came knocking at their doors, leftist and liberal organizations knew this meant challenging their own use and abuse of women.

> *Transgenderism* bastardises the core feminist insight that 'woman' is a politically defined social category generated by male violence and the exclusion, expropriation and colonisation of female human beings. Rendered as a Leftist wedge issue, this insight becomes the distorted proposition that 'woman' is a flexible human 'identity' with which any individual might associate themselves — even fully-grown rational male human beings. Rather than being a designator of subordinated social class membership, 'woman' is a feeling that can swell in any man's breast (Norma, 2015).

Norma asserts that prostitution was a "particularly cynical choice" as a wedge issue because the left had traditionally been opposed to it and called for its abolition — its sacred source being the *Manifesto of the Communist Party*. The left's turnaround on prostitution is displayed in Amnesty International's prostitution policy, which protects men's right to use women in prostitution and is a primary example of how progressive organizations have totally sold out women.

As Andrea Dworkin has written, "The Left cannot have its whores and its politics too" (Dworkin, 1979). Yet leftist men continue to try. On issues of prostitution and pornography, they have not only abandoned women but also abandoned their anti-capitalist politics. Capitulating to a market model, the left sold pornography as an expression of women's (read men's) sexual freedom. The discourse of the left now accepts prostitution as 'sex work', not sexual exploitation. In this corporate-centered view, pimps are third-party business agents who women 'choose' to protect themselves and their interests, not first-class exploiters. And male sex buyers are cordial clients who provide women with needed income, not abusers.

Bolstered by trans activists, progressive organizations have now found their way out of defending natal women and women's rights by promoting the notion that men can be women, that is, the 'women' they can do business with. Trans-identified women are much more acceptable to men than those tedious radical feminists who are always talking about male violence against women, male entitlement and male accountability! So why not redirect the conversation to a version of women's rights that the left can accept and control — a version of 'women's rights' that requires only that they accept their male counterparts as 'women'? But just wait until these self-declared women start swinging their 'lady sticks' around and demanding sex with heterosexual males if they dare to try.

Transgender principles have infected Democratic political campaigns in the United States. For example, during the Democratic primary in 2020, Senator Elizabeth Warren spoke at a town hall, sponsored by CNN and a mainstream LGBT+ organization called the Human Rights Campaign. Warren became a major spokeswoman for LGBT+ policy, which during the town hall discussion was largely devoted to issues of transgender.

Beginning with language, Warren's advocacy for transgender rights used the demeaning language of 'cisgender women'. Before the town hall meeting, the then-surging Democratic presidential candidate announced plans to end the policy of assigning prisoners to facilities based on their biological sex. She also said she would spend taxpayer dollars supporting 'sex-reassignment surgery':

> I will direct the Bureau of Prisons (BOP) to end the Trump Administration's dangerous policy of imprisoning transgender people in facilities based on their sex assigned at birth and ensure that all facilities meet the needs of transgender people, she writes on her campaign website, including by providing medically necessary care, like transition-related surgeries while incarcerated (Warren, 2020).

Censorship in the Major Mainstream Media Giants

Any writer or journalist who has been critical of trans ideology and practices has long been subject to censorship in the media. Whether it's mainstream or progressive, the purging of dissent has been the same. For example, it is difficult to find, in the archives of the illustrious *The New York Times,* even a handful of gender critical articles published since Elinor Burkett's 2015 cutting-edge piece entitled 'What Makes a Woman?' Now we are deluged with *Times* opinion pieces and news reports of uncritical writing favorable to all aspects of the transgender issue, even giving the reader information about 'transwomen's underwear'.

You won't find any major news coverage of a 2020 landmark victory in the UK case brought by Keira Bell in which the High Court compelled Britain's largest gender identity clinic to shut down its hormone treatments program for youth. Bell had sued the Tavistock Clinic for prescribing puberty blockers, testosterone and a double mastectomy as part of its gender affirmation 'care' when she was in her teens. The Court decision found that the clinic's gender program was not based on credible evidence, and expert witnesses testified that the treatments given to youth at Tavistock amounted to a "live experiment on children and adolescents" (Manning, 2021). But don't look for any critical reports on the UK's High Court decision or other critical stories of transgenderism in *The New York Times* or the *Washington Post*.

Readers have noticed and indicted *The Times* for its steady stream of positive articles on the topic of transgender and the silencing of women that this achieves. One commentator wrote:

> The constant publishing of articles on this very same topic, day after day, week after week, in the NYTimes, in an attempt to force people to share the opinion that biological sex is some vague mental construct. Please, NYTimes, stop trying to silence women's voices and tell readers what to think. Move on to other subjects.

As an informal exercise in a content analysis search of articles in *The New York Times* on the subject of transgender over the last decade, I sought to estimate the number of articles that offer a critical view of trans-centered narratives, whether in a direct or indirect way. The exercise overwhelmingly revealed media bias in favor of publishing multiple articles that turn a positive lens on trans-centered narratives focused on a variety of issues including sports, legislation, philosophy, education, and fashion.

Once the trans posses descend on any gender-critical article, media back off and cave in to a broadside of insistent threats and boycotts. Even mild criticism of transgender issues can cause an explosion of mobbing and bullying of editors. And it works. One editor told Julie Bindel that it is just too much trouble to touch the trans issue and no matter how balanced the piece, the complaints overwhelmed the positives. When Bindel contacted writers for a quote about being censored, they insisted on anonymity "… for fear that they will be blacklisted from publications if identified" (Bindel, 2018a).

Discussion, debate and any questioning of transgenderism and its dogmas are impossible because sensible interchange of opinions is rigged right from the beginning. There is no starting line for discussion because, as trans activists maintain, discussion of trans dogmas constitutes 'violence' and questioning the very existence of trans-identified persons.

To question any trans precept is to question trans existence. One writer, Samantha Allen, contends, "There are not two sides to a debate about whether a group of people should exist" (Allen, 2013). Trans-identified woman, Parker Molly, reiterates Allen's position. When Molly is invited to appear on a TV program, she wonders

> … whether I'm going to get roped into a debate over my very existence … if debate starts from the premise that trans people are and will always be whatever happens to be stamped on our original birth certificates … each conversation is handled as a referendum on our legitimacy and existence (Molloy, 2018).

But refusing to accept that men can be women is not disputing transpersons' existence; it's disputing their gender identity and their claim to be women.

When the transgenderist position is 'no discussion of our very existence,' this censors legitimate questions about what that very existence means. It promotes a fundamentalist belief system, a doctrinaire faith of trans evangelists who punish misgendering and mispronouning as blasphemy and that consigns doubters to damnation.

The disease of censorship has also infected Amazon Books. When Ryan Anderson published his book entitled *When Harry Became Sally, Responding to the Transgender Moment* (2018), Amazon delisted his book. His publisher was flabbergasted that Amazon would seek to censor a bestseller. Not only Anderson but Scott Howard's *The Transgender Industrial Complex*, Maria Keffler's *Desist-Detrans-Detox: Getting Your Child Out of the Gender Cult* and Abigail Shrier's *Irreversible Damage: The Transgender Craze Seducing Our Daughters* have also withstood periods of being banned by

Amazon. Searching on Amazon for these three books, I couldn't find *The Transgender Industrial Complex,* but I was able to find Adolf Hitler's *Mein Kampf.*

When I looked for my own first book entitled *The Transsexual Empire: The Making of the She-Male,* it was there, but priced out of sight with the hardback costing $578.99 and the paperback ranging between $166 and $596!

It remains to be seen whether Amazon will continue this censorship. As I write, undoubtedly if the 'book burning' continues, *Doublethink: A Feminist Challenge to Transgenderism* may be another victim relegated to the Index of Forbidden Books, a list of historically banned books by the Roman Catholic Church that has now become secularized in the woke canon of the trans church.

Conclusion

Women's lack of choosiness about who may be called a woman strengthens the impression that women do not see their sex as real, and suggests that perhaps they too identify themselves as not-male, the other, any other.

— Germaine Greer, *The Whole Woman*

No one — women, men, children, or trans-identified persons — should be subjected to any form of exploitation or targeted for discrimination. Trans-identified persons are entitled to the same human and civil rights as others. Recognizing these rights, however, does not mean that we must accept that hormones and surgery transform men into women and women into men; or that persons who self-declare as members of the opposite sex are what they subjectively claim to be; or that hormones and surgery are 'life-saving and necessary treatments' for those seeking transition.

Transgender activists champion the 'right' to hormones and surgery for every child who presents as 'dysphoric', treatments they define as 'emergency medical care'. This rhetoric of dysphoria allows accusers to assert that opponents are depriving children of necessary health care, as if hormones are an issue of life and death comparable to insulin needed by diabetics.

By defining these treatments as a right, trans activists can brand both opponents of affirmation treatment and questioning parents as biased, allegedly depriving children of their civil liberties. Instead of supporting a child's right to protection from the health risks of such procedures, trans activists claim that robbing children of quick affirmation of treatment is life-threatening and may cause suicide.

The suicide alarm is used as a cudgel to hammer trans tenets into truths. Suicide numbers are blown out of proportion and invoked widely within trans circles, especially to defend certain medical procedures for young people.

Keira Bell, the brave young woman who brought a successful legal case against the UK Tavistock Clinic, has written:

> I was adamant that I needed to transition. It was the kind of brash assertion that's typical of teenagers. What was really going on was that I was a girl insecure in my body who had experienced parental abandonment, felt alienated from my peers, suffered from anxiety and depression, and struggled with my sexual orientation.

As she grew older, Bell understood, "I recognized that gender dysphoria was a symptom of my overall misery, not its cause" (Bell, 2021).

After a round of "superficial conversations" with social workers, Bell was given puberty blockers at age 16, testosterone shots at 17, and at 20, she had a double mastectomy. Five years later, she de-transitioned. The health consequences, however, were not superficial: infertility, loss of breasts with inability to breastfeed, atrophied genitals and a permanently changed voice (Bell, 2021).

Writer Max Robinson quotes a friend who argues that

> ... if the top priority of all providers of transgender health-care services was really to help people feel their best, they'd be banging on the doors of the many women talking about alternative strategies for coping with feelings currently or formerly diagnosable as gender dysphoria (2021, p. 14).

Quick gender affirmation treatment for children reverses the Hippocratic medical principle to 'do no harm' when clinicians subject young patients to iatrogenic or doctor-induced risks that include infertility or chemical sterilization, vaginal atrophy in girls and heart problems. Even the notion of harm is inverted when trans activists and clinicians claim the actual damage done to young patients is due to parents and others who *reject* quick affirmation treatment, a rejection they label as child abuse.

Transgenderism has even taken root in US medical schools. Professors, besieged by woke medical students, are apologizing, for example, for using the term 'pregnant woman' instead of 'pregnant person'. Some schools are conceding that "the notion of sex … is just a man-made creation" (in Herzog, 2021), an admission that can have disastrous effects if doctors and patients ignore the material reality of sex and its consequences for diagnosis and treatment.

Transgenderism is undermining medical training. One student, Lauren, gives an example: "Take abdominal aortic aneurysms … These are four times as likely to occur in males than females." But when discussed, this sex difference wasn't emphasized. Other sex differences such as heart attack symptoms manifest differently in males and females. But sex differences that impact treatment are not part of the curriculum. Lauren continues, "I'm not even sure what I'm being taught, and unless my classmates are as skeptical as I am, they probably aren't aware either" (in Herzog, 2021).

In spite of what Lauren sees happening in medical schools, she is "both hopeful for the future and not." She observes that the transgender movement "is portrayed as a civil rights movement … it seems virtuous … So how can you fight against something that's being marketed as a fight for human rights?" (in Herzog, 2021).

Rejecting Trans Ideology and Affirming Gender Non-Conformity

Transgenderism would not prevail if the constraints of sex roles and the demands of toxic masculinity and femininity did not dominate many lives. This is a position I espoused in *The Transsexual Empire* where I wrote there would be less need for injurious body modifications, including hormone treatment, mastectomies, and penectomies, if the trans canopy had not become the reference point for what is actually sex role dissatisfaction and gender non-conformity.

Trans advocates have no monopoly on gender non-conformity. Why should gender non-conforming behavior be confined to the realm of transgender and turned into an object of medical attention? Transgenderism depoliticizes non-compliant behavior and restricts it to a so-called gender identity, thus making it a question of individual behavior amenable to hormone treatments, surgery and self-identification. Clinicians should be encouraging young people to challenge sex roles without rejecting their natal bodies.

Gender non-conformity is just what it says — the practice of not conforming to role-defined rules and regulations, no matter whether they are traditionally or progressively presented. People shouldn't need to identify as transgender or transsexual to live a gender non-compliant life.

Feminists invented gender non-conformity, and we have fought for decades to break out of traditional sex roles and to combat toxic masculinity and femininity, only to see them reappear as variations of transgenderism. Women have battled many gendered restrictions in the professions, higher education, politics and government: roles traditionally reserved for men but historically considered off-limits to women because of our alleged natures. There is nothing innate about sex roles, in contrast to the claims of trans activists, and there should be nothing wrong with people expressing a range of so-called masculine and feminine behaviors and appearances, without having to alter their sex.

With the spread of the transgender movement, gender abolitionists are now facing another challenge generated by a new world of gender expectations. Feminism seemed to lose its way when trans definitions and the gender industry gained ground, and gender non-conforming behavior was confined to the fictional category of trans persons.

The 'transing' of men, women and children is the new 'progressive' version of traditional sex role socialization now supported by a huge gender industry spreading its vast tentacles in influential places.

The 'transing' of the history of women, gay men and lesbians is also rampant, when our very history is appropriated as trans.

Traditional sex role socialization makes it difficult to be a girl, and the contemporary transgender movement tells girls it has a simple answer to their troubles: "just transition, it's easy." Lisa Selin Davis, a freelance journalist and mother, illustrates the straight-jacket of reducing gender non-conforming behavior to transgender, especially in K-9 (primary and middle) schools. In an article called 'My Daughter is Not Transgender. She is a Tomboy', Davis describes a query from her daughter's teacher obviously wanting to properly identify the girl who doesn't act like most girls. The teacher asks, "Your child wants to be called a boy, right? Or is she a boy that wants to be called a girl? Which is it?" (Selin Davis, 2017).

The mother responds, "I love correcting them, making them reconsider their perception of what a girl looks like. She's a girl," I said. The teacher looked unconvinced. The mother reiterates, "Really she's a girl. My daughter wears track pants and T-shirts. She has shaggy short hair … sporty and strong, incredibly sweet, and a girl."

And yet her daughter is asked by her teachers, by her pediatrician and by people who have known her for many years, if she feels like or wants to be a boy. Davis states, "the initial question might be considerate but when they keep questioning her and are skeptical of her response, the message they send is that a girl cannot look and act like her and still be a girl … we've narrowed what we think a boy or a girl can look like and do." In other words, she must be a "trans boy" (Selin Davis, 2017).

When feminists are vilified as bigots for maintaining that the trans movement is erasing women, here is one mother's testimony of how girlhood erasure happens when transing takes over and infects law, education, sports, corporations, medicine and universities. What a travesty that the girl's gender non-conformity is measured by whether or not she fits a trans standard and not the standard of being an independent girl.

What a disturbing turnaround that gender non-conforming girls are presumed to be 'transboys' — not simply ordinary girls if they do not kowtow to this new version of sex-role stereotyping. 'Transing' the gender non-conforming lives of girls is in fact a new demand for gender compliance that operates in the same old way as traditional sex-role socialization, especially by urging young girls into identifying as 'trans boys' rather than as girls. As Abigail Shrier has admonished, "Stop pathologizing girlhood" (2020, p. 215).

The transing of any kind of gender non-conformity is a given in many school systems, where the curriculum has the power to erase children who do not identify as trans, yet also do not conform to traditional roles of masculinity or femininity. The message Davis sends to her daughter is: "You are an awesome girl for not giving in to pressure to be and look a certain way. I want her to be proud to be a girl" (Selin Davis, 2017).

When teachers show films that 'explore gender' and use trans-gender teaching manuals to instruct kids about gender identity, they are encouraging a substantial number of children to question their sex, particularly when the message is 'you might have been born in the wrong body'. These 'teachings' may channel many vulnerable gay and lesbian kids into becoming trans or influence those who are uncertain — what writer and publisher Susan Hawthorne has called the 'Trans Scam' (Hawthorne, 2021).

Attorney Maya Dillard Smith, formerly head of Georgia's ACLU chapter, has said:

> From what I can see, the transgender narrative very much reinforces patriarchy … I've never heard a trans narrative that does not rely on sexual stereotypes to explain how someone knew they were actually born in the wrong body. I'd like to return to the old feminist war cry: Start a revolution and stop hating your body (in Hedges, 2017).

Radical feminists reject identities such as transgender or transsexual. That some men wear makeup, or have long hair and are nurturing, and that some women don't wear makeup or have short hair, and are non-nurturing, should be unexceptional. If we expand the bandwidth of what it is to be a man or a woman, we don't need to seek a change in sex but rather a change in society's codes of femininity or masculinity. If we expand the bandwidth of what it is to be a man or a woman, trans terms would have little meaning and certainly, we wouldn't need the medicalizing of young bodies in order to live in a gender non-conforming way.

Learning from the Survivors of Transgenderism

It's time that we recognize women returning to themselves — post trans — not only as women making a personal choice but also as members of a *feminist political movement of survivors*. The increasing numbers of girls and women who transitioned to trans male but who later de-transitioned have not been fully acknowledged, researched, and written about.

For over 30 years, I have worked to combat the sexual exploitation and trafficking of girls and women. In my capacity as co-director of an international NGO whose mission is to abolish prostitution (The Coalition against Trafficking in Women), I have spoken with hundreds of women in systems of prostitution who have testified that prostitution is not a choice nor is it a job: it is sexual exploitation. In writing this book on transgender, I have learned that there are many instructive parallels that are expressed in the testimonies of survivors of prostitution and survivors of transgender. De-transitioners are the survivors of transgenderism.

Survivors of prostitution have taught us that there is no essentializing of prostitution — that women are not prostitutes by nature, and that there is no psychological essentialism that claims women who are prostituted enjoy sex. Just as survivors of prostitution have rejected the rationalizations of prostitution as sexual freedom and sex work, survivors of transgenderism — especially young women survivors who are now de-transitioning — are also telling us that they have rejected the system of transgender that has kept them in a situation that exploits them biologically, psychologically, sexually, and economically.

By accepting the pro-sex work position that prostitution is a 'choice', advocates have consigned prostituted women to a segregated class of women who are kept in systems of sexual exploitation that pass for benevolent institutions, especially in those countries and states where the prostitution industry is legalized or decriminalized. So-called 'progressive' LGBT+ organizations are in the vanguard of advocating the decriminalizing of prostitution, where brothels, pimping and sex buyers are the building blocks of an ever-expanding sexual exploitation industry that has ravaged the lives of women through a romanticizing of 'free choice', a 'choice' that is not free for the thousands of women who are abused in the industry.

As the sex industry idealizes prostitution as beneficial and liberating for women, so too does a transgender industry that capitalizes on glamorizing transgender as hip, cool, and transgressive. The transgender industry encompasses the trans fashion industry, the trans pornography and trans prostitution industries, and the medical industry that is now mutilating young children with puberty blockers and opposite-sex hormones: all a part of what is now the vast transgender empire.

Like the sex industry, the transgender industry feeds on sexual exploitation, especially of young women who have been sexually objectified, harassed, and abused. When we review the narratives of young girls who reject toxic femininity and who endure breast binders, hormones and surgery in their quest to become boys, we find multiple narratives of sexual abuse in their lives, abuse they were attempting to overcome by transitioning to trans manhood. Women de-transitioners speak about their flights from toxic femininity that require women and girls to 'act like a woman should act' and the degrading sexual exploitation widespread in LGBT+ circles (see Chapter 4).

The decision to stop hormone treatments for children in gender identity clinics in the UK, Finland and Sweden is a step in the right direction. And as more researchers begin to speak out about their findings of harm, hopefully more researchers will come together like the Society for Evidence Based Gender Medicine (SEGM) to urge clinicians and researchers to stop these treatments.

As rising numbers of young de-transitioners speak out, publish testimonies, and use the law to sue their doctors and clinics for malpractice, it will become harder to ignore this 'clinical house of horrors' that has medicalized the gender dissatisfaction of young children.

We have seen the global prostitution survivor movement take a leading role in the campaign to end prostitution. Likewise, I am optimistic about the impact of de-transitioning women as they begin to write about their journeys of returning to their selves.

Moving Forward

How is it that critics of the transgender system have been demonized, threatened and attacked for calling out the lies and stating the truth? For one thing, self-declared women, as the men that they are, are not listening to de-transitioning women. Instead trans activists seek to downplay the numbers of de-transitioners and brand them as traitors. Men who identify as women and their allies have seized the public stage and set in motion the trans policing of those with whom they disagree, harassing and attacking both de-transitioners and natal women.

Young women who identified formerly as 'trans men' and are now de-transitioning are asking perceptive questions that challenge trans dogma. Men who self-identify as women could take a page from their female counterparts and begin this kind of personal and political reflection.

Transsexualism and its more recent incarnation, transgenderism, raise half-truths that highlight the situation of those individuals in society who feel uniquely body-bound by gender constrictions — but individual distress is not the whole truth. Although transgenderism poses the question of gender dissatisfaction, it fails to give a social and political answer. Instead it reinforces the society and social norms that produced transgender to begin with. And too often, it offers no solution to the individual's gender dissatisfaction. Rachel Hewitt has tweeted:

> The cis/trans linguistic binary implies there's only 1 way to reject gender stereotypes associated w sex: you either accept them or you reject them by transitioning. It doesn't allow a third way: eg rejecting stereotypes by changing society, not the individual body (aka feminism) (Hewitt, 2018).

As I have written elsewhere, many people, especially feminists, have faced dissatisfaction with their bodies. However, feminists have raised questions and given answers to gender dissatisfaction that go far beyond the transsexual and transgender context — questions about body mutilation and integrity, medical research priorities, definitions of maleness and femaleness and the expansion of the industrialization of gender. Any woman who has experienced the agony of not fitting into a society where 'gender hurts' (Jeffreys, 2014) is hardly insensitive to the plight of trans identified persons.

Many trans identified persons speak compellingly about their own experience. Many experience acute body dissatisfaction. Having experienced dissatisfaction with one's body, however, does not make anyone an authority on the larger social, political and medical contexts that generate trans identification. This kind of reflection requires looking beyond the individual self at the ways in which social and political structures influence identity.

Given the damage that transgenderism is doing to children who are being processed through gender identity clinics, seeking to change their bodies through hormones and surgery, the most honest, informed and sensitive position one can take is to be openly gender critical. Otherwise, we engage in a passive tolerance, a laissez-faire attitude that reinforces a gender-defined society and a gender industry that prolongs the harm.

Misplaced sympathy will only strengthen a society in which new sex roles are the norm, where gender crises become subject to medicalization, and where self-declaration of sex is epidemic. Such a tolerance encourages children and adults to alter their bodies or their appearance rather than to join together in altering societal standards. In the long run, this kind of tolerance, sensitivity, or sympathy does not aid those who suffer but rather creates more victims.

What is at stake in the transgender conflict is not just an individual person's 'feeling'. Rather, this anti-woman and anti-feminist ideology is having a far-reaching impact on legislation normalizing that men can be women, often with no input from women who would be harmed by the legislation. Unfortunately, where transgender legislation is placed on the docket, public opinion lags behind public policy.

Trans activists have taken their ideology and practice to absurd lengths, and people have played along with it giving anything that passes for trans their support. We are in the grip of a repudiation of reality that is responsible for much harm, especially to children. Every day, there are new revelations about transgender intrusions into the educational system and women's sports, the proliferation of gender identity clinics, and legislation that is pending or has passed that institutionalizes transgenderism. Principled people must be willing to speak out and say 'enough'.

I hope that more people will come to see gender dissatisfaction not as a disorder requiring medical treatment, or as a matter of self-identification, but as an issue that will not be resolved until we challenge both the traditional and 'progressive' gender-defined culture and the denialism that perpetuates it. I hope that the trans survivor movement will become a strong political movement that will contribute to changing what is now a men's rights movement to a gender-abolitionist movement that honors women and women's rights.

References

AAP. n.d. American Academy of Pediatrics. *Advocacy and Policy, AAP Health Initiatives.* <https://www.aap.org/en-us/Pages/Default.aspx>

Abeni, Cleis. 2016, Feb, 3. 'New History Project'. *The Trans Advocate.* <https://www.advocate.com/think-trans/2016/2/03/new-history-project-unearths-radical-feminisms-trans-affirming-roots>

ACLU. n.d. 'Changing the Game: The GLSEN Sports Project'. *American Civil Liberties Association.* <https://www.aclu.org/library-lgbt-youth-schools-resources-and-links>

Aitkenhead, Decca. 2017, Feb. 25. 'I'm Not Going to Stoop and Apologise and Grovel'. *The Guardian.* <https://www.theguardian.com/us-news/2017/feb/25/rachel-dolezal-not-going-stoop-apologise-grovel>

Allen, Charlotte. 2019, March 4. 'Trans Men Erase Women'. *First Things.* <https://www.firstthings.com/web-exclusives/2019/03/trans-men-erase-women>

Allen, Samantha. 2013, July 12. 'The Hate Group Masquerading as Feminists'. *Salon.* <https://www.salon.com/2013/07/11/the_hate_group_masquerading_as_inclusive_feminists_partner>

Alter, Charlotte. n.d. 'Transgender Men See Sexism from Both Sides'. *Time Magazine.* <https://time.com/transgender-men-sexism/>

American Society of Plastic Surgeons. 2017, May 22. 'Gender Confirmation Surgeries Rise 20% in First Ever Report'. <https://www.plasticsurgery.org/news/press-releases/gender-confirmation-surgeries-rise-20-percent-in-first-ever-report>

Angum, Fariha, Tahir Khan, Jasndeep Kaler, Lena Siddiqui and Azhar Hussain. 2020, May 12. 'The Prevalence of Autoimmune Disorders in Women: A Narrative Review'. Pub Med 12(5): e8094. *National Library of Medicine* (NIH). <https://pubmed.ncbi.nlm.nih.gov/32542149/>

Archive. 2016, Sept. 3. 'Female Detransition and Reidentification: Survey Results and Interpretation'. *Tumblr.com.* <https://guideonragingstars.

tumblr.com/post/149877706175/female-detransition-and-reidentification-survey>

Atkinson, CJ. 2018, July 17. 'Trans Masculine People Are Being Excluded from the Conversation'. *The Economist*. <https://www.economist.com/open-future/2018/07/17/trans-masculine-people-are-being-excluded-from-the-conversation>

Autonomous Womyn's Press. 2015. *Blood and Visions: Womyn Reconciling with Being Female*. <https://www.goodreads.com/book/show/30792924-blood-and-visions>

Avery, Dan. 2021, Jan. 5. 'Trans Women Retain Athletic Edge After a Year of Hormone Therapy'. *NBC News*. <https://www.nbcnews.com/feature/nbc-out/trans-women-retain-athletic-edge-after-year-hormone-therapy-study-n1252764>

Bannerman, Lucy. 2018, Sept. 8. 'Trans Goldsmiths Lecturer Natacha Kennedy Behind Smear Campaign Against Academics'. *The Times* and *Reddit*. <https://www.reddit.com/r/GGdiscussion/comments/9e3vzp/trans_goldsmiths_lecturer_natacha_kennedy_behind/>

Bartlett, Tom. 2019, March 19. 'Journal Issues Revised Version of Controversial Paper that Questioned Why Some Teens Identify as Trangender'. *The Chronicle of Higher Education*. <https://www.chronicle.com/article/journal-issues-revised-version-of-controversial-paper-that-questioned-why-some-teens-identify-as-transgender/>

Bartosch, Josephine. 2021, Apr. 3. 'America's Creation of the Transgender Child'. *PM, The Post Milennial*. <https://thepostmillennial.com/americas-creation-of-the-transgender-child>

Batty, David. 2004, July 29. 'Sex Changes Are Not Effective, Say Researchers'. *The Guardian*. <https://www.theguardian.com/society/2004/jul/30/health.mentalhealth>

BBC. 2019a, June 26. 'Martina Navratilova Explores Issues Faced by Trans Athletes in BBC Documentary'. <https://www.bbc.com/sport/48777660>

BBC. 2019b, Dec. 19. 'Maya Forstater: Woman Loses Tribunal over Transgender Tweets'. <https://www.bbc.com/news/uk-50858919>

Beale, Charlotte. 2016, Apr. 17. 'Feminists Mock Green Party Young Women's Group for Invite to "Non-men"'. *Independent*. <https://www.independent.co.uk/news/uk/feminists-mock-green-party-young-women-s-invite-non-men-a6987061.html>

Beauchamp, Zack. 2019, Apr. 23. 'Our Incel Problem'. *Vox*. <https://www.vox.com/the-highlight/2019/4/16/18287446/incel-definition-reddit>

Bell, Keira. 2021, Apr. 7. 'Keira Bell: My Story'. *Persuasion*. <https://www.persuasion.community/p/keira-bell-my-story>

Bilek, Jennifer. 2018a, Feb. 2. 'Who Are the Rich White Men Institutionalizing Transgender Ideology'. *The Federalist*. <https://thefederalist.com/2018/02/20/rich-white-men-institutionalizing-transgender-ideology/>

Bilek, Jennifer. 2018b, July 5. 'Transgenderism Just Big Business Dressed up in Pretend Civil Rights Clothes'. *The Federalist*. <https://thefederalist.com/2018/07/05/transgenderism-just-big-business-dressed-pretend-civil-rights-clothes/>

Bilek, Jennifer. 2020a, May 6. 'Deconstructing the "Good Transwomen"'. *Uncommon Ground*. <https://uncommongroundmedia.com/deconstructing-the-good-transwomen/>

Bilek, Jennifer. 2020b, Nov. 3. 'The Gender Identity Industry: What We're Up against'. *The 11th Hour Blog*. <https://www.the11thhourblog.com/post/the-gender-identity-industry-what-we-re-up-against>

Bilek, Jennifer. 2020c, Nov. 13. 'The Body Industry'. *Iai News*. <https://iai.tv/articles/the-body-industry-auid-168>

Bindel, Julie. 2018a, March 19. 'Why You Can't Rely on the News Media to Understand Trans Issues'. *UnHerd*. <https://unherd.com/2018/03/cant-rely-news-media-understand-trans-issues/>

Bindel, Julie. 2018b, Aug. 29. 'Why Are so Many LGBT Organizations Caving to Trans Activists and Losing Lesbians?' *Feminist Current*. <https://www.feministcurrent.com/2018/08/29/many-lgbt-organizations-caving-trans-activists-losing-lesbians/>

Bindel, Julie. 2019a. Interview with Max Robinson.

Bindel, Julie. 2019b, June 9. 'The Man in a Skirt Called Me a Nazi –Then Attacked'. *The Sunday Times*. <https://www.thetimes.co.uk/article/julie-bindel-the-man-in-a-skirt-called-me-a-nazi-then-attacked-8dfwk8jft>

Bindel, Julie. 2020, Sept. 9. 'If Offensive Inclusivity Dictates that Women Are Now "Womxn" – Then Men Must Be "Mxn"'. *The Telegraph*. <https://www.telegraph.co.uk/women/life/offensive-inclusivity-dictates-women-now-womxn-men-must-mxn/>

BJJ World. 2018, Oct. 21. 'MMA Fighter Breaks Skull of Her Female Opponent. Are We Becoming Too Careful Not to Offend Any Group of People?' *BJJ World*. <https://bjj-world.com/transgender-mma-fighter-fallon-fox-breaks-skull-of-her-female-opponent/>

Bowcott, Owen. 2019, Dec. 18. 'Judge Rules Against Researcher Who Lost Job Over Transgender Tweets'. *The Guardian*. <https://www.theguardian.com/society/2019/dec/18/judge-rules-against-charity-worker-who-lost-job-over-transgender-tweets>

Brennan, Christine. 2021, Feb. 1. 'Sports Leaders Seek to Protect Women's Sports While Accommodating Transgender Girls and Women'. *USA Today*.

<https://www.usatoday.com/story/sports/2021/02/01/group-protect-womens-sports-accommodate-transgender-athletes/4345854001/>

Brunskell-Evans, Heather. 2018, Dec. 5. 'The Ministry of Trans Truth'. *Spiked.* <https://www.spiked-online.com/2018/12/05/the-ministry-of-trans-truth/>

Brunskell-Evans, Heather. 2020. *Transgender Body Politics*. Mission Beach, Australia: Spinifex Press.

Burkett, Elinor. 2015, June 6. 'What Makes a Woman?' *The New York Times.* <https://www.nytimes.com/2015/06/07/opinion/sunday/what-makes-a-woman.html>

Campbell, Beatrix. 2015, Feb. 14. 'We Cannot Allow Censorship and Silencing of Individuals'. *The Observer/Guardian.* <https://www.theguardian.com/theobserver/2015/feb/14/letters-censorship>

Cantor, James. 2018. 'American Academy of Pediatrics and Trans-kids: Fact-checking Rafferty'. <http://www.jamescantor.org/uploads/6/2/9/3/62939641/cantor_fact-check_of_aap.pdf>

Carmichael, Polly, Gary Butler, Una Masic, Tim J. Cole, Bianca L. De Stavola, Sarah Davidson, Elin M. Skageberg, Sophie Khadr and Russell M. Viner. 2021, Feb. 2. 'Short-term Outcomes of Pubertal Suppression in a Selected Cohort of 12 to 15 Year Old Young People with Persistent Gender Dysphoria in the UK'. *PLOS One.* <https://journals.plos.org/plosone/article?id=10.1371/journal.pone.0243894>

Change.org. 2015. 'Drop the T'. Change.org. Petition. <https://www.change.org/p/human-rights-campaign-glaad-lambda-legal-the-advocate-out-magazine-huffpost-gay-voices-drop-the-t >

Change.org. 2018. 'Tell San Francisco Public Library to Remove Exhibit of Weapons Intended to Kill Feminists'. <https://www.change.org/p/tell-san-francisco-public-library-to-remove-exhibit-of-weapons-intended-to-kill-feminists>

Change.org. 2021. 'The University Must Support Professor Donna Hughes' Right to Free Speech'. <https://www.change.org/p/tell-the-univ-of-rhode-island-to-support-professor-donna-hughes-right-to-free-speech>

Clary, Sasha. 2018, May 10. 'Facial Feminization Surgery: What You Should Know'. *Healthline.* <https://www.healthline.com/health/transgender/facial-feminization-surgery#cost>

Cook, Michael. 2018, Nov. 7. 'Are the Wheels Falling off the Transgender Juggernaut?' *Mercatornet.* <https://mercatornet.com/are-the-wheels-falling-off-the-transgender-juggernaut/23777/>

Crashchaoscats. 2016. 'Women Transition'. Article Deactivated in 2020 by Tumbir.

Crashchaoscats. 2019, Jan. 29. 'Letting Go of Gender'. *Redress Alerts*. <https://redressalert.tumblr.com/post/182390280355/letting-go-of-gender>

Cummings, Mark. 2006. *The Mirror Makes No Sense*. Bloomington, Indiana: Authorhouse.

Dank, Meredith, P. Mitchell Downey, Cybele Kotonias, Debbie Mayer, Colleen Owens, Laura Pacifici and Lilly Yu. 2014, March 12. 'Estimating the Size and Structure of the Underground Commercial Sex Economy in Eight Major US Cities'. Urban Institute. <https://www.urban.org/research/publication/estimating-size-and-structure-underground-commercial-sex-economy-eight-major-us-cities>

Davidson, Gina. 2019, June 6. 'Feminist Speaker Julie Bindel "Attacked by a Trans Person" at Edinburgh University After Talk'. *The Scotsman*. <https://www.scotsman.com/news/scottish-news/feminist-speaker-julie-bindel-attacked-transgender-person-edinburgh-university-after-talk-545841>

Daz, Chrissie. 2013, March 26. 'Trans: The Phoniest Community in Britain'. *Spiked*. <https://www.spiked-online.com/2013/03/26/trans-the-phoniest-community-in-britain/>

de Beauvoir, Simone. 1949. *The Second Sex*. Translated by H.M. Parshley. Harmondsworth, Middlesex: Penguin Books.

Dhejne, Cecilia, Paul Lichtenstein, Marcus Boman, Anna L.V. Johansson, Niklas Långström and Mikael Landén. 2011, Feb 22. 'Long-term Follow-up of Transsexual Persons Undergoing Sex Reassignment Surgery: Cohort Study in Sweden'. *PLoS One* 6 (2). <http://www.ncbi.nlm.nih.gov/pubmed/21364939>

Ditum, Sarah. 2014, March 18. '"No Platform" Was Once Reserved for Violent Fascists. Now It's Being Used to Silence Debate'. *New Statesman*. <https://www.newstatesman.com/sarah-ditum/2014/03/when-did-no-platform-become-about-attacking-individuals-deemed-disagreeable>

Ditum, Sarah. 2018a, May 13. 'Genderquake Failed. Now for a Proper Trans Debate'. *The Guardian*. <https://www.theguardian.com/commentisfree/2018/may/13/genderquake-failed-now-for-a-proper-trans-debate>

Ditum, Sarah. 2018b, July 5. 'Trans Rights Should Not Come at the Cost of Women's Fragile Gains'. *The Economist*. <https://www.economist.com/open-future/2018/07/05/trans-rights-should-not-come-at-the-cost-of-womens-fragile-gains>

Dobkin, Alix. 1998, July 8. 'The Philadelphia Story, Part One'. *Minstrel Blood*.

Dobkin, Alix. 2000a, March. 'Are We an Endangered Species?' *Lesbian News*.

Dobkin, Alix. 2000b, December. 'Victim Politics: The Tyranny of Hurt Feelings'. *Lesbian News*. <https://www.feminist-reprise.org/docs/victimalix.html>

Dockray, Heather. 2019, March 15. 'The Trans Meme Community on Reddit is about So Much More than Jokes'. *Mashable*. <https://mashable.com/article/trans-meme-subreddits/>

Dodworth, Laura. 2020, Nov. 18. 'The Detransitioners'. *Medium*. <https://medium.com/@barereality/the-detransitioners-72a4e01a10f9>

Douglas, Angela. 1977, Aug-Sept. *Sister*. Referenced in 'A Gender Variance Who's Who. Angela Douglas (1943–2007), musician, activist'. <https://zagria.blogspot.com/2007/06/angela-douglas-1943-2007-musician.html#.YF_VFy2ZNXg>

Doyle, Michael. 2021, Aug. 2. 'Transgender Weightlifter Laurel Hubbard out of Competition after Being Unsuccessful on All Lift Attempts'. *ABC News*. <https://www.abc.net.au/news/2021-08-02/transgender-weightlifter-laurel-hubbard-out-of-competition/100344174>

Duberman, Martin. 2020. *Andrea Dworkin: The Feminist as Revolutionary*. New York: The New Press.

Dugan, Emily and Sam Griffiths. 2021, June 20. 'Tavistock Gender Clinic "Converting" Gay Children'. *The Sunday Times*. <https://www.thetimes.co.uk/article/tavistock-gender-clinic-converting-gay-children-tz8cs77p3>

Dumas, Daisy. 2015. 'The In-betweeners'. *The Sydney Morning Herald*. <https://www.smh.com.au/lifestyle/the-inbetweeners-20150730-ginojq.html>

Dworkin, Andrea. 1974. *Woman Hating*. New York: G.P. Putnam's Sons.

Dworkin, Andrea. 1979. *Pornography: Men Possessing Women*. New York: Perigee Books, E.F. Dutton & Co.

Dworkin, Andrea. 1983. *Right-Wing Women*. New York: Perigee Books,

Dworkin, Andrea. 1987. *Intercourse*. New York: The Free Press.

Editorial. 2018, Oct. 30. 'US Proposal for Defining Gender Has No Basis in Science; A Move to Classify People on the Basis of Anatomy or Genetics Should Be Abandoned'. *Nature*. <https://www.nature.com/articles/d41586-018-07238-8>

Elizabethwarren.com. 2020. Plans. 'Securing LGBTQ+Rights and Equality'. <https://elizabethwarren.com/plans/lgbtq-equality>

Eve. 2021. 'Grotesque'. In Kitty Robinson, ed. *You Told Me You Were Different: An Anthology of Harm*. Ugly Truths Publishing Collective.

Fair Play for Women. 2017, Nov. 9. 'Half of all Transgender Prisoners Are Sex Offenders or Dangerous Category A Inmates'. *Fair Play for Women*. <https://fairplayforwomen.com/transgender-prisoners/>

Fair Play for Women. 2018, Dec. 13. 'Open Letter to the International Olympic Committee by Ana Paula Henkel'. *Fair Play for Women*. <https://fairplayforwomen.com/ana_paula_henkel/>

Fake cisgirl. n.d. *Radtransfem blog, Tumbir.* <https://radtransfem.tumblr.com/post/69255599985/fakecisgirl-biyuti-realsubtle>

Farr, Tom. 2019, June 7. 'Male Silence and Male Violence: A Marriage of Complicity'. *Medium.* <https://medium.com/@tom_farr/male-silence-and-male-violence-a-marriage-of-complicity-ad669b87c800>

Fazackerley, Anna. 2018, Oct. 30. 'UK Universities Struggle to Deal with "Toxic" Trans Rights Row'. *The Guardian.* <https://www.theguardian.com/education/2018/oct/30/uk-universities-struggle-to-deal-with-toxic-trans-rights-row>

Fisher, Dan. 2019, June 7. 'Open Letter to the British Media: You Are Complicit in Male Violence Against Feminists'. *Uncommon Ground.* <https://uncommongroundmedia.com/british-media-complicit-male-violence/>

Fitzgerald, Erin, Sarah Elspeth, Darby Hickey, with Cherno Biko, 2015, December. 'Meaningful Work: Transgender Experience in the Sex Trade'. *Transgender National Center for Transgender Equality.* <https://www.transequality.org/sites/default/files/Meaningful Experiences in the Sex Trade." %20Work-Full%20Report_FINAL_3.pdf>

Fleming, Pippa. 2018, July 3. 'The Gender-identity Movement Undermines Lesbians'. *The Economist.* <https://www.economist.com/open-future/2018/07/03/the-gender-identity-movement-undermines-lesbians>

Fox, Angus. 2021, Apr. 12. 'When Sons Become Daughters, Part III: Parents of Transitioning Boys Speak Out on Their Own Suffering'. *Quillette.* <https://quillette.com/2021/04/12/when-sons-become-daughters-part-iii-parents-of-transitioning-boys-speak-out-on-their-own-suffering/>

Garelick, Rhoda. 2015, June 3. 'The Price of Caitlyn Jenner's Heroism'. *The New York Times.* <https://www.nytimes.com/2015/06/03/opinion/the-price-of-jenners-heroism.html>

Gender Apostates. n.d. 'Narcissistic Rage'. *Gender Apostates.* <http://genderapostates.com/transwomen-and-narcissistic-rage/>

Gerlich, Renee. 2018, Oct. 30. 'New Zealand is Greenlighting Gender Identity Ideology and Policy without Considering the Consequences'. *Feminist Current.* <https://www.feministcurrent.com/2018/10/30/new-zealand-green-lighting-gender-identity-ideology-policy-without-considering-consequences/>

Gessen, Masha. 2021, March 21. 'The Movement to Exclude Trans Girls From Sports'. *The New Yorker.* <https://www.newyorker.com/news/our-columnists/the-movement-to-exclude-trans-girls-from-sports>

Gluck, Genevieve. 2020, Nov. 29. 'Why Isn't Anyone Talking About the Influence of Porn on the Trans Trend?' *Feminist Current.* <https://www.

feministcurrent.com/2020/11/29/why-isnt-anyone-talking-about-the-influence-of-porn-on-the-trans-trend/>

Gold, Ronald. 2009, Dec. 13. '"No" to the Notion of Transgender'. *Dyneslines.* <http://dyneslines.blogspot.com/2009/12/ordeal-of-ronald-gold.html>

Goldberg, Michelle. 2015, Dec. 9. 'The Trans Women Who Say That Trans Women Aren't Women'. *Slate.* <https://slate.com/human-interest/2015/12/gender-critical-trans-women-the-apostates-of-the-trans-rights-movement.html>

Gragg, Frances, Ian Petta, Hardee Bernstein, Karla Eisen and Liz Quinn. 2007, Apr. 18. *New York Prevalence Study of Commercially Sexually Exploited Children: Final Report.* Rensselaer, New York: New York State Office of Children and Family Services. <http://www.ocfs.state.ny.us/main/reports/csec-2007.pdf>

Greenberg, Steve. 1993, July 13. 'The Next Wave'. *The Advocate.*

Greep, Monica. 2021, Jan. 8. 'Philosophy Professor Vows Not to Be Silenced …' *Daily Mail.* <https://www.dailymail.co.uk/femail/article-9123083/Academics-slam-government-awarding-OBE-anti-trans-professor.html>

Greer, Germaine. 2000. *The Whole Woman.* New York: Random House.

Grey, Alex. 2018, Jan. 10. 'Academics Say Research Is Being Hindered by Universities' Fear of Online Backlash'. Association of Internet Research Specialists. <https://aofirs.org/articles/academics-say-research-is-being-hindered-by-universities-fear-of-online-backlash>

Hamby, Mark. 2017, Apr. 15. 'Johns Hopkins Hospital Opens Center for Transgender Health'. *American Bar Association.* <https://www.americanbar.org/groups/litigation/committees/lgbt-law-litigator/practice/2017/johns-hopkins-hospital-opens-center-for-trangender-health/>

Harris, Tamara Winfrey. 2015, June 16. 'Black Like Who? Rachel Dolezal's Harmful Masquerade'. *The New York Times.* <https://www.nytimes.com/2015/06/16/opinion/rachel-dolezals-harmful-masquerade.html>

Harrison, Kristina. 2018, July 3. 'A System of Gender Self-identification Would Put Women at Risk'. *The Economist.* <https://www.economist.com/open-future/2018/07/03/a-system-of-gender-self-identification-would-put-women-at-risk>

Hawthorne, Susan. 2020. *Vortex: The Crisis of Patriarchy.* Mission Beach, Australia: Spinifex Press.

Hawthorne, Susan. 2021, June 23. 'The Trans Scam Is Sweeping over Australia and Australian Women Are Not Having It'. *4W Newsletter.* <https://4w.pub/transcam-and-australia>

Hay, Carol. 2019, Apr. 1. 'Who Counts as a Woman'. *The New York Times.* <https://www.nytimes.com/2019/04/01/opinion/trans-women-feminism.html>

Hayton, Debbie. 2018, July 3. 'Gender Identity Needs to Be Based on Objective Evidence Rather than Feelings'. *The Economist.* <https://www.economist.com/open-future/2018/07/03/gender-identity-needs-to-be-based-on-objective-evidence-rather-than-feelings>

Hedges, Chris. 2015, March 8. 'The Whoredom of the Left'. *Truthdig.* <https://www.truthdig.com/articles/the-whoredom-of-the-left/>

Hedges, Chris. 2017, July 3. 'The Battle Over What It Means to Be Female'. *Truthdig.* <https://www.truthdig.com/articles/the-battle-over-what-it-means-to-be-female/>

Henkel, Ana Paula. 2018. 'Open Letter to the International Olympic Committee by Ana Paula Henkel'. *Fair Play for Women.* <https://fairplayforwomen.com/ana_paula_henkel/>

Herzog, Katie. 2017, June 28. 'The Detransitioners: They Were Transgender until They Weren't'. *The Stranger.* <https://www.thestranger.com/features/2017/06/28/25252342/the-detransitioners-they-were-transgender-until-they-werent>

Herzog, Katie. 2021, July 27. 'Med Schools Are Now Denying Biological Sex'. *Common Sense with Bari Weiss.* <https://bariweiss.substack.com/p/med-schools-are-now-denying-biological sex>

Hewitt, Rachel. 2018, July 3. Twitter Thread. <https://twitter.com/drrachelhewitt/status/1015270919881797633?lang=en>

Hill, Amelia. 2019, March 30. 'Mother Drops Action Against Woman Who Said She "Mutilated" Trans Daughter. *The Guardian.* <https://www.theguardian.com/society/2019/mar/20/catholic-journalist-investigated-by-police-after-misgendering-trans-woman>

Hilton Emma, Pam Thompson, Colin Wright and David Curtis. 2021, Jan 15. 'The Reality of Sex'. Letter to the Editor. *Irish Journal of Medical Science.* <https://link.springer.com/article/10.1007/s11845-020-02464-4>

History.com. 2009, Nov. 16. Updated 2020, June 22. 'Title IX Enacted'. *History.* <https://www.history.com/this-day-in-history/title-ix-enacted>

Holston-Zannell, LaLa. 2020, June 10. 'Sex Work is Real Work, and It's Time to Treat It That Way'. *ACLU Trans Justice Campaign.* <https://www.aclu.org/news/lgbt-rights/sex-work-is-real-work-and-its-time-to-treat-it-that-way/>

Horvath, Hacsi. 2018, December 19. 'The Theatre of the Body: A Detransitioned Epidemiologist Examines Suicidality, Affirmation, and Transgender Identity'. *4W Newsletter.* <https://4thwavenow.com/2018/12/19/the-

theatre-of-the-body-a-detransitioned-epidemiologist-examines-suicidality-affirmation-and-transgender-identity/>

Hughes, Donna M. 2021, Feb 28. 'Fantasy Worlds on the Political Right and Left: Qanon and Trans-Sex Beliefs'. Featured Posts, *4W Newsletter*. <https://4w.pub/fantasy-worlds-on-the-political-right-and-left-qanon-and-trans-sex-beliefs-2/>

Hughes, Donna M. 2021, Apr. 28. Personal Communication.

Human Rights Campaign. 2020a. 'Marking the Deadliest Year on Record, HRC Releases Report on Violence Against Transgender and Gender Non-Conforming People'. <https://www.hrc.org/press-releases/marking-the-deadliest-year-on-record-hrc-releases-report-on-violence-against-transgender-and-gender-non-conforming-people>

Human Rights Campaign. 2020b. 'Affirming Gender in Elementary School. Social Transitioning'. *Welcoming Schools*. <www.welcomingschools.org>

Internet Society. 2017, March 24. 'Internet Society Perspectives on Internet Content Blocking: An Overview'. <https://www.internetsociety.org/resources/doc/2017/internet-content-blocking/>

James, Sandy E., Jody L. Herman, Susan Rankin, Mara Keisling, Lisa Mottet and Ma'ayan Anafi. 2016. 'The Report of the 2015 U.S. Transgender Survey'. *National Center for Transgender Equality*, Washington, D.C. <https://transequality.org/sites/default/files/docs/usts/USTS-Full-Report-Dec17.pdf>

Jeffreys, Sheila. 2014. *Gender Hurts: A Feminist Analysis of the Politics of Transgenderism*. London: Routledge.

Jeffreys, Sheila. 2020. *Trigger Warning: My Lesbian Feminist Life*. Mission Beach, Australia: Spinifex Press.

Jeffreys, Sheila. 2021, Feb. 18. Personal Communication.

Jenefsky, Cindy with Ann Russo. 1998. *Without Apology: Andrea Dworkin's Art and Politics*. Boulder, Colorado: Westview Press.

Jensen, Robert. 2016, July 19. 'Is the Ideology of the Transgender Movement Open to Debate?' *Voice Male*. <https://voicemalemagazine.org/is-the-ideology-of-the-transgender-movement-open-to-debate/>

Jensen, Robert. 2017. *The End of Patriarchy: Radical Feminism for Men*. North Melbourne, Australia: Spinifex Press.

JMW. n.d. *Malicious Communications Act*. JMW Solicitors. <https://www.jmw.co.uk/services-for-business/business-crime/malicious-communications-act-offences>

Joyce, Helen. 2020, Jan. 30. 'Speaking up for Female Eunuchs'. *Standpoint*. <https://standpointmag.co.uk/speaking-up-for-female-eunuchs/>

Justice, Tristan. 2021, March 10. 'Poll: Letting Transgender Athletes Compete in Women's Sports Is an Unpopular, Fringe Viewpoint'. *The Federalist.* <https://thefederalist.com/2021/03/10/poll-letting-transgender-athletes-compete-in-womens-sports-is-an-unpopular-fringe-viewpoint/>

Kay, Jonathan. 2021, March 18. 'The Campaign of Lies against Journalist Jesse Singal –And Why It Matters'. *Quillette.* <https://quillette.com/2021/03/18/the-campaign-of-lies-against-journalist-jesse-singal-and-why-it-matters/>

Kearns, Madeleine. 2019a, March 30. 'The "Woke" Police'. *Yahoo News.* <https://news.yahoo.com/woke-police-192735383.html>

Kearns, Madeleine. 2019b, Aug. 28. 'Women-Only Rape-Shelter Defunded, Then Vandalized'. *National Review.* <https://www.nationalreview.com/2019/08/women-only-rape-relief-shelter-defunded-then-vandalized/>

Keith, Lierre and Derrick Jensen. 2013, June 21. 'The Emperor's New Penis'. *Counterpunch.* <https://www.counterpunch.org/2013/06/21/55123/>

Kersten, Katherine. 2019, June 20. 'Pediatric Gender Clinics: We May Look Back and Ask 'What Were We Thinking'''. Opinion Exchange. *Star Tribune.* <https://www.startribune.com/pediatric-gender-clinics-we-may-look-back-and-ask-what-were-we-thinking/511596442/>

Kirkup, James. 2019a, Feb. 5. 'Why Are the Police Stopping a 74-year-old Tweeting about Transgenderism?' *The Spectator.* <https://www.spectator.co.uk/article/why-are-the-police-stopping-a-74-year-old-tweeting-about-transgenderism-5-february-2019>

Kirkup, James. 2019b, Dec. 2. 'The Document that Reveals the Remarkable Tactics of Trans Lobbyists'. *The Spectator.* <https://www.spectator.co.uk/article/the-document-that-reveals-the-remarkable-tactics-of-trans-lobbyists>

Kitchener, Caroline. 2019, June 27. 'Why It Matters that Julián Castro Used the Term Reproductive Justice'. *The Lily.* <https://www.thelily.com/why-it-matters-that-julian-castro-used-the-term-reproductive-justice/>

Knox, Liam. 2019, Dec. 19. 'Media's "Detransition" Narrative Is Fueling Misconceptions, Trans Advocates Say'. <https://www.nbcnews.com/feature/nbc-out/media-s-detransition-narrative-fueling-misconceptions-trans-advocates-say-n1102686>

Kuhr, Elizabeth. 2020, Sept. 8. 'High Schools Must Teach LGBTQ-Inclusive Sex Education in England'. *NBC Out News.* <https://www.nbcnews.com/feature/nbc-out/high-schools-must-teach-lgbtq-inclusive-sex-education-england-n1239514>

Labine, Jeff. 2020, June 9. 'U of A Professor Says She Was Dismissed over Views that Biological Sex Trumps Transgender Identity for Policy Decisions'. *Edmonton Journal.* <https://edmontonjournal.com/news/local-news/u-

of-a-professor-says-she-was-dismissed-over-views-that-biological-sex-trumps-transgender-identity-for-policy-decisions>

Lane, Bernard. 2019a, Oct. 14. 'Regretful Transitioners on Rise'. *The Australian.* <https://www.theaustralian.com.au/nation/regretful-detransitioners-on-rise/news-story/627a9cc0f42d700be7dfab435c0522a9>

Lane, Bernard. 2019b, Nov. 2. 'Reason Lost to Suicide in Trans Debate'. *The Australian.* <https://www.theaustralian.com.au/inquirer/reason-lost-to-suicide-in-trans-debate/news-story/af31e3357a4ec08f9a3e91227b3424bf>

Lavender, Jane. 2019. 'Transgender Women "Should be Entitled to Womb Transplants" So They Can Have a Baby'. *Daily Mirror.* <https://www.mirror.co.uk/news/uk-news/transgender-women-should-entitled-womb-13972102>

Lewis, Helen. 2018, Apr. 20. 'The Madness of Our Gender Debate, Where Feminists Defend Slapping a 60-year-old Woman'. *New Statesman America.* <https://www.newstatesman.com/politics/feminism/2018/04/madness-our-gender-debate-where-feminists-defend-slapping-60-year-old>

Littman, Lisa. 2018, Aug. 16. 'Parent Reports of Adolescents and Young Adults Perceived to Show Signs of a Rapid Onset of Gender Dysphoria'. *PLOS One.* <https://journals.plos.org/plosone/article?id=10.1371/journal.pone.0202330>

Litzcke, Karin. 2021, May 19. 'Gender Activists Co-Opted British Columbia's Courts: Meet the Woman Who Stood up to Them'. *Quillette.* <https://quillette.com/2021/05/19/gender-activists-co-opted-british-columbias-courts-meet-the-woman-who-stood-up-to-them/>

Longman, Jeré. 2020, Sept. 8. 'Track's Caster Semenya Loses Appeal to Defend 800-Meter Title'. *The New York Times.* <https://www.nytimes.com/2020/09/08/sports/olympics/caster-semenya-court-ruling.html>

Lukianoff, Greg and Jonathan Haidt. 2015, Sept. 'The Coddling of the American Mind'. *The Atlantic.* <https://www.theatlantic.com/magazine/archive/2015/09/the-coddling-of-the-american-mind/399356/>

MacKinnon, Catharine A. 1987. *Feminism Unmodified: Discourses on Life and Law.* Cambridge MA: Harvard University Press.

Manning, Sanchez. 2021, Jan. 9. '"A Live Experiment on Children": The Shocking Physicians' Testimony that Led a High Court Judge to Ban NHS's Tavistock Clinic from Giving Puberty Blocking Drugs to Youngsters as Young as 10 Who Want to Change Sex. *Daily Mail.* <https://www.dailymail.co.uk/news/article-9130157/The-physicians-testimony-led-High-Court-judge-ban-child-puberty-blocker-drugs.html>

Marchiano, Lisa. 2017, Oct. 6. 'Misunderstanding a New Kind of Gender Dysphoria'. *Quillette*. <https://quillette.com/2017/10/06/misunderstanding-new-kind-of-gender-dysphoria/>

Marchiano, Lisa. 2020, Jan. 2. 'The Ranks of Gender Detransitioners Are Growing. We Need to Understand Why'. *Quillette*. <https://quillette.com/2020/01/02/the-ranks-of-gender-detransitioners-are-growing-we-need-to-understand-why/>

Market Watch. 2021, June 21. 'Sex Reassignment Surgery Market Analysis and Forecast by Key Players, Share and Trend to 2026'. Press Release. <https://www.marketwatch.com/press-release/sex-reassignment-surgery-market-analysis-and-forecast-by-key-players-share-and-trend-to-2026-2021-06-21>

Marr, Rhuaridh. 2021, May 3. 'Caitlin Jenner Says Trans Girls Should Be Blocked from Girls' Sports'. *MetroWeekly*. <https://www.metroweekly.com/2021/05/caitlyn-jenner-says-trans-girls-should-be-blocked-from-girls-sports/>

Mazzoni Center. 2017. 'Detransitioning Issues'. *Wikipedia*. <https://en.wikipedia.org/wiki/Mazzoni_Center>

Miller, Leila. 2021, Apr. 5. 'California Prisons Grapple with Hundreds of Transgender Inmates Requesting New Housing'. *Los Angeles Times*. <https://www.latimes.com/california/story/2021-04-05/california-prisons-consider-gender-identity-housing-requests>

Mitchell, Charlotte and Chris Jewers. 2021, May 7. 'Fury over Decision to Let Transsexual Enter Tokyo Olympics: New Zealand's Female Weightlifters Reveal They Are "Told to Be Quiet" When They Complain that a Woman "Will Lose Out"'. *Daily Mail*. <https://www.dailymail.co.uk/news/article-9553101/Fury-decision-let-transsexual-enter-Tokyo-Olympics.html>

Molloy, Parker. 2018, Nov. 29. 'How Twitter's Ban on "Deadnaming" Promotes Free Speech'. *The New York Times*. <https://www.nytimes.com/2018/11/29/opinion/twitter-deadnaming-ban-free-speech.html>

Moore, Suzanne. 2020, Aug. 29. 'How Progressive Misogyny Works'. *The Spectator*. <https://www.spectator.co.uk/article/how-progressive-misogyny-works>

Morris, Steven. 2015, Nov. 18. 'Germaine Greer Gives University Lecture despite Campaign to Silence Her'. *The Guardian*. <https://www.theguardian.com/books/2015/nov/18/transgender-activists-protest-germaine-greer-lecture-cardiff-university>

Murphy, Meghan. 2017, Feb. 7. 'Vancouver Women's Library Opens amid Anti-Feminist Backlash'. *Feminist Current*. <https://www.feministcurrent.

com/2017/02/07/vancouver-womens-library-opens-amid-anti-feminist-backlash/>

Murphy, Simon and Libby Brooks. 2020, Sept. 22. 'UK Government Drops Gender Self-Identification Plan for Trans People'. *The Guardian.* <https://www.theguardian.com/society/2020/sep/22/uk-government-drops-gender-self-identification-plan-for-trans-people>

Muzima, Jeanette. 1978, Summer/Fall. 'Thoughts on Transsexualism'. *The Second Wave.* Vol. V, No. 2.

N.A. 2015. Feb.14. 'We Cannot Allow Censorship and Silencing of Individuals'. *The Guardian.* <https://www.theguardian.com/theobserver/2015/feb/14/letters-censorship>

N.A. 2019, May 22. 'Twitter-ban Feminist Defends Transgender Views ahead of Holyrood Meeting'. *BBC News.* <https://www.bbc.com/news/uk-scotland-48366184>

National Action Alliance for Suicide Prevention. n.d. 'Public Messaging'. <https://theactionalliance.org/messaging/public-messaging>

National Center for Transgender Equality. 2015. *National Transgender Survey.* <https://www.ustranssurvey.org>

Newgent, Scott. 2020, Oct. 6. 'Forget What Gender Activists Tell You. Here's What Medical Transition Looks Like'. *Quillette.* <https://quillette.com/2020/10/06/forget-what-gender-activists-tell-you-heres-what-medical-transition-looks-like/>

New York City Commission on Human Rights. 2002.'Legal Enforcement Guidance on Discrimination on the Basis of Gender Identity or Expression': Local Law No. 3 (2002); N.Y.C. Admin. Code § 8-102(23). <https://www1.nyc.gov/site/cchr/law/legal-guidances-gender-identity-expression.page>

Noanodyne. 2013, Aug. 4. 'There is No T in Lesbian'. *Liberation Collective.* <https://liberationcollective.wordpress.com/2013/08/04/there-is-no-t-in-lesbian/>

Norma, Caroline. 2015, Oct. 28. 'Transgenderism: The Latest Anti-Feminist Wedge of the Left'. *ABC Religion and Ethics.* <https://www.abc.net.au/religion/transgenderism-the-latest-anti-feminist-wedge-of-the-left/10097710>

NYAAF. 'About – Mission Statement.' <https://www.nyaaf.org/about/>

Odling, George. 2020, Dec. 11. 'Mother Who Called Trans Woman "He" on Twitter Is CLEARED of Wrongdoing after Appealing Against Conviction'. *Daily Mail.* <https://www.dailymail.co.uk/news/article-9041725/Mum-called-trans-woman-Twitter-CLEARED-wrongdoing.html>

Olson-Kennedy, Johanna, Jonathan Warus, Vivian Okonta, Marvin Belzer and Leslie F. Clark. 2018a, May. 'Chest Reconstruction and Chest

Dysphoria in Transmasculine Minors and Young Adults Comparisons of Nonsurgical and Postsurgical Cohorts'. *JAMA Pediatrics*. Vol. 172, No. 5, pp. 431–436. <https://jamanetwork.com/journals/jamapediatrics/fullarticle/2674039?resultClick=1>

Olson-Kennedy, Johanna. 2018b, Nov. 5. 'Dr. Johanna Olson-Kennedy Explains why Mastectomies for Healthy Teen Girls is no Big Deal'. *YouTube*. <https://www.youtube.com/watch?v=5Y6espcXPJk>

Olson-Kennedy, Johanna. 2019. July 8. 'The Impact of Early Medical Treatment in Transgender Youth. Protocol for the Longitudinal, Observational Trans Youth Care Study'. *Journal Research Protocols (JMIR)*. <https://docs.wixstatic.com/ugd/3f4f51_a929d049f7fb46c7a72c4c86ba43869a.pdf>

Ontario Human Rights Commission. 2014. 'Questions and Answers About Gender Identity and Pronouns'. <http://www.ohrc.on.ca/en/questions-and-answers-about-gender-identity-and-pronouns>

Onyenucheya, Adaku. 2020. 'UK Doctors Resigning over Transgender Lunacy Targeting Children'. *The Guardian* Features (Nigeria). <https://guardian.ng/features/health/uk-doctors-resigning-over-transgender-lunacy-targeting-children/>

Orwell, George. 1949. *1984*. New York: Harcourt, Brace and Company.

Pajer, Nicole. 2019, May 1. 'There are New Options in Trans Underwear'. *The New York Times*. <https://www.nytimes.com/2019/05/01/fashion/transgender-underwear.html>

Peitzmeier, Sarah, Ivy Gardner, Jamie Weinand, Alexandra Corbet and Kimberlynn Acevedo. 2017. *Culture, Health & Sexuality*, 19:1, pp. 64–75. <https://www.tandfonline.com/doi/abs/10.1080/13691058.2016.1191675?journalCode=tchs20> Full text also available at <https://queerdoc.com/wp-content/uploads/2018/05/Binding-Health-Project-Results.pdf>

Peter, Jeremy W. 2021, May 3. 'Transgender Girls in Sports: G.O.P. Pushes New Front in Culture War'. *The New York Times*. <https://www.nytimes.com/2021/03/29/us/politics/transgender-girls-sports.html>

Platine, Cathryn. 2007. 'Was Janice Raymond Right? Why Trans People Are Often Their Own Worst Enemies'. <http://gallae.com/cathy/essay22.html>

Pollock, Nicolas. 2018, June 18. 'I Wanted to Take My Body off: Detransitioned'. *The Atlantic*. <https://www.theatlantic.com/video/index/562988/detransitioned-film/>

Polumbo, Brad. 2019, Oct. 26. 'It's Time for "LGB" and "T" to Go Their Separate Ways'. *Quillette*. <https://quillette.com/2019/10/26/its-time-for-lgb-and-t-to-go-their-separate-ways/>

Post Trans. n. d. *Detransition Stories*. <https://post-trans.com/Detransition-English>

Public Policy Institute of California (PPIC). 2019, July 19. 'California's Prison Population'. <https://www.ppic.org/publication/californias-prison-population/>

Radical Girlsss Young Women Movement of the European Network of Migrant Women. 2020, June 12. 'Radical Girlsss Statement in Support of JK Rowling: Migrant Perspectives'. *Medium*. <https://medium.com/@radicalgirlsss/radical-girlsss-statement-in-support-of-jk-rowling-f5e5a5ac9922>

Rankin, Laura. 2013, July 31. 'Not Everyone Who Has an Abortion Is a Woman — How to Frame the Abortion Rights Issue'. *Truthout*. <https://truthout.org/articles/not-everyone-who-has-an-abortion-is-a-woman-how-to-frame-the-abortion-rights-issue/>

Raymond, Janice G. 1977. 'Transsexualism: The Ultimate Homage to Sex-Role Power'. *Chrysalis*. No. 3, pp. 11–23.

Raymond, Janice G. 1979/1994. *The Transsexual Empire: The Making of the She-Male*. Boston: Beacon Press; New York: Teachers College Press. Available at janiceraymond.com

Raymond, Janice G. 2013, Sept. 14. 'Letter to the Editor'. *Klassekampen*. (A Norwegian-language paper.)

Raymond, Janice G. 2014. 'Fictions and Facts about The Transsexual Empire'. <https://janiceraymond.com/fictions-and-facts-about-the-transsexual-empire/>

Raymond, Janice G. 2015. Letter to the Intelligence Report. Unpublished.

Rippon, Gina. 2019. *Gender and Our Brains: How New Neuroscience Explodes the Myths of the Male and Female Minds*. New York: Random House.

Rivers, Jan. 2021, Feb. 15. Personal Communication.

Rivers, Jan and Jill Abigail. 2020, Dec. 2. 'Another Unfortunate Experiment? New Zealand's Transgender Health Policy and Its Impact on Children'. *Public Good*. <https://www.publicgood.org.nz/2020/12/02/another-unfortunate-experiment/>

Robinson, Kitty. 2019, March 30. 'Re Twitter Terms of Service'. *Medium*. <https://medium.com/@kittyit/re-twitter-terms-of-service-c681356d0809>

Robinson, Kitty, ed. 2021. *You Told Me You Were Different: An Anthology of Harm*. Ugly Truths Publishing Collective.

Robinson, Max. 2020. Personal Communication.

Robinson, Max. 2021. *Detransition: Beyond Before and After*. Mission Beach, Australia: Spinifex Press.

Romboy, Dennis. 2021, Feb. 24. 'Does Allowing Transgender Women to Compete Spell the End to Women's Sports?'. *Deseret News*. <https://www.

deseret.com/utah/2021/2/24/22299922/allowing-transgender-women-compete-end-womens-sports-mike-lee>

Rosario Sanchez, Raquel. 2019, Apr. 2. Interviewing and Translating Maira and Ana (FRIA). 'Attacks on Radical Feminists Reach Argentina'. *Feminist Current.* <https://www.feministcurrent.com/2019/04/02/interview-radical-feminism-and-trans-activism-clash-violently-in-argentina/>

Rosario Sanchez, Raquel. 2020, May 20. 'Bullying and Harassment Permitted by Bristol University'. *Crowd Justice.* <https://www.crowdjustice.com/case/bullying-and-harassment-permit-bristol-university/>

Rosario Sanchez, Raquel. 2021. 'Update on Bullying and Harassment Permitted by Bristol University'. *Crowd Justice.* <http://r.mail.crowd justice.co.uk/mk/mr/7ogOG8NVz_zZ66U2qavn426XbWttbxlDSI USZxY4toYgAHHYFQtDpwwxzSZeuol7tZVhXSu1DZESovxIXtni LqDa_qCv4-2PEifWWvSYnjiy76Lsx4BQYA>

Sadeghi, McKenzie. 2020b, Feb. 2. 'Fact Check: Posts Criticizing Biden Order on Gender Discrimination Lack Context'. *USA Today.* <https://www.usatoday.com/story/news/factcheck/2021/02/02/fact-check-biden-executive-order-discrimination-transgender-women-sports/6686171002/>

Sampson, Amani, Laura L. Kimberly, Kara N. Goldman, David L. Keefe and Gwendolyn P. Quinn. 2019. 'Uterus Transplantation in Women Who Are Genetically XY'. Vol. 45, pp. 687–689. *British Medical Journal* (BMJ). <https://jme.bmj.com/content/45/10/687>

San Francisco Public Library. 2018, May 24. 'The Terf Exhibit'. San Francisco. <https://wlrnmedia.wordpress.com/2018/05/24/wlrn-participates-in-terf-art-exhibit-called-by-anonymous-gender-critical-activists>

SEGM. Society for Evidence Based Gender Medicine. 2020. 'The Dutch Protocol: the Basis of the Gender-Affirmative Treatment'. <https://segm.org>

SEGM. Society for Evidence Based Gender Medicine. 2021, May 5. 'Sweden's Karolinska Ends All Use of Puberty Blockers and Cross-Sex Hormones for Minors outside of Clinical Studies'. <https://segm.org/Sweden_ends_use_of_Dutch_protocol>

Selin Davis, Lisa. 2017, Apr. 18. 'My Daughter Is Not Transgender. She's a Tomboy'. *The New York Times.* <https://www.nytimes.com/2017/04/18/opinion/my-daughter-is-not-transgender-shes-a-tomboy.html>

Shaw, Diana. 2020, Feb. 15. 'Women Interrogated by Police, One Thrown in Jail, for Disbelief in Gender Identity'. In *Women Are Human.* <https://www.womenarehuman.com/women-interrogated-by-police-one-thrown-in-jail-for-disbelief-in-gender-identity-theory/>

Shrier, Abigail. 2020. *Irreversible Damage: The Transgender Craze Seducing Our Daughters*. Washington DC: Regnery Publishing.

Shuster, Allison. 2020, July 28. 'Speaker: Most Parents Have No Idea Their Kids' Schools Are Pushing Insane Transgender Ideology'. *The Federalist*. <https://thefederalist.com/2020/07/28/speaker-most-parents-have-no-idea-their-kids-schools-are-pushing-insane-transgender-ideology/>

Shute 2017. Findings by Shute quoted in Wikpedia Article.'Detransition, Occurrence'. <https://en.wikipedia.org/wiki/Detransition>

Siddique, Haroon. 2021a, June 5. 'Stonewall Is at the Centre of a Toxic Debate on Trans Rights and Gender Identity'. *The Guardian*. <https://www.theguardian.com/society/2021/jun/05/stonewall-trans-debate-toxic-gender-identity>

Siddique, Haroon. 2021b, June 10. 'Gender-critical Views Are a Protected Belief, Appeal Tribunal Rules'. *The Guardian*. <https://www.theguardian.com/law/2021/jun/10/gender-critical-views-protected-belief-appeal-tribunal-rules-maya-forstater>

Singal, Jesse. 2016, July 25. 'What's Missing from the Conversation about Transgender Kids'. *New York Magazine*. <https://www.thecut.com/2016/07/whats-missing-from-the-conversation-about-transgender-kids.html>

Sinnott, Christopher. 2019, Apr. 8. 'Oxford Professor Criticises Use of Gender Hormones as "Unregulated Live Experiment on Children"'. *Cherwell News*. <https://cherwell.org/2019/04/08/oxford-professor-criticises-use-of-gender-hormones-as-unregulated-live-experiment-on-children/>

Slater, Tom. 2020, Jan. 24. 'The Trans-Sceptic Academic Who Now Needs Bodyguards for Protection'. *The Spectator*. <https://www.spectator.co.uk/article/the-trans-sceptic-academic-who-now-needs-bodyguards-for-protection>

Spangenberg, Mia. 2001. 'Prostituted Youth in New York City: An Overview'. ECPAT-USA. <https://d1qkyo3pi1c9bx.cloudfront.net/00028B1B-B0DB-4FCD-A991-219527535DAB/7922f23e-a266-44f4-aae4-0f525f3dbe7d.pdf>

Stanescu, Bianca. 2020, June 19. 'Transgender Athletes Don't Belong in Girls' Sports. Let My Daughter Compete Fairly'. *USA Today*. <https://www.usatoday.com/story/opinion/2020/06/19/transgender-athletes-robbing-girls-chance-win-sports-column/4856486002/>

Starr, Michelle. 2017, Oct. 18. 'Blood Transfusions from Some Women Can Be More Dangerous for Men, According to a New Study'. *Business Insider*. <https://www.businessinsider.com/blood-transfusions-women-dangerous-for-men-2017-10>

Stoltenberg, John. 2020, Apr. 8. 'Andrea Dworkin Was a Trans Ally'. *Boston Review.* <http://bostonreview.net/gender-sexuality/john-stoltenberg-andrea-dworkin-was-trans-ally>

Stratford, Brandon. 2019, June 26. 'The Majority of Schools in 15 States and DC Offer LGBTQ-inclusive Sex-ed Curricula'. *Child Trends.* <https://www.childtrends.org/blog/the-majority-of-schools-in-15-states-and-dc-offer-lgbtq-inclusive-sex-ed-curricula>

Strauss, Penelope, Ashleigh Lin, Sam Winter, Angus Cook, Vanessa Watson and Dani Wright Toussaint. 2017. 'Trans Pathways: The Mental Health Experiences and Care Pathways of Trans Young People'. Summary of Results. Telethon Kids Institute, Perth, Australia. <https://www.telethonkids.org.au/projects/trans-pathways/>

Suerth, Jennifer. 2020, May 31. 'What is Antifa'. *CNN News*, <https://www.wxii12.com/article/what-is-antifa-2020/32723769#>

Sullivan, Andrew. 2021, Apr. 9. 'A Truce Proposal in the Trans Wars'. *The Weekly Dish.* <https://andrewsullivan.substack.com/p/a-truce-proposal-in-the-trans-wars-c49>

Talk. 2018. 'Sussex Students Union Defames Dr. Kathleen Stock'. *Mumsnet.* <https://www.mumsnet.com/Talk/womens_rights/3301937-Sussex-Students-Union-defames-Dr-Kathleen-Stock-Title-Edited-by-MNHQ>

TaylanUB. 2017, Dec. 16. 'Documenting Bias in Transgender-related Articles'. *Wikipedia.* <https://en.wikipedia.org/w/index.php?title=User:Taylan UB&oldid=815735606>

Terisi, Dick and Kathleen McAuliffe. 1985. "Male Pregnancy." *Omni.* <https://academic.csuohio.edu/neuendorf_ka/com370/370_male_pregnancy.pdf>

Teresi, Dick. 1994, Nov. 27. 'How to Get a Man Pregnant'. *The New York Times.* <https://www.nytimes.com/1994/11/27/magazine/how-to-get-a-man-pregnant.html>

Terf Is a Slur. n.d. 'Terf Is a Slur: Documenting the Violence, Harrassment and Misogyny of Transgender Identity Politics'. <https://terfisaslur.com>

Terry, Don. 2015, Summer. 'In the Crossshairs. LGBT People Are More Victimized than Any Other Minority'. *Intelligence Report,* Southern Poverty Law Center. <https://medium.com/hatewatch-blog/in-the-crosshairs-3700fbf2203d>

The Economist. 2020, Dec. 10. 'An English Ruling on Transgender Teens Could Have Global Repercussion'. *The Economist.* <https://www.economist.com/international/2020/12/12/an-english-ruling-on-transgender-teens-could-have-global-repercussions?gclsrc=aw.ds&gclid=Cj0KCQiAj9iBB hCJARIsAE9qRtBaiV7KuWhK8Sla3m2PchIH8-HwwawDv1Y3rGbe_d4yai_8i32lyFMaAi-NEALw_wcB&gclsrc=aw.ds>

The Gender Map. 2021. 'The Transgender Medical Scandal'. <https://www.transgenderabuse.org/name-and-shame-doctors>

The TERFs. n.d. 'TERFs & Trans Healthcare'. <https://theterfs.com/terfs-trans-healthcare/>

37 Radical Feminists. 2013, August 12. 'Forbidden Discourse: The Silencing of Feminist Criticism of "Gender"'. *An Open Statement*. <http://meeting groundonline.org/wp-content/uploads/2013/10/GENDER-Statement-InterActive-930.pdf>

Transgender Trend. 2019, April 17. 'Johanna Olson-Kennedy and the US Gender Affirmative Approach'. *Blog*. <https://www.transgendertrend.com/johanna-olson-kennedy-gender-affirmative-approach/>

Turner, Janice. 2020, March 3. 'The Battle over Gender Has Turned Bloody'. *The Times*. (Reprinted by Peak Trans). <https://www.peaktrans.org/the-battle-over-gender-has-turned-bloody-janice-turner-in-the-times/>

Twitter Help Center. 2019, July. 'Hateful Conduct Policy'. <https://help.twitter.com/en/rules-and-policies/hateful-conduct-policy>

Urquhart, Evan. 2018, Feb. 27. 'Decriminalizing Prostitution Is Central to Transgender Rights'. *Slate*. <https://slate.com/human-interest/2018/02/decriminalizing-prostitution-is-central-to-transgender-rights.html>

Urquhart, Evan. 2021, Feb. 2. 'An "Ex-Detransitioner" Disavows the Anti-Trans Movement She Helped Start'. *Slate*. <https://slate.com/human-interest/2021/02/detransition-movement-star-ex-gay-explained.html>

U.S. Department of Education, 2021. 'Fact Sheet on U.S. Department of Education Policy'. <https://transequality.org/sites/default/files/ED-DCL-Fact-Sheet.pdf>

Vigo, Julian. 2013, June 7. 'The Left Hand of Darkness'. *Counterpunch*. <https://www.counterpunch.org/2013/06/07/the-left-hand-of-darkness/>

Vigo, Julian. 2018, June 3. 'The Degenderettes: The Transgender Hate Group Taking Aim at Women'. *Public Discourse*. <https://www.thepublicdiscourse.com/2018/06/21574/>

Wakefield, Lily. 2020, Dec. 11. 'Troll Arrested after Targeting Trans Woman with "Campaign of Harassment" wins Appeal to Overturn Conviction'. *Pink News*. <https://www.pinknews.co.uk/2020/12/11/kate-scottow-appeal-conviction-trans-woman-abuse-twitter-troll/>

Wallace, Andrew and Lyle Matthew Kan. 2020. '2018 Tracking Report: Lesbian, Gay, Bisexual, Transgender and Queer Grantmaking by U.S. Foundations'. <https://lgbtfunders.org/research-item/2018-tracking-report/>

Walsh, Joani. 2019, Nov. 10. 'Meet the Detransitioners: The Women Who Became Men – and Now Want to Go Back'. *The Telegraph*. <https://www.

telegraph.co.uk/women/life/meet-detransitioners-women-became-men-now-want-go-back/>

Warren, Elizabeth. 2015. 'Criminalization of LGBTQ+People'. <https://elizabethwarren.com/plans/lgbtq-equality/?>

Weale, Sally. 2017, Sept. 25. 'University Turned Down Politically Incorrect Transgender Research'. *The Guardian*. <https://www.theguardian.com/education/2017/sep/25/bath-spa-university-transgender-gender-reassignment-reversal-research>

WHRC. n.d. *Declaration on Women's Sex Based Rights*. Women's Human Rights Campaign. <https://www.womensdeclaration.com/en/>

Wikipedia. n.d. 'Detransiton: Occurrence'. <https://en.wikipedia.org/wiki/Detransition>

Wild, Angela C. 2019, Mar. 'Lesbians at Ground Zero: How Transgenderism Is Conquering the Lesbian Body'. <http://www.gettheloutuk.com/attachments/lesbiansatgroundzero.pdf>

Williams, Sophie. 2019, Aug. 11. 'Are Women Better Ultra-endurance Athletes than Men?' *BBC News*. <https://www.bbc.com/news/world-49284389>

Windust, Jamie. 2018, Oct. 9. 'A Guide to the Best Porn for Trans and Non-binary People'. *Cosmopolitan*. <https://www.cosmopolitan.com/uk/love-sex/sex/a23676859/trans-porn/>

WoLF. n.d. 'Declaration of No Confidence in LGB Movement Leadership'. <https://www.womensliberationfront.org/declaration-of-no-confidence-in-lgb-movement-leadership>

WoLF. 2021a, Feb. 5. 'Women's Sports are Under Attack in the United States'. <https://www.womensliberationfront.org/take-action/protection-of-women-and-girls-in-sports-senate>

WoLF. 2021b, Apr. 9. 'Ed Dept Responds to WoLF Petition for Rulemaking on Title IX, Annouces Hearing'. <https://www.womensliberationfront.org/news/ed-dept-petition-response>

WoLF. 2021c, Apr. 14. 'ACLU Sues Private Citizen to Suppress Public Records Request in Washington State'. <https://www.womensliberationfront.org/news/aclu-sues-private-citizen-to-suppress-public-records-request-in-washington-state>

WoLF. 2021d, Apr. 26. 'Judge Dismisses Female Student Athletes' Case in Connecticut'. <https://www.womensliberationfront.org/news/judge-dissmissal-soule-sports-ct-case>

WoLF. 2021e, May 19. 'Male Rapists Housed in Wash. Women's Prison Confirmed'. <https://www.womensliberationfront.org/news/washington-aclu-male-rapists-confirmed>

WoLF. 2021f, June 17. 'FAQ: Dept. of Ed Changes to Title IX Interpretation'. <https://www.womensliberationfront.org/news/faq-dept-of-ed-changes-to-title-ix-interpretation>

WoLF. 2021g, July 15. 'CA Women's Prisons Anticipate Pregnancy after Forcing Women to Be Housed with Men'. <https://www.womensliberationfront.org/news/ca-womens-prisons-anticipate-pregnancy-sb123>

Woodstock, Tuck. 2020, Oct. 2. 'Who Is Committing Violence against Trans Women?' *Portland Monthly*. <https://www.pdxmonthly.com/news-and-city-life/2020/10/who-is-committing-violence-against-trans-women>

Woolf, Virginia. 1929. *A Room of One's Own*. New York: Harcourt, Brace & World.

Wright, Colin M. and Emma N. Hilton. 2020, Feb. 13. 'The Dangerous Denial of Sex'. *Wall Street Journal*. <https://www.wsj.com/articles/the-dangerous-denial-of-sex-11581638089>

Yang, Avery. 2020, Feb. 1. '"Black History Month" Florence Griffith Joyner Smashed Records and Stereotypes'. <https://www.si.com/olympics/2020/02/01/black-history-month-florence-griffith-joyner>

York, Harry. 2017, Dec. 23. 'Academics Say Research Is Being Hindered by Universities' Fear of Online Backlash'. *The Telegraph*. <https://kaleistyleguide.com/news/2017/12/23/academics-say-research-hindered-universities-fear-online-backlash/>

Index

Other books by Spinifex Press

Detransition: Beyond Before and After
Max Robinson

Many feminists are concerned about the way transgender ideology naturalizes patriarchal views of sex stereotypes, and encourages transition as a way of attempting to escape misogyny.

In this brave and thoughtful book, Max Robinson goes beyond the 'before' and 'after' of the transition she underwent and takes us through the processes that led her, first, to transition in an attempt to get relief from her distress, and then to detransition, as she discovered feminist thought and community.

The author makes a case for a world in which all medical interventions for the purpose of assimilation are open to criticism. This book is a far-reaching discussion of women's struggles to survive under patriarchy, which draws upon a legacy of radical and lesbian feminist ideas to arrive at conclusions.

Robinson's bold discussion of both transition and detransition is meant to provoke a much-needed conversation about who benefits from transgender medicine and who has to bear the hidden cost of these interventions.

ISBN 9781925950403

Transgender Body Politics

Heather Brunskell-Evans

At a time when supposedly enlightened attitudes are championed by the mainstream, philosopher and activist Heather Brunskell-Evans shows how, in plain view under the guise of liberalism, a regressive men's rights movement is posing a massive threat to the human rights of women and children everywhere.

Everyone, including every trans person, has the right to live freely without discrimination. But the transgender movement has been hijacked by misogynists who are appropriating and inverting the struggles of feminism to deliver an agenda devoid of feminist principles.

In a chilling twist, when feminists critique the patriarchal status quo it is now they who are alleged to be extremists for not allowing men's interests to control the political narrative. Institutions whose purpose is to defend human rights now interpret truth speech as hate speech, and endorse the no-platforming of women as ethical.

This brave, truthful and eye-opening book does not shirk from the challenge of meeting the politics of liberalism and transgender rights head on. Everyone who cares about the future of women's and children's rights must read it.

ISBN 9781925950229

Vortex: The Crisis of Patriarchy
Susan Hawthorne

In this enlightening yet devastating book, Susan Hawthorne writes with clarity and incisiveness on how patriarchy is wreaking destruction on the planet and on communities. The twin mantras of globalisation and growth, expounded by neoliberalists who have hijacked the planet, are revealed in all their shabby deception.

Backed by meticulous research, the author shows how so-called advances in technology are, like a Trojan horse, used to mask sinister political agendas that sacrifice the common good for the shallow profiteering of corporations and mega-rich individuals. She argues that transgenderism via its war on biology is a means to breaking the spirit of the Women's Liberation Movement.

Susan Hawthorne details how women, lesbians, people with disabilities, Indigenous peoples, the poor, refugees and the very earth itself are being damaged by the crisis of patriarchy that is sucking everyone into its vortex.

The book shows a way out of the vortex: it is now up to the collective imagination and action of people everywhere to take up the challenges Susan Hawthorne pinpoints. This is a vital book for a world in crisis.

ISBN 9781925950168

*If you would like to know more about Spinifex Press,
write to us for a free catalogue, visit our website
and subscribe to our monthly newsletter.*

Spinifex Press
PO Box 105
Mission Beach QLD 4852
Australia

www.spinifexpress.com.au
women@spinifexpress.com.au